# Grant Writing

for
## dummies®
A Wiley Brand

6th edition

## by Dr. Beverly A. Browning, MPA, DBA

for
dummies®
A Wiley Brand

# Grant Writing For Dummies®, 6th Edition

Published by: **John Wiley & Sons, Inc.,** 111 River Street, Hoboken, NJ 07030-5774, www.wiley.com

Copyright © 2016 by John Wiley & Sons, Inc., Hoboken, New Jersey

Published simultaneously in Canada

For general information on our other products and services, please contact our Customer Care Department within the U.S. at 877-762-2974, outside the U.S. at 317-572-3993, or fax 317-572-4002. For technical support, please visit https://hub.wiley.com/community/support/dummies.

Wiley publishes in a variety of print and electronic formats and by print-on-demand. Some material included with standard print versions of this book may not be included in e-books or in print-on-demand. If this book refers to media such as a CD or DVD that is not included in the version you purchased, you may download this material at http://booksupport.wiley.com. For more information about Wiley products, visit www.wiley.com.

Library of Congress Control Number: 2016950787

ISBN 978-1-119-28012-5 (pbk); ISBN 978-1-119-28013-2 (ebk); ISBN 978-1-119-28014-9 (ebk)

Manufactured in the United States of America

10  9  8  7  6  5  4  3  2  1

# Contents at a Glance

# Table of Contents

# Introduction

When I wrote the first edition of *Grant Writing For Dummies* in 2001, a lot of my grant professional colleagues thought I was giving away "our" secrets. However, I didn't feel that way. I just wanted everyone who had an interest in finding grant-funding opportunities and writing grant proposals to have access to a handy reference tool filled with expert-driven insight and information. (After all, if I didn't know anything about this process, I would certainly look to a leading reference tool to teach me.) With each new edition of this book, I work diligently to provide fresh perspectives and updated information on grant writing.

By using this book daily, you can achieve your highest goals, which probably include winning almost everything you submit for funding or award consideration. You can even build your funding success rate. And, if you want to dive even further into grant writing with me, you may want to consider enrolling in one of my online classes or sponsoring one of my two-day Grant Writing Boot Camps.

## About This Book

The structure of *Grant Writing For Dummies*, 6th Edition, is designed to help you get in and get out of the text with just the information you were looking for. Consider this book your ultimate grant-writing reference tool. Read it in any order you want and bookmark sections you expect to return to again and again.

You don't need to read the sidebars sprinkled throughout the text. You can identify them by their gray-shaded boxes. They're simply extra tidbits of information that are interesting but not critical to your understanding of grant writing.

# Foolish Assumptions

As I wrote this book, I assumed it would serve as a desktop and online reference for

>> Individuals seeking research and education on grant-writing sources and approaches

>> New grant writers looking to be guided through every step of the process, from understanding the definition of a grant to planning, researching, writing, and submitting

>> Veteran grant writers seeking to increase their funding success rates

*Note:* Although I address grant opportunities for individuals, the majority of this book focuses on winning grants on behalf of nonprofit organizations, government agencies, and other eligible applicants in the eyes and minds of the funders.

# Icons Used in This Book

The little pictures in the margins throughout this book are designed to highlight information that's special and important for one reason or another. *Grant Writing For Dummies,* 6th Edition, uses the following icons:

REMEMBER

This icon points to pieces of information you shouldn't forget.

TIP

Wherever you see this icon, you're sure to find a good idea, trick, or shortcut that can save you time and trouble.

WARNING

Make sure to read the paragraphs marked with this icon; it indicates information that can help you avoid disasters.

# Beyond the Book

In addition to the material in the print or e-book you're reading right now, this product also comes with some access-anywhere goodies on the web. Check out the free Cheat Sheet for tips on writing effective grant proposals, where to look for grant funding, and grant research websites worth your time. To get this Cheat Sheet, simply go to www.dummies.com and type **Grant Writing For Dummies Cheat Sheet** in the Search box.

You can also go to www.dummies.com/go/grantwritingfd6e for templates you can use to make your next grant-writing experience a little easier.

# Where to Go from Here

Where you start reading this latest edition of *Grant Writing For Dummies* is up to you. You can begin by perusing the table of contents and then hitting sections of interest. Or you can head to the chapter that addresses an area of grant writing you're currently struggling with. If, however, you're brand-new to the grant research and writing game, I suggest you begin with Chapter 1, which gives you an overview of this book's tips and strategies for finding grant-funding opportunities and winning grant awards.

# 1

# Getting Started with Grant Writing

Distinguish between the two main types of funders that provide grant monies: public-sector funders (federal, state, city, and local governments) and private-sector funders (foundations and corporations).

Become acquainted with the basic elements of the typical grant application.

Create a strategic plan to drive your organization's decision-making process for now and in the future.

Get familiar with the basics funders expect to see in a grant request — and numerous ways to give your application an edge over the competition.

Chapter 1

# Grant-Writing Basics

I f I had a dollar for every call and email I've received from everyone and every organization wanting to pursue grant funding, I'd be super rich. I can actually recite the response that I regretfully have to give most inquirers.

In this chapter, I guide you through all the essentials of grant-writing basics. I flush out the whats, hows, whys, whens, and ifs to help new grant writers, new nonprofits, and grant professionals returning to active grant seeking and grant writing. Let's get started!

## Getting Up to Speed on Grant-Seeking Basics

In order to hone your "find a grant now" skill set, you need a lot of basic information. First things first: what a grant is *not*. A grant is *not* a way to pay off your debts, like mortgages, student loans, government loans, or utility bills. A grant also is *not* a way to get a free vacation. You won't be able to find a grant funder that will send you on an trip where you propose to take photographs of historical sites when you're not at the local bar celebrating happy hour.

In this section, I explain common terms and lay out the basic information you need to know before you toss your hat (and hopes) into the grant-seeking arena.

# Defining common grant-writing terminology

Basically speaking, a *grant* (sometimes labeled a *cooperative agreement* by government funding agencies) is a monetary award of financial assistance. The principal purpose of the grant is to transfer dollars from a funding agency or entity *(grantor)* to a recipient *(grantee)* who undertakes to carry out the proposed objectives (your written implementation plans in the grant application narrative) that you committed to when you submitted your grant application. Here are some common grant-writing terms and their definitions:

>> **Grant/cooperative agreement:** The distinguishing factor between a grant and a cooperative agreement is the degree of government (state, federal, or local) participation or involvement during the grantee's actual startup and implementation of the proposed activities.

**REMEMBER**

A grant award is made via a contract or agreement between the funding agency (the *grantor*) and the recipient (the *grantee*), with the grant supporting the activities and deliverables (implementation strategies and measurable time-bound objectives or benchmarks) detailed in the proposal/application (and finalized during the process of confirming the grant award). Reading the grant application's guidelines thoroughly (and multiple times) is critical to being funded. (Refer to Part 2 for tips on finding grant-funding opportunities.)

>> **Grantor:** A *grantor* (also known as a *grant maker* or *funder*) is the organization or agency that receives your funding request and decides to fund it or reject it. Grantors include the grant-making agencies of the federal government, tons of state and local government agencies (including in the US territories), and more than 100,000 foundations and corporate grant makers. Two categories of grantors exist:

- **Public sector funder:** Any government grant maker (federal, state, county, or local unit of government) that awards grants with money that comes from congressional allocations, federal pass-through dollars to states and municipalities, or taxpayer dollars — the public sector.

- **Private sector funder:** A foundation or corporate grant maker (independent of private foundation, operating foundations, corporate foundations, and community foundations) that uses funds from private sources — investments, contributions, donations, or grants — to fund eligible grant applicants.

>> **Grantee:** The eligible grant applicant designated to receive a grant award. All grants require the grantee to use the funds as written (and promised) in the grant application. The required grant award paperwork is considered a contract between the grantor and the grantee. Up until you're awarded the grant, you're a *grant applicant;* you become a grantee only if you are approved for funding and agree to accept the award.

**REMEMBER**

Be certain you are an eligible grantee before applying for the grant.

So, how do you get a grantor to give you a grant and make you a grantee? After you've reviewed the guidelines (at least three times) for submitting an application and made initial contact with the potential funder, you're ready to research, write, and submit your *grant application* or *proposal* (also known as a *funding request*). I fill you in on the pieces or sections of a grant application/proposal in the section "Looking at the components of a grant application," later in this chapter.

## Looking at different types of grants

Almost every grant-funding agency publishes specific types of funding it awards to prospective grant seekers. When you know what you want to use grant monies for, you can evaluate whether your request fits with the type of funding the grantor has available. For example, if you want money for architectural fees related to a historical preservation project, you can skip applying to a grantor that's only accepting grant requests for small technology-related equipment.

Look long and hard at the different categories of funding offered:

>> **Annual campaigns:** Grants to support annual operating expenses, infrastructure improvements, program expansion, and, in some cases, one-time-only expenses (such as a cooling-system replacement).

>> **Building/renovation funds:** Grants to build a new facility or renovate an existing facility. These projects are often referred to as *bricks-and-mortar projects.* Building funds are the most difficult to secure; only a small percentage of foundations and corporations award grants for this type of project.

>> **Capital support:** Grants for equipment, buildings, construction, and endowments. This type of request is a major undertaking by the applicant organization because this type of large-scale project isn't quickly funded. An organization often needs two to three years to secure total funding for such a project.

>> **Challenge monies:** Grants that act as leverage to secure additional grants from foundations and corporations. They're awarded by grant makers that specifically include *challenge grants* or *challenge funds* in their grant-making priorities.

These grants are contingent upon you raising additional funds from other sources. Typically, a challenge grant award letter directs you to raise the remaining funding from other grantors; however, that typically excludes government grants.

>> **Conferences/seminars:** Grants to cover the cost of attending, planning, and/or hosting conferences and seminars. You can use the funding to pay for all the conference expenses, including securing a keynote speaker, traveling, printing, advertising, and taking care of facility expenses such as meals.

>> **Consulting services:** Grants to strengthen an organization's capacity can be used to retain the services of a consultant or consulting firm. For example, if you bring in a consultant to do a long-range strategic plan or an architect to develop plans for a historical preservation project, you can apply for a grant to cover these types of expenses.

>> **Continuing support/continuation:** Grants additional funds to your organization after you've already received an initial grant award from that same grantor. These monies are intended to continue the program or project initially funded.

>> **Endowments:** Grants to develop long-term, permanent investment income to ensure the continuing presence and financial stability of your nonprofit organization. If your organization is always operating in crisis-management mode, one of your goals should be to develop an endowment fund for long-term viability.

>> **Fellowships:** Grants to support graduate and postgraduate students in specific fields. These funds are typically awarded to institutions and not directly to individuals, with the exception of some international fellowship funders.

>> **General/operating expenses:** Grants for general line-item budget expenses. You may use these funds for salaries, fringe benefits, travel, consultants, utilities, equipment, and other expenses necessary to support agency operations.

>> **Matching funds:** Grants awarded with the requirement that you must match the grant award with your own monies or with in-kind contributions.

>> **Program development:** Grants to pay for expenses related to the expansion of existing programs or the development of new programs.

>> **Research:** Grants to support medical and educational research. Monies are usually awarded to the institutions that employ the individuals conducting the research.

>> **Scholarship funds:** Grants to eligible organizations seeking to award scholarships to eligible individuals. Remember that when funds are awarded

directly to an individual, they're considered taxable income (that is, the recipient owes taxes on them).

>> **Seed money:** Grants awarded for a pilot program not yet in full-scale operation. Seed money gets a program underway, but other monies are necessary to continue the program in its expansion phase.

>> **Technical (consulting) assistance:** Grants to improve your internal program operations as a whole (versus consulting on one specific program). Often, this type of grant is awarded to hire an individual or firm that can provide the needed technical assistance.

# Understanding your eligibility for grants

The types of organizations or entities eligible to apply for a grant vary from grantor to grantor. Each type of grantor — government (public) or foundation (private) — always includes clear, published grant-making guidelines that indicate who or what type of entity is eligible to apply for those specific grant funds. To access these grant-making guidelines, simply visit the grantor's website.

Funders typically include one or more of the following types of grant applicants in their *eligible applicant* language:

>> State government

>> County government

>> City or township government

>> Federally recognized Native American tribal governments

>> Independent school districts

>> Nonprofits with and without Internal Revenue Service (IRS) 501(c)(3) (non-profit) status

>> Private, public, and state-controlled institutions of higher education

>> Public and Native American housing authorities

>> For-profit businesses

>> For-profit organizations other than businesses

>> International nonprofits (called *nongovernmental organizations* or NGOs)

>> Individuals

**TIP**

Always check with the funder in advance to make sure that the entity that you're applying for is an eligible grant applicant. For example, funders view a nonprofit as an IRS-approved 501(c)(3) designated tax-exempt organization. Just being incorporated as a nonprofit in your state (for US-based grant makers) is not going to qualify you to apply for funds. You'll definitely need IRS approval in writing.

**REMEMBER**

Familiarize yourself with Grants.gov before you actually have plan on applying for funding. All federal grant applicants have to do a lot of upfront work before they can submit an application for funding consideration.

Grants are awarded to organizations that have applied to the IRS for nonprofit status and have received the 501(c)(3) designation as well as to units of government (state agencies, counties, cities, towns, and villages) and government agencies, including state colleges and universities. Foundation and corporate grantors focus predominantly on nonprofit organizations and aren't inclined to fund for-profits. However, a few grants are given to individuals (see Chapter 7 for details).

In some instances, government agencies have set up separate 501(c)(3) nonprofit structures in order to scoop up more private sector (foundation and corporate) grant awards.

# Recognizing the Value of a Funding Development Plan

**REMEMBER**

If you're looking for funding to support an entire organization or a specific program, the first rule in grant seeking is that you don't write a grant request without first completing a comprehensive planning process that involves the grant applicant organization's key stakeholders: *target population* members (the people your organization serves), administrative staff, and the board of directors.

Without key stakeholder input on what your target population needs and the plan for closing the gap on these needs, you're fishing without the right bait. You must have an organized *funding development plan* to guide your organization in adopting priority programs and services and then identifying all potential grantors you plan to approach with grant requests. A funding development plan answers questions such as the following:

> » What programs are strong and already have regular funding to keep them going and are they likely to be refunded?

>> What community needs aren't being addressed by our organization or other organizations providing similar services?

>> What new programs need funding and is there evidence of the needs?

>> What opportunities exist to find new funding partners and who will be responsible for making the initial contact with each funder?

>> What existing grants expire soon and can we reapply or will we have to find new funding?

When you answer these questions, you can begin to look at the multitude of areas where grants are awarded and start prioritizing the type of funding you need. (For more information on funding development plans, see Chapter 2.)

# Connecting to Public Sector Grant-Making Agencies

I receive dozens of emails every week asking about grants. Everyone wants grants! If you're feeling clueless as to how to find potential funding for your organization, you simply need to use the Internet. You can search for potential sources interested in what your organization needs in the way of goods and services. Fire up your computer and start searching for the monies that may be waiting for your organization. While you're at it, why not start with the nation's wealthiest relative, Uncle Sam?

Did you know that the US government is one of the largest grant-making entities? If you want to score big in grant awards, you may want to consider targeting federal grant-making agencies.

REMEMBER

Two types of government grant awards exist:

>> A *competitive grant* is one where applicants compete against each other for a limited amount of funding.

>> A *formula grant* is awarded based on a predetermined formula (a set amount of money per person) established by the funding agency. Formula grants aren't considered competitive. For example, community action agencies are funded formula grants, in part, through the Community Services Block Grant (CSBG) program. These grants are awarded on a service-population-based formula. The agencies receive these funds year after year by merely updating the previous year's application and resubmitting.

In the following sections, I help you understand what type of public sector grant money (or grantor) will pay you to implement your idea, project, or program.

## Federal funding: Raiding Uncle Sam's stash

The first place to look for big pots of money is in Uncle Sam's closet of federal funding agencies. In Chapters 4 and 5, I explain public sector grants and wade through the main federal e-grant portal, Grants.gov.

Many newly established nonprofit organizations think that they should apply for government grants before raising seed funding from local foundations and corporations. Your organization needs to have established a credible track record for implementing, evaluating, and prudently managing funding from smaller fish in the sea before jumping into the federal grant application process.

If you're interested in looking at what the feds have to offer, take some time to browse the Catalog of Federal Domestic Assistance (CFDA), which you can find at www.cfda.gov. The CFDA is the directory of grant-funding programs. Although it doesn't tell you about open grant competitions you can apply for at a particular time, the CFDA does give you an overview of grant programs. To find active or current grant-funding opportunities from Uncle Sam, go to www.grants.gov, which gives you daily funding announcements on money you can apply for *now*, providing your organization is an eligible grant applicant.

## State and local government funding: Seeking public dollars closer to home

Each state receives grant monies from the feds and from tax revenues that are funneled into and out of the state's general funds. After taking their fair (or unfair) share for administrative overhead, states re-grant the money to eligible agencies and organizations in the form of competitive grants or formula grants.

You can search the Internet to find state agencies that award grants. Examples of some of the state agencies that re-grant federal monies are agriculture, commerce, education, health, housing development, natural resources, and transportation. You can also contact your state legislator's local office for assistance in identifying grant opportunities within your state.

There's a wide variation in state grant making. It's always best to meet with your state-level elected officials and funding agency representatives to pave the way for successful grant seeking.

# Scoping Out Sources of Private Sector Grants

Foundation and corporate grant makers are private sector funders. The rainfall of private-sector grant money continues to be conservative, but it's also continuously available to grant seekers who meet this type of grantor's area of interest.

Where can you find out more about these grants? You can locate sources by visiting a Foundation Center Cooperating Collections site (usually at a state university library, community foundation, or other nonprofit information center). These sites are the only places where you can access the Foundation Center's *Foundation Directory Online* for free. Otherwise, you need to subscribe at one of the levels that best fits your grant research needs. (To find a Cooperating Collections site, visit www.foundationcenter.org.)

TIP

If you're targeting private sector funders, start with local organizations first to improve your odds of receiving funds.

## Finding foundations that award grants

*Private foundations* typically get their monies from a single-donor source, such as an individual, a family, or a corporation. Others raise funds from a variety of donor sources. You can find hundreds of private foundations in the Foundation Center's *Foundation Directory Online* or by typing "list of private foundations" or "private foundations" plus your state's name into your favorite search engine.

*Public foundations,* on the other hand, are supported primarily through donations from the general public. That's a no-brainer, right? Public foundations also receive funding from foundation and corporate grants, as well as individual donors. Again, the Foundation Center's website can give you loads of information on these types of foundations.

REMEMBER

The grant-seeking and grant-making processes may differ for public and private foundations. Always contact potential foundation funders to introduce your organization, start to build a communications bridge, and inquire about their grant-making processes.

## Scoping out corporations that award grants and in-kind donations

Did you know that many of the biggest businesses in the nation set 5 percent or more of their profits aside for grants? Why is that, you ask? The reason is *corporate social responsibility* and *community engagement* — which are the approaches that successful businesses take when they decide to make a financial commitment to the community where they're headquartered or where they have operating locations.

Corporations that award grants usually have a website link labeled Community, Community Relations, Social Responsibility, Local Initiatives, Grants, or Corporate Giving. Use the *Foundation Directory Online* to view corporations with giving programs.

# Understanding Grant Submission Requirements

One of the biggest keys in grant writing is recognizing the different application formats that funders require you to submit. Some grantors require more information than others. Today, at least 50 percent of funders with websites require online e-grant applications. Others require traditional paper-written narratives, forms, budgets, and mandatory attachments. In Chapter 22, I cover e-grant tips.

REMEMBER

Determine the writing format for each funding source you identify. Carefully view each private sector funder's website, and if you're still not sure about what to write or how to write it, make a quick call or send an email to the listed contact person. Governmental agencies have their own application kits, and you can submit applications for these agencies only at certain times in the year when there is a specific funding deadline published.

## Looking at the components of a grant application

A *government grant* or *cooperative agreement application* is a written funding request you use to ask for money from a government agency. Government grant applications are specific to each of the federal grant-making agencies. Even state agency grant applications that are funded with federal pass-through dollars closely mirror federal grant application guidelines and grantee requirements. Each federal agency has dozens of agencies under its wing that release Notices of Funding Availability (NOFAs), Request for Applications (RFAs), Funding Opportunity Announcements (FOAs), or Request for Proposals (RFPs). Each NOFA, RFA, FOA, and RFP has different funding priorities and guidelines for what you need to write in order to submit a responsive and reviewable grant application.

Government and other types of grant applications generally require that you write narrative responses for the following sections (each of which I cover in more depth in Part 4):

>> Executive summary or abstract

>> Statement of need

>> Program design or methodology

>> Adequacy of resources or key personnel

>> Evaluation plan

>> Organization background/history or organization capability

>> Sustainability statement

>> Budget

A foundation or corporate grant application typically takes the form of a proposal. A *proposal* is a structured document that must follow each grant maker's specific guidelines. Writing a proposal to a foundation or corporation requires the same adherence to the guidelines and incorporation of relevant information as completing government grant applications.

*Note:* Some foundations and corporate grant makers accept the Common Grant Application format; see the later "Getting your request in the door at foundations and corporations" section for more details on this format.

## Perusing government grant application guidelines

Although government grant application formats vary from agency to agency and department to department, some common threads exist in the highly detailed, structured, military-like regimen that's commonly referred to as an *application package.* These common threads include a standard cover form, certification and assurances forms, narrative sections, and the budget narratives and related forms. And of course, all government grant applications require mandatory attachments or appendixes, such as résumés of project staff and copies of your nonprofit status determination letter from the IRS. (Head to Chapter 5 for more about the application package.)

REMEMBER

Always follow the pagination, order of information, and review or evaluation criteria guidelines. All government grants are awarded on the basis of your meeting point-weighted review criteria, which are written and published in each funding agency's grant application guidelines. (Most grants use a 100-point system.) The review criteria tell you what the peer reviewers will base their ratings on in the application package. With the competition being so hot and heavy for all government grants, you want to carefully craft an award-winning narrative that scores at least 95 points or higher. The grant applications recommended for funding typically score in the mid- to high 90s.

TIP

As you read through the application guidelines, highlight all narrative writing requirements and look for sections that tell you how the grant reviewers rate or evaluate each section of the narrative. By formatting and writing your narrative sections to meet the review criteria, you can edge out the competition and increase your funding success rate. (I tell you how to prepare and write for the review criteria in Chapter 10.)

## Getting your request in the door at foundations and corporations

Before you even consider approaching a foundation or corporation with a grant request, you absolutely must research each and every potential foundation and corporate funding source. Don't rely solely on online grant research databases. Let your fingers do the typing to find each potential funder's website. Read every link and become highly familiar with each source. Find out the organization's funding priorities, the number of grants it awards annually, and the grant request range. Become very fluent in who they are, what they fund, when they fund, and their mission statement.

REMEMBER

Whenever contract information is available, be sure to go out of your way to introduce your organization to the grantor before applying. It's critical that you get a green light before submitting your grant application. Building a relationship before asking for a grant is the first step in this introductory process.

TIP

As a new grant seeker of a particular funder, make sure your grant request is near the low end of the grantor's grant range. Private sector funders don't want to award mid- to high-funding award range amounts until after they test the waters with a small grant award. After you've demonstrated ethics, cost-effective grants management, and accountability to the funder, you can then ask for larger grants in future requests.

In the past, some private sector funders have been swamped daily with large volumes of unsolicited grant proposals. To circumvent this influx of steady reading and decision making, more and more private sector funders have moved toward requiring an initial *letter of inquiry,* which is a brief letter asking about the foundation's interest in your project. If the organization is interested, it then asks you to submit a full grant proposal. If you fail to submit the letter of inquiry, you may find the door closed to your unsolicited grant proposal. I give you a link to an online letter of inquiry template at the end of Chapter 2.

Whether the private sector funder is large or small, it most likely requires a cover letter as well as a variety of attachments. The attachments are a major portion of what counts with this group of grantors. The private sector funder may ask for the project's evaluation plan, your organization's structure or administration, your finances, and other supporting material.

TIP

A generic grant proposal template still in use with some funders is known as the Common Grant Application (CGA). The CGA format contains all the essentials: a cover sheet, a two-section narrative, and multiple attachments. Even if a grantor requests a different order of information, you can do a lot of cutting and pasting from a grant application written in the CGA format to create a non-CGA grant request. To determine whether using the CGA is appropriate in your situation, check the grantor's guidelines by contacting it directly or seeking information in one of the many available grantor directories. Here's a trustworthy website to download the CGA: http://chfs.ky.gov/nr/rdonlyres/635f46a0-8ef6-4ce7-a6ae-b33d3dbe35a6/0/nngcommongrantapplication.pdf.

WARNING

Before you start writing in a generic format such as the CGA, check to see whether the region you operate in requires you to use a different format. The Forum of Regional Associations of Grantmakers, a national network of local leaders and organizations across the United States that supports effective charitable giving, should be your first stop. Most of the regional groups of foundation grant makers you can find at this site have likely designed their own specific grant application formats.

TIP

To find contact information for the various Regional Associations of Grantmakers, head to www.givingforum.org/directory.

I strongly encourage you to build a relationship with any potential private sector funder before you start begging for a grant. Courtesy and protocol mean everything in the private sector funding environment, so always establish communications via email, a letter of inquiry, or a face-to-face meeting before sticking your hand out. In Chapter 21, I give you lots of tips on how to build relationships with potential funders.

**TIP**

If a board member at your organization happens to know a board member at the foundation or corporation you're targeting for funding, board-member-to-board-member contact can help a ton. Foundations and corporations make decisions based on specific funding priorities, which change periodically, sometimes even annually, based on the direction that the board of directors wants to take the foundation or corporation. Although the program staff initially reviews your grant proposal and makes recommendations to the board of directors, the board has the final approval or veto. Remember, board members can override staff decisions.

## Making a List and Checking It Twice

**REMEMBER**

Whether you're submitting a hard copy of your grant application or a digital (e-grant) version, always follow the funder's instructions. I can't stress this enough! Here are some additional must-do's when preparing a grant application:

>> Read the guidelines three times: one time to understand the general instructions, a second time to focus on the technical formatting requirements, and a third time to note the narrative content requirements.

>> Highlight all technical and content requirements.

>> Call the funder (if permissible) to clarify any conflicting instructions and ask questions in general.

>> Write in chronological order (the same order that the funder asks for the information in its guidelines).

>> Get a second and third set of eyes to read the guidelines and check your application document line for line. Your readers should be looking at grammar, punctuation, formatting, content, clarity, connection between the narrative sections, budget accuracy, and inclusion of all mandatory attachments.

## Tracking Your Submission Status

After you submit all your funding requests, you need to develop a tracking system that helps you keep up with their progress and cues you when the period of silence from grantors has been too long. Most public and private sector grantors specify a time frame for when they will announce grant awards somewhere in the application packet or in the published description of their application process. At the federal and state levels, you can even enlist tracking support from your legislative team. To do this, you can directly call or write. However, at the corporate and foundation levels, you're on your own (unless, of course, members of your board of directors have friends and associates on the grantor's board of trustees).

The old-school approach is to develop a manual or electronic tracking system to monitor what you've written, who received it, and the status of your funding request (pending, funded, or rejected). However, the new and easier way to keep track of submitted requests is to purchase grant management or tracking software. Look at lots of cloud-based grants management options to meet your needs. You can find out what's available by typing **grant management systems** into your favorite web browser. These systems can cost thousands of dollars. However, many offer a free trial or demonstration, so you can see whether the program suits your needs before you buy.

TIP

Keeping track of how many grant requests you submit on an annual basis is a best practice. You also want to know how many of those requests were funded. For example, if you wrote 20 grant applications and 10 were funded (at any level), one-half or 50 percent of your requests were successful. Your success percentage is interpreted as your *funding success rate.* When you're looking for a raise or promotion, or simply trying to start your own grant-writing consulting business, everyone who has control over your future will ask you for your funding success rate. Track it; know it!

# Jumping for Joy or Starting All Over?

When you win, you celebrate, right? Well, yes, you celebrate, but you also notify your stakeholders of your success in winning a grant award. And you prepare for the implementation phase now that monies are on the way.

When you win a grant award, it's important to remember to thank the funder (by a letter, resolution, invitation to your board meeting to acknowledge their monetary gift, and so on) and determine if you can issue a press release or if their contribution is confidential.

REMEMBER

If your grant request wasn't awarded, you have some critical steps to take to determine why your funding request was denied and when you can resubmit it. Follow these steps (and refer to Chapter 20 for more details):

1. **Contact the funding agency and ask why your grant application wasn't recommended for funding and ask for a review of your application or the reviewer's remarks.**

   You may have to ask for this feedback in writing so the grantors have a paper trail of whom they release information to and why.

2. **When you know where the weakness is in your grant application, develop a plan for rewriting.**

   You want to rewrite the weak sections of your narrative and ready it for submission to other grantors and even for future resubmission to the same grant-making agency that rejected the first request. Grantors usually allow you to reapply in the next funding cycle (next year).

# Chapter 2

# Preparing for the World of Grant Seeking

Typically, organizations spend weeks working on their long-range strategic plans. However, when it comes to developing a *grant-funding plan* — the road map for identifying the dollars that will support your existing and new programs — their efforts are significantly less or nonexistent. A grant-funding plan is a working document that identifies potential funders for each program, their funding range, application deadlines, contact information, action steps required, and who is responsible for carrying out the action steps. Finally, it includes a status column to keep everyone involved updated on what has been completed, what's still pending, and what hasn't been started to help track follow-through red flags.

In this chapter, I show you how to create a work-in-progress grant-funding plan and manage the plan on an ongoing basis. In addition, I show you how to track multiple potential funders for one project.

# Creating a Grant-Funding Plan

Your grant-funding plan is really a guide and a road map for where the dollars will come from for two years to support your programs. Just a few years ago, the trend was to create three- to five-year long-range funding plans. Today, if an organization wants to be on the cutting edge and able to roll with the economic punches, as well as the shifts in priorities by existing funding sources, its strategy needs to focus on two fiscal years. Yes, that's it — 24 months.

If you have current funders that traditionally fund your organization year after year, their decision-making processes will be shorter. For example, if you have a track record for implementation success (carrying out the program's goals and activities that you committed to in writing), then there is likely a turnaround time of six months or less from the time your organization requests funding until you get the check in the mail.

On the other hand, if you're planning to approach new funders, which means building a relationship before asking, the time between the grant application's submission and the funding decision could be longer than 12 months. What you thought would be awarded in this fiscal year won't be coming into your bank account until the *next* fiscal year. This means you need to track funding priorities and decision-making time frames so you don't build your annual organizational operating budget on dollars that won't come in for 12 to 24 months.

**REMEMBER**

This is a grant-funding plan for your *grant-seeking* goals. But there are also funding plans for securing dollars from individual contributions, special events, and miscellaneous sources. Because this is *Grant Writing For Dummies*, I want you to focus on developing a plan for going after grants from all types of grantors.

In the following sections, I get you acquainted with the components of a typical grant-funding plan, show you an example of one, and give you a checklist of how to keep your plan in tiptop shape.

## Looking at the plan components

The grant-funding plan (created in table format) that I use the most for grant seeking captures eight fields in this order (see Figure 2-1):

>> **Program, Service, or Activity:** This is where you list the program, service, or activity priorities that are written in your organization's strategic plan.

>> **Funding Source:** In this column, you identify the funding source(s) that you plan to approach to support your programs, services, or activities in the current and next fiscal years.

Most recent modification date:

| Program, Service or Activity | Funding Source | Address, Telephone, Email, and Website | Contact Person/Title | Request | Application Deadline/Giving Cycle | Assigned To | Status/Results |
|---|---|---|---|---|---|---|---|
| Nonprofit Capacity Building Services | Mt. Morris Community Foundation | 7777 S. 77th Rd., Branson, MI 85341 No website published info@mtmorris@gmail.com | Dr. Bev Browning, Program Officer for Community Capacity Building Initiatives | $50,000 | February 3 Notification letters will be sent out September 1. | New funder contact team: Board President and Grant Writer | Face-to-face meeting scheduled for November 4, 2016. |
| | Miracle Bank Corporate Giving Program | 555 W. Wonderland Dr., Browning, AR 55555 jbrowning@mb.com www.mb.com | Mr. John Browning, Corporate Giving Director | $10,000 | February 10 Award letters will be sent within six weeks of submission date; rejected requests will not be notified. | Board Treasurer and Executive Director | Conference call scheduled for January 10 (Board Treasurer's wife works at this bank). |
| After School Academic Enhancement | Specifica Department of Education Services— 21st Century Community Learnings Centers grant program | 4243 S. State Funding Ave., Specifica, MO 87878 sjones@specificadoe.mo.gov www.spedificadoe.mo.ogv | Dr. Sydney Jones, Director 21st Century Community Learning Centers Program | $150,000 per year for three years | March 5 Notification emails will be sent by July 15. | Grant writing consultant specializing in writing this specific grant application | Grant writer attending new applicant orientation meeting on January 28. She will report back to the Executive Director before starting work on the application. |
| | Grant Writing Training Foundation | P.O. Box 9999, Goodyear, AZ 77777 ascott@gwtf.org www.gwtf.org | Ms. Aaliyah Scott, Executive Director | $25,000 | Continuation application due April 4. This money is already committed to our organization and a request for Year 2 of 4 funding. Check will be issued within four weeks of continuation application submission date. | Grant writing consultant | Annual funding supporter. Needs to receive a letter of appreciation from the Board of Directors and be included in our annual partnership luncheon. Board will take action at next meeting. |

Funding Plan: ABC Nonprofit Organization
January 2, 2017–December 31, 2018

© John Wiley & Sons, Inc.

**FIGURE 2-1:** An example of a funding plan.

**TIP**

You can have multiple funding sources that you contact for one program. Putting all your eggs in one basket (applying to only one funder) and then receiving a rejection letter nine months later if not your goal. If you did that, you would have to start all over with only three months left in the year. Approach multiple funders for every program, service, or activity in need of funding.

>> **Address, Telephone, Email, and Website:** By incorporating this column into your funding plan, you have clickable links to quickly email or review the websites of current and potential funders. Adding the mailing address reduces your time-on-task when sending out a letter of inquiry (I provide an example of this type of document later in this chapter). And, most important, the phone number is handy when you need to speak with the designated contact person for the funder.

>> **Contact Person/Title:** Research the funder's website and even call their office to make sure that you have the correct name of the contact person and their title. Make sure to ask if the contract person is female or male, if there's any chance of confusion. Names like Chris and Pat can belong to men and women.

>> **Request:** The amount of grant funding that you plan to request goes in this column. Make sure to review the funder's profile for their grant-making range. Stay below the top of the range if you're a first-time grant applicant with the funder.

>> **Application Deadline/Giving Cycle:** This column captures the grant application's deadline(s) and when grants are awarded by the funder. Some funders only accept and award grants once a year, while others may have multiple grant application submission deadlines and giving cycles.

>> **Assigned To:** In this column, you add the name(s) of the board member(s) or administrative-level staff that are assigned to making contact with the funder to continue previous funding conversations or begin initial conversations with new funders. In Chapter 21, I explain more about this process.

>> **Status/Results:** This is where you insert the status of the funding request — for example: "Contacting in September," "First contact meeting went well on September 5, 2016," "Grant application submitted on September 5, 2016," or "Funding declined for September 2016 giving cycle; letter indicated to apply again next year (2017); follow-up meeting requested to discuss problems with grant application."

## Updating critical information

The Status/Results column of your funding plan (refer to Figure 2-1) must be updated continuously. After you meet with the funder and can assess their level of interest in supporting your organization, you'll need to change the meeting status note to the feedback received and add the next step (for example, "Apply this cycle," "Wait until next year," or "Not interested in this project"). Here are some essential activities needed on your part to keep the funding plan a working document:

>> **Write it down.** You need to officially document your funding plan ideas. Create funding plan templates and hand one to everyone at the meeting. This way, all parties are onboard and writing/talking about the same things in the same sequence.

>> **Use it.** The funding plan must become a daily guide to help your organization decide what programs or services have funding priority and how to most logically fund them.

>> **Keep it up to date.** Update your funding plan's Status/Results column every time you apply for grant funding or receive the results of your efforts. Record whether you're being funded, and if so, the funding amount. If you don't secure the money, find out why your efforts failed.

>> **Review and revise it annually.** Why? Both your needs and funders' priorities change, sometimes as often as annually. For instance, just because a lot of money is available for programs for after-school academic programs this year doesn't mean that this funding area will still be the focus next year.

Your plan must change to reflect what funders want to fund. In other words, your funding plan isn't just about what your organization wants or needs; it's about what funders want to fund within the parameters of your organization's mission.

REMEMBER

REMEMBER

Involve both your board of directors and your administrative staff in fleshing out the funding plan and updating it. Sit down and have a brainstorming session to determine your funding priorities. Ask administrative staff about unmet needs, waiting lists, or any feedback from frontline employees. Ask board members to assess programmatic weaknesses from their viewpoint as well. When the Status/Results column changes, update it immediately and get a copy of the modified plan document out to all who need it as their road map for assignments.

TIP

Keep your funding plan flexible. Funders change their priorities often, and your target population's needs are likely to change as well. So be willing to review previous evaluation reports or results from funded programs and stay on top of newly released community needs assessments. Update the funding plan by removing and adding programs and services, and then incorporate these changes into your revised document.

# Increasing Your Chances for Success

When you're ready to start your grant-funding research, keep your funding plan template close at hand. You're likely to find a lot of potential funding opportunities, so reading the opportunity and then perusing the plan to make sure the opportunity fits is a smart move. You're searching for perfect fits between what you need and what the funder wants to fund.

**REMEMBER**

The best way to sustain a high funding success rate is to identify multiple funding sources for each project initiative in your funding plan. Then submit your grant proposals to all of them.

**TIP**

Sending out multiple proposals is standard practice as long as you tell all the funders that you plan to approach other sources. Providing each proposal with a simple one-page attachment labeled "Funding Sources Receiving This Request" is the most ethical way to inform all funders of your strategy. (I provide an example of such a document in Chapter 18.) Or you can list other sources you've approached on the actual grant application, if such a section exists.

In the sections that follow, I explain what you need to know to find a broad range of potential funding sources.

## Looking for needles in a haystack

To identify as many potential grant-funding sources as possible for your organization, you need to carefully research the primary sources of funding: the public sector (federal, state, and local government) and the private sector (foundations and corporations).

As you read information on each funder, you see few, if any, funders want to receive a grant proposal without any warning from the applicant. For many, you need to, in a sense, be invited to submit a full grant request after you've met each funder's initial contact requirements. That's why your *initial approach* (your first contact with the funder) is so important.

Review each funder's initial approach preference using their website or funding database subscription to find what *initial contact* or *approach document* they require. In Chapter 6, I tell you how to find private-sector funders and mine the right information. You can find more information regarding these documents in the later section "Using a letter of inquiry."

**REMEMBER**

Focus on finding open or current grant-funding opportunities first. Then you can print out expired notices and contact the grant-making agency to see whether the funding will be available again in the future.

**TIP**

Create a day-to-day work plan to monitor a project that will require multiple funding requests. When you're juggling multiple funders, developing a work plan using a table or spreadsheet format and plotting this information, as I show in Figure 2-2, is a good way to stay organized and on top of everything. Your work plan is an extension of all the details plotted out in your funding plan. The work plan is an ancillary document to track all potential funders for one program. Make sure the funder number listed on your table matches up with the correct grant proposal. Also, as you move through the application process, fill in the last two columns on the right-hand side. In the status column, you can enter: writing scheduled, writing in progress, submitted, and pending decision. For the outcome column, you can fill in funded or rejected when you know.

| Tracking Multiple Potential Funders | | | | | | | |
|---|---|---|---|---|---|---|---|
| Funder | Initial Approach | Deadline | Average Range of Funding | Anticipated Notification Date | Date Submitted | Status | Outcome |
| 1 | E-grant application | Rolling annually | Up to $5,000 | 90 days from submission | | | |
| 2 | Letter proposal | June 15 & December 15 annually | Up to $15,000 | 60 days following deadline | | | |
| 3 | Common Grant Application | April 1 annually | Up to $12,000 | 60 days following deadline | | | |
| 4 | Letter of inquiry | 1st of each month annually | Up to $15,000 | 30 days from submission | | | |
| 5 | Online letter of inquiry | Rolling annually | Up to $25,000 | 90 days from submission | | | |
| 6 | E-grant application | December 31 | Up to $10,000 | 90 days following deadline | | | |
| 7 | E-grant application | April & October | Up to $25,000 | 60 days from submission | | | |
| 8 | E-grant application | Quarterly | Up to $1,000 | 45 days from submission | | | |
| 9 | Letter of inquiry | May 15 annually | Up to $2,500 | 45 days following deadline | | | |
| 10 | Letter of inquiry | Rolling annually | Up to $5,000 | 60 days from submission | | | |

**FIGURE 2-2:** Make a chart to track multiple potential funders for one program.

*Illustration by Ryan Sneed*

## Conducting a federal funding search

Thankfully, the federal government aids your federal funding search with its one-stop grant opportunity information website, Grants.gov (www.grants.gov). Visiting this site is the quickest way to conduct a federal funding search.

After you log on to Grants.gov, click Search Grants. Then type your search terms in the Keyword(s) Search field. Sample keywords include "after school," "capacity building," "rural telecommunications," and "prevention." Your search should produce a list of federal grant opportunity announcements that contain your keyword(s). Simply click each one to read the announcement and determine whether it fits your specific funding needs.

You may want to search Grants.gov on a weekly or monthly basis because the federal government releases new grant opportunity announcements daily (except for federal holidays). Or simply sign up for Grants.gov alerts under Manage Subscriptions (in the upper-right corner of the home page) to get free alerts by email.

## Performing a foundation or corporate funding search

When you're ready to conduct a foundation or corporate funding search, the place to turn to is the Foundation Center (www.foundationcenter.org). This center's publications and online databases provide grant seekers, grant makers, researchers, policymakers, the media, and the general public with up-to-date information on grant funding and other nonprofit-related issues.

Through the Foundation Center's *Foundation Directory Online* you can download profiles of foundations whose interests, priorities, and types of funding support match your funding needs. These profiles include the foundation's address, website, contact person, funding priorities, award range, preferred method of initial approach, and much more. To conduct your search, you can either subscribe to the directory (varying levels of subscriptions are available, beginning at as little as $39.95 per month) or use the Center's website to locate a library near you that has a subscription to the directory.

When you start using the Foundation Center's resources, you see several information fields for entering your keywords. Keep it simple. If you're looking for money to provide housing for the homeless, first search for "housing" and screen the results. For the second search, type in "homeless" and again screen the results, eliminating duplicate funders found in the first search. I use this search approach, and it yields far more potential grant sources than typing in a search string made of two or more words. Be sure to check the box to exclude foundations that don't accept unsolicited grant proposals to save yourself considerable time and disappointment. (Refer to Chapter 6 for more about foundation and corporate grants.)

To find out more about researching foundation or corporate funding sources located outside the United States, visit Fundsnet Services.com's website (http://fundsnetservices.com). It's accessible, free of charge, and has pages of international funders listed.

# Using a letter of inquiry

Many foundations state in their published guidelines that they prefer the initial approach to be a *letter of inquiry*, which is a one- to three-page letter in which you ask about their interest in receiving a full grant proposal from your organization. This letter allows the funder to make sure that what you're requesting is within its area of interest and funding award range. Nowadays, some foundation funders require a brief letter of inquiry because they're overwhelmed with requests for funding and the letter is a way to weed out applicants.

The Foundation Center is one source for linking to foundation websites to view their funding guidelines. Another way is to use your favorite Internet search engine to locate the funder's website. Checking a funder's website provides you with the most current guidelines. You may also find that some foundation funders have online inquiry forms; others request a letter of inquiry. However, not all foundations, particularly smaller local foundations, have websites. If the foundation doesn't have a website, be sure to get in touch with the contact person identified in the Foundation Center's foundation profile.

Utilize the following sentence count suggestions to practice crafting your own Letter of Intent:

>> **All requests for funding must be on grant applicant letterhead.** This presentation gives the funder agency a clear visual affirmation of the applicant organization, its location, and how to contact the applicant in writing, by telephone, or by email.

>> **Call the funder to verify the gender, name, title, and address of the contact person.** After all, to make a professional impression with the letter of inquiry, the contact person's information must be correct.

Verifying contact information is especially important when you're contacting a funder whose first name is gender ambiguous, such as Terry, Pat, or Kim. Find out whether that person is a Ms., Mrs., Mr., or Dr. Respect titles and use them to reach the right person the first time.

>> **In the first two sentences, introduce your organization.** Tell the funding agency who's sending the letter, your nonprofit status, and why. For example:

The Grant Writing Training Foundation is a 501(c)(3) private operating foundation located in Arizona. As director, I am writing to invite your organization to be a financial stakeholder in the foundation's mission to provide affordable training programs.

>> **In the next two to four sentences, plant the seeds for your needs.** Share startling facts and statistics about the problem your organization seeks to address with grant funds:

> Annually, the foundation is approached by approximately 40 small- to mid-size nonprofit organizations that want to host a Grant Writing Boot Camp at their location. The typical potential site host is an intermediary agency like the United Way or the state-level association of nonprofits. Given this discouraging economy, board members, volunteers, and inexperienced staff members at many organizations are all given the task of grant writing; few, if any, have experience and most don't know how to begin this massive technical process.

>> **In one sentence, note how you want the recipient to be involved.** Ask for the funding agency's investment or partnership in your efforts to provide specific programs and services to the target population:

> Our board realizes that the foundation cannot financially afford to accept all invitations for training partnerships; however, with your assistance, we can at least develop a productive training schedule to meet the demand for our programs.

>> **In no more than three sentences, show the funder your plans by writing futuristic global goals.** For the example here, I'd write something like "The foundation's goals are to" and then add the goals.

>> **In no more than seven sentences, sell, tell, and ask directly for help.** For instance, sell the funder on the problem or need that the grant funds will address, tell the story in plain language, and ask for grant-funding support, including the amount of funding needed:

> Other nationally accredited grant-seeking and proposal-writing training programs are often three to five days in length and charge $1,000+ per registrant. Feedback from previous attendees at these types of workshops (survey conducted annually for the past five years by the Foundation) shows that the trainer is reading from a script and unable to answer critical questions on the spot. In addition, the elongated training time frame is not appealing for anyone who has to take a full week off from work at his or her employer's expense. The Grant Writing Training Foundation's two-day Grant Writing Boot Camp is comprehensive, compressed, and internationally accredited by several national grants industry associations . Registrants receive 14 continuing education units, a *Grant Writing For Dummies* reference book, and a notebook full of writing exercises and resources. Our board is asking you to consider underwriting at least 10 Boot Camps next year at a cost of $10,000 each (20 registrants will attend each of the ten two-day sessions free of charge).

>> **In one sentence, ask for technical assistance if the funder can't fund your project.** Some needs your organization identifies may be instructional rather than monetary. For example, you may ask the funder to show you how to do a specific task, and then you can combine that knowledge with the resources that you have:

> If you cannot consider awarding grant funds at this time, the board is asking for technical assistance in connecting with state-level nonprofit associations, councils, and foundations that may be potential site hosts.

>> **In one sentence, show hope in your closing.** Sign off with "Waiting to hear from you," "Hopefully," or some other impactful closing.

>> **In one line of type, make sure the CEO signs the letter of inquiry.** This step shows that the top administrator for your organization is aware of your request for grant funding.

>> **Remember to proofread the letter yourself, as well as have someone else provide input on the content and character of the letter.**

TIP

I include a template for a letter of inquiry at www.dummies.com/go/grant writingfd6e.

## Using a letter of intent

Some government grant-making agencies and a handful of foundations request a *letter of intent* (a document that states you intend to apply for a grant in an open/active funding cycle). Just about all the funders that request a letter of intent have their own specific online format.

Here are some examples of letter of intent formats that various funders require:

>> **Charlotte Community Foundation** (https://charlottecommunity foundation.org/pdfs/sample-LOI.pdf): This foundation requires a very simple one-page letter of intent.

>> **National Science Foundation** (www.nsf.gov/pubs/policydocs/pappguide/nsf08_1/gpg_1.jsp): This quasi-government funding agency provides specific instructions for submitting a letter of intent.

# Chapter 3

# Understanding What It Takes to Get Funded

M ost private and public sector funding sources all have funding-request guidelines for your perusal on the Internet. I urge you to use these guidelines — they're the golden key to opening doors for funding consideration. In this chapter, I help you understand grant-related terms and guide you through how to tell and sell your story to potential funders. (Think of this chapter as a warm-up to the heavy lifting you do when you write your proposal. More about that in Part 4.)

## Delivering the Information Funders Ask For

Potential funding sources for your well-deserved grant award have been trying hard to help grant seekers, including you, understand what they want to read in an award-winning grant proposal. Although the funders' guidelines may vary in how they order the requested information or word the headings/subheadings, in the end they all want to see commonly organized, written presentations of information.

Shift your focus from the excitement of finding grant-funding opportunities for your organization to gearing up to write the following blocks of information:

>> Factual information about your organization and its qualifications

>> Compelling information about the specific project for which you're seeking funding

>> Planning-savvy narrative about what you intend to do with the money if you receive it

As you read through each section of the funder's guidelines, make sure you understand how the funder defines its terms. You need to consider whether you can interpret what it's asking for in more than one way in order to avoid accidentally giving the wrong info.

TIP

What do you do if you don't understand what the funder really wants? Make a call or send an email, of course. When in doubt, ask! When confused, ask!

In the following sections, I review the basic facts you're required to provide on most grant applications. I also give you an overview of the project details funders expect you to provide, and I offer suggestions on how to win over the application reviewers, also known as decision makers. After all, you do want to get funded, right?

## Providing the facts about your organization

Any funding source you approach will have questions about the grant applicant organization's legal name and structure, such as nonprofit, *unit of government* (village, town, township, city, county, or state government agency), association, or membership-based organization. Although the wording may vary slightly from one application to another, the cover documents (if applicable) and narratives of grant applications generally ask for the same basic information. Understanding exactly what the application is asking for and knowing how to reply in the right language is critical.

REMEMBER

Don't hesitate to call the funding source for assistance if you have questions about any portion of the application. Asking a funder for help won't hurt your chances of getting a grant. In fact, doing so may even help because you're filling out forms in the best possible way. Calling or emailing with queries is another way to connect on a higher level with potential funder communications.

If you're trying to enter your responses into an online electronic (e-grant) application, pay special attention to any word, character, or space limitations and stay within those limits. Also, don't try to copy and paste any graphics or other non-transferable formatting like bullets, underlining, italics, or bold font from Microsoft Word to an e-grant application template. I tell you more about e-grants in Chapter 22.

The basic applicant information requested by all funders includes the following:

>> **Legal name of the grant applicant:** Be sure to list your organization's *legal* name here. For charitable organizations, associations, and foundations, the legal name is the one that appears on the organization's IRS 501(c)(3) or 501(c)(6) letter of nonprofit determination. (If you're not sure, 501(c)(3) is the charitable designation, and 501(c)(6) is the association or membership designation.) For cities, townships, villages, county units of government, and public schools, which have a different classification of nonprofit status, the legal name is the incorporated name.

>> **Type of grant applicant:** Check the box that best describes your organization's forming structure. For example, you can choose from state agency, county, municipal, township, interstate, intermunicipal, special district, independent school district, public college or university, Native American tribe, nonprofit, individual, private, profit-making organization, and other (which you have to specify).

Is your organization a type of applicant that isn't eligible? Search for a partner (government agency or nonprofit) that can be the lead grant application responder. Doing so gets dollars into the front door of your organization because you're incorporated into the funding request as a subcontracting partner.

>> **Year the grant applicant organization was founded:** Enter the year your organization was incorporated or created. Often, the year of incorporation differs from the creation date because many nonprofit founders start providing programs and services first and seek incorporation several years later. You need to explain any such discrepancy in your opening narrative, which is the background/history narrative section.

>> **Current grant applicant operating budget:** Supply the organization's 12-month operating budget total for the current fiscal year. Note that some funders also request the operating budget for the time period that the grant would cover. Always comply with whatever information is requested.

When it comes to money, be sure to supply information that portrays the truth and nothing but the truth.

>> **Grant applicant organization's employer identification number (EIN) or taxpayer identification number (TIN):** This portion of the form asks for the seven-digit EIN/TIN assigned to your organization by the IRS. The EIN/TIN is also called a *taxpayer reporting number*. You can find the EIN/TIN on your IRS letter of nonprofit determination or by calling your organization's financial person/department.

>> **Grant applicant organization's fiscal year:** Indicate the 12-month time frame that your organization considers to be its operating, or *fiscal,* year. The fiscal year is defined by the organization's bylaws and can correspond with the calendar year or some other period, such as July 1 to June 30.

>> **Grant applicant organization's contact person information:** Name the primary contact in your organization for grant or cooperative agreement negotiations, questions, and written correspondence. This person should be your executive director, board of directors' president, or program director — not the grant writer. Why? Because you, the grant writer, have no legal or financial authority to act as the contact person. Communications clearly need to be with the governing body or the authorized executive-level staff.

>> **Grant applicant organization's address:** Provide the current street and/or mailing address for the applicant organization.

**WARNING**

Potential funders view a post office box address as a red flag because these addresses tend to be used by grassroots nonprofits and fly-by-night (here today, gone tomorrow) grant applicants. Stick with a street address on your grant application.

>> **Grant applicant organization's telephone/fax/email information:** List the contact person's telephone and fax numbers (with area code) as well as an email address.

>> **Grant applicant organization's website address:** Organizations seeking grant funds are wise to have a website that funders can refer to that includes an overview of the organization.

If you're applying to a federal funder, you also need to provide the following information:

>> **D-U-N-S number:** Federal grant-making agencies require that all grant applicants have a D-U-N-S number that lets others more easily recognize and learn about their organizations. The *D-U-N-S number* is a nine-digit identification sequence that provides a unique identifier of a single business entity while linking corporate family structures together. You can register for a unique D-U-N-S number by visiting the Grants.gov website (www.grants.gov/web/grants/applicants/organization-registration/step-1-obtain-duns-number.html) and following the on-screen instructions.

You'll need to register with SAMS.gov to have your DUNS fully integrated for government grant identification purposes.

>> **Grant applicant's congressional districts:** On a federal grant application, you need to list all the congressional districts in which your organization is located and your grant-funded services will be implemented. You can get this information by calling the public library or surfing the Internet to locate your legislator's website, which will contain his or her district numbers.

Knowing and developing ties with representatives in Washington, DC, and at your state capital is critical. You always need friends in high places. (See Chapter 4 for more on connecting to government officials.)

## Writing about the project in need of funding

Filling in all the blanks on paper or electronic grant application and cooperative agreement cover forms and budget forms is critical. Leaving any field related to applicant agency and project details blank makes you look nonresponsive, and this impression alone may stop a reviewer from reading your document any further.

Luckily, most electronic grants and letters of inquiry are programmed to alert you to missing information and won't let you upload the document until you supply the missing information. Just in case, though, I use the following sections to highlight the blanks you must pay particular attention to so the reviewer doesn't lose interest in your organization.

### Project name

List your project name on the cover letter, the cover form, and any other funder-requested documents. A project name enhances the storytelling (personalized) approach necessary in today's highly competitive grant-seeking arena.

Project names should be memorable, but stay away from long names. Here's a great example for a project name: Project CII–PHTR. What does it stand for? Changing the Insurance Industry–Physicians for Holistic Treatment Reimbursements. And that's just one possibility. Whatever you do, use your imagination and don't use a name that translates into an offensive abbreviation or acronym.

### Organization mission

When funders ask for the grant applicant organization's mission statement, they want to see the vision-driving string of words that communicates to the world your organization's purpose. Be sure to limit your mission statement to a single sentence or a very brief paragraph.

## Purpose of the request

Compose a short, one-sentence statement about why you're approaching this particular funding source. Does its mission align with your organization's? Has it funded your organization previously? For example, "The purpose of this request is to seek your initial and ongoing funding for Project CII–PHTR (Changing the Insurance Industry–Physicians for Holistic Treatment Reimbursements)."

## Give dates for the project

Provide the proposed starting and ending dates of the project. You don't have to figure exact days; just express the project dates according to month and year. Don't forget to give the project a start date that's at least six months into the future; funders need time to review and make decisions about who receives grant awards. Many funders specify when (month/year) they anticipate announcing awards. If a time frame is specified in the application materials, target your start date to correspond with it.

## Amount requested

Enter the amount you're requesting from the funder (round off to the nearest dollar). *Tip:* Do your homework by reading the funder's instructions — they usually contain a funding range minimum and maximum along with the grant award amount number. For example, "In order to implement and expand this new holistic treatment reimbursement initiative, the American Holistic Care Providers Network is seeking $100,000."

## Total project cost

Include the total cost of the proposed project. Double- and triple-check to make sure the number you enter here matches the total cost of the project listed in the budget narrative and on the budget forms. (For more about budgets, check out Chapter 17.) For example, "The total project cost is $100,000."

## Geographic area served

Describe the location of your project in this order: city, county, state. You can even narrow your target population area down to census tract numbers, specific names of neighborhoods, or congressional districts. (Some funding is designated for specific geographic regions within a state.) For example, "The geographic area to be served includes 48 states and 6 territories. The census tracts impacted are listed in Attachment 1."

## Signatures

Practically all federal government applications are submitted online now through one of the feds' e-grant portals, Grants.gov, so you type the requested contact information for the authorized contact person for your organization into a signature field box instead of submitting an original signature. Even foundations and corporations are using typed names for e-grant signature boxes.

TIP

If you end up submitting a paper/hard copy of your grant application (which will likely only happen with state agencies and foundations that have not embraced e-grant technology), all signatures should be in blue ink. Using this color makes differentiating the original document from the copied documents easy for the funder.

# Telling your project's story

Over the years, the field of grant writing has shifted from technical "just the facts and nothing more" writing to a kinder, friendlier way of cozying up to the grant maker's decision-making staff. Now, if you want to secure a grant, you must put life, personality, and compassion into your request. This type of writing approach is referred to as *storytelling*.

TIP

Here, I give you some great tips on the type of information to include in each section of your funding request and how to turn the ordinary into the extraordinary in each narrative section you're likely to see in any funder's grant application format (I provide more in-depth advice and examples for these narrative sections in Part 4):

>> **Background/history of the grant applicant organization:** Write with passion about your organization: its founding date, its purpose, its mission, and its location. Include quaint, not-so-common information about the founder and his reason for creating a nonprofit organization.

If you're writing about a unit of municipal government (city, town, township, village, hamlet, or county subdivision of government), include trivia on how the community was named, started, incorporated, and so forth. Also, include information on any major grant-topic-related accomplishments the grant applicant organization has achieved.

>> **Current programs and activities:** Write with excitement about the current initiatives the grant applicant organization is involved in. List in chronological order all the organization's programs and activities.

Include specific program names, dates started, and outcomes-to-date, such as the number of participants who have received services and the benefits they gained because of their involvement in the program.

>> **Description/demographics of your constituency:** Write with accuracy about the population the grant applicant organization provides services to. Include age range, gender, ethnicity, economic status, educational level, and other characteristic descriptors. The funder needs to know whom you serve and what's special about your target population.

Include a *case scenario*, a story about how a participant has encountered multiple life barriers and is now on a waiting list to be served by the grant applicant organization.

>> **Description of community:** Write with innate knowledge about your community's makeup where the grant applicant organization is located or where its services will be provided. Describe the community by providing a combination of city and county information. This section is about the virtual picture of your community — facts and statistics — not trivia, which belongs in the background section.

Use compelling words and colorful (but true!) descriptions; funders don't want to read a book report about your town. Don't just copy and paste census information from the Internet. Where you do use statistics, incorporate them into tables, graphics, and figures.

Cite your sources, and don't use statistics that are more than five years old. Copying and pasting information you find on the Internet is okay as long as you include a reference citation (footnote by copying the website address where you found the information). Just make sure your online sources are reliable.

>> **Description of work with partnership agencies:** Write about the grant applicant organization's demonstrated partnership experiences with community, regional, state, and national partners. Create a table with header rows for partners and their roles with the grant applicant organization. You can even add a third column to the table for years of affiliation.

**REMEMBER**

You can't copy and paste tables or other graphics into online e-grant templates. You can only include them if the funder allows you to upload Microsoft Word files or PDFs. Chapter 22 includes more tips on e-grants.

Add shading to the table's header row and to each column. Just be sure to keep it legible and not distracting.

>> **Proposed initiative:** Write with certainty about what the grant applicant organization plans to do with the grant or cooperative agreement award. State the intentions simply and directly in one or two sentences.

Write something like "The purpose of this request is to secure the necessary financial infusion to change the lives of 300 or more chronically unemployed individuals who have long given up hope for ever securing gainful employment."

>> **Statement of need:** Write with compassion about the problem the grant applicant organization will combat with the awarded funds.

Use gripping words to relay the gloom, doom, drama, and trauma of your situation and why your organization needs the requested funds. Be honest, cite hard data that demonstrates your need, and don't just use anecdotal observations.

>> **Program design/plan of action:** Write with the knowledge of demonstrated best practices about the process you'll implement to solve the problem or need. Incorporate evidence-based practices (proven intervention/prevention best practices models, which you can find on the Internet); by doing so, you demonstrate to the funder that you're relying on proven research to design your program. You let the funder know that you've taken steps to avoid reinventing the wheel. (No funder wants to pay for a clueless process of discovery when the intervention process has been perfected elsewhere.)

- **Goals:** In futuristic and global terms, create numbered project goals.

  Detail where the target population will be when the grant funds have been expended.

- **SMART objectives:** These **s**pecific, **m**easurable, **a**ttainable, **r**ealistic, and **t**imebound objectives show the funder how you'll measure the program's success.

  Write percentage-driven benchmarks for your target population or program that are achievable within the grant period (including annual benchmarks for multiyear requests).

- **Activities/strategies:** Write about the proposed activities, tasks, or strategies you'll implement to reach your goals.

  Put this information into table format and shade each row and column differently (but don't use too many colors).

- **Timeline:** Incorporate target dates for your objectives and activities/strategies. Note when the objectives will happen and when the activities will start and end. A timeline presented in a table looks great to readers. This timeline chart or table is often referred to as a *Gantt* or *implementation chart*. When the applications indicate required elements in the timeline, be sure to include every required element in your final timeline chart.

  Shade your rows and columns.

- **Impact on problem:** Write about how the grant applicant organization's proposed action will reduce the problems discussed in the statement of need.

  Note how similar interventions or preventions in other locales demonstrated impact and resolution of the problem(s).

- **Project significance:** Write about the impact the grant applicant organization's project will have on the target population from a wide viewpoint.

  Write this section in italics. When you incorporate italics, you're speaking more directly to the grant reader/decision maker. Project significance can be stated in a brief paragraph.

- **Systemic change:** Write about how the program the grant applicant organization plans to develop with funding support will positively change society or improve rigid and antiquated systems.

  Use futuristic, hopeful language.

- **Performance evaluation plan:** Write about who will conduct the performance evaluation, what it will cover, and the time frame for evaluation activities. Keep in mind that the collection of frequent and unbiased feedback from members of the grant's target population is critical to an accurate performance evaluation.

  Create tables that incorporate the previously written SMART objectives (see the earlier bullet) and how they will be measured.

- **Dissemination of evaluation findings:** Write about who will receive a copy of the evaluation findings. Dissemination of evaluation materials is important for reporting to current funders and can sway future funding sources when you attach them to grant applications and cooperative agreements.

  Propose to disseminate findings beyond your local areas. For example, present the findings at a national conference or regional round table where other organizations will benefit from your experiences and results.

>> **Key personnel/staffing:** Write with familiarity about the staff, contracted consultants, and volunteers needed to carry out the program or project. For each position, indicate what percentage of the person's time will be allocated to the project and which budget — cash match, in-kind, or requested — his salary will come from. (*Cash match* refers to cash your organization has available to allocate to the grant-funded program, when funded.)

Format position titles and time allocated to the projects in bold.

>> **Management plan/organizational structure/administration:** Write with confidence about who will report to whom and where the built-in assurances of administrative and financial responsibility will be established. Be sure to add your financial staff to the management plan. Funders want to see that your organization has strong financial accounting and stewardship practices in place.

Incorporate this information into a table.

>> **Sustainability:** Write with accountability about how the grant applicant organization will continue some or most of the grant-funded program components after the initial grant-funding time frame has ended.

Tell funders about the funding plan your board of directors and administrative staff or development office staff have in place. Let them know that you'll be working hard to identify continuation funding for their starting grant investments.

>> **Adequacy of resources:** Write with confirmation about any financial, physical, and personnel resources the grant applicant organization already owns or has access to that can be used for program activities.

Bullet the resources list.

# Providing the Required Documents

Virtually all grant applications require a few standard *attachments* that provide additional information about the grant applicant organization. These attachments follow the grant or cooperative agreement narrative. The following list outlines some of the things you'll likely attach to your grant request. Keep in mind that each funder has its own instructions on how to order these attachments, so the order here isn't necessarily standard.

WARNING

Funders are often very specific with regard to attachments. Many accept only the attachments they specifically list. If the funding source's guidelines indicate that the funder accepts no attachments or that submitting any material besides the grant application results in the application not being reviewed, omit the standard attachments covered in this list:

>> **Budget summary/cost summary:** Fill in the blanks on a standard worksheet listing line items and expense amounts as required by the grant guidelines or directions. (Head to Chapter 17 for more about budgets and financial stuff.)

>> **Budget detail/budget narrative/cost justification:** Write a detailed narrative on each proposed expense.

>> **Up-to-date financial statement:** Attach a copy of the grant applicant organization's most recent financial statement. Whether audited or unaudited, the financial statement should explain any findings of concern.

>> **Proof of tax-exempt status (if applicable):** Proof is a copy of the grant applicant organization's 501(c)(3) letter of nonprofit determination from the IRS, with the date on which a certifying agency recognized the status.

>> **Board of directors with affiliations:** This attachment lists the names and board positions of the organization's governing body along with their position within the community (board of directors, city council members, village trustees, and so on). This document also should mention the lengths of their board terms and amount of time remaining to be served.

>> **Letters of commitment:** A *letter of commitment* comes from a partner organization and states that the partner is committed to providing leveraging assets to your grant-funded program when funded. Partner organizations can commit to providing cash, facilities, technical assistance, equipment, supplies and materials, or loaned staff. Ask for letters of commitment from affiliates early in the writing process, and include at least three such letters with all grant applications you send out.

>> **Memorandum of Agreement (MOA) and Memoranda of Understanding (MOU):** The names for these requested documents can be interchangeable depending on the type of funding agency. Typically, they're multipage formal contracts between the grant applicant and its program implementation partners. These documents detail the role of each party in the agreement and include their specific committed tasks when the funding is awarded.

>> **Annual report:** Include an annual report (brochure, booklet, or newsletter).

>> **Other documentation:** Submit one-page summaries or complete résumés of key program personnel, as the funding source prefers. Also, if your organization has memorandums of agreement or memorandums of understanding signed by partner or collaborating agencies, attach these documents last. (Go to Chapter 9 for more information on these documents.)

# 2

# Digging Up Grant-Funding Opportunities

**IN THIS PART . . .**

Begin your search for public sector funds with your local or state government. Aim for bigger bucks by applying for funds from one of the 26 federal grant-making agencies. Create a grant-funding plan.

Become best friends with the main federal e-grant portal, Grants.gov, in order to find critical funding opportunities and submit applications.

Browse online grant databases to identify private-sector funding opportunities and figure out whether your organization fits a funder's organizational, geographic, and programming criteria so you don't pursue an opportunity that's not realistic.

Understand the types of individual and for-profit business grants available. Dispel infomercial-based myths, and discover what's really out there for you or your organization.

Locate the grants set aside for organizations that provide programs and/or services outside the United States, and follow the rules of the international funder you're applying to.

Know what funders expect to read in your funding requests.

Chapter 4

# Wading into Public-Sector Grants

L et me set the record straight when it comes to government money: There is no such thing as a "free" grant. Every grant award comes with strings attached. Either you have to spend your own money first (reimbursement grant) and submit receipts to actually get grant funds, or you have to file reams of electronic paperwork to generate an electronic funds transfer into your organization's bank account.

In this chapter, I take you on a journey down the government's grant-making highway, which starts in Congress and ends in your state, county, town, village, or city. I also reveal how to get your elected officials to support your grant-seeking efforts.

## Researching Local Funding First

Washington, DC, is a funding epicenter for US government grant-making agencies. Congress creates legislation and then votes to allocate funding to hundreds of grant-making programs annually. This funding then trickles down to your state capital. (Note that there are plentiful opportunities for nonprofits and units of local government to apply directly to a federal funding agency for a grant.)

Federal dollars trickle down in three forms:

» **Formula:** This money is paid based on a preset head-count (enrollments and population) formula.

» **Entitlement:** State agencies get these monies because federal legislation entitles them to receive it every fiscal year.

An entitlement grant is one in which funds are provided to specific grantees on the basis of a formula, prescribed in legislation or regulation, rather than on the basis of an individual project. The formula is usually based on such factors as population, enrollment, per-capita income, or a specific need. Entitlement grants often result in pass-through grants to municipalities and nonprofits.

» **Competitive grant or cooperative agreement awards:** The state, munici-pality, nonprofit, or other grant applicant with the best grant application wins this money.

Some states post all the state funding and re-granting announcement links on one website. (*Re-granting* refers to grants made from the monies a state has received from the federal government.) In addition, some states develop their own grant programs funded entirely through state dollars. If you're fortunate enough to live in a state that does so, check out the relevant website for a mailing list. You may be able to sign up for email grant notice alerts from the agencies. However, most states don't post these announcements, so you have to be a really great Internet detective to find the monies in your state (not to mention in Washington, DC). You need to surf a bit each day to catch all the new postings for grant-funding opportunities. When I'm searching for state grants in Arkansas, I use Google and type in **grants, state of Arkansas agencies**. The results are a list of state agencies in Arkansas that have grant-funding opportunities posted on their websites.

**REMEMBER**

Most state grants usually award less money and require just as much paperwork as federal grants. But the odds of winning a grant are better at the state level than at the federal level. It's a no-brainer: The main reason you face better odds is that fewer grant applicants are competing for the state-level monies.

The next sections reveal how to find grant monies available at the state and local government levels.

## Finding out where the money is in your state

To find grant opportunities at the state level:

>> **Visit your state government's website.** Use a search engine, such as Bing or Google, if you need help locating the address. If you search the state site and can't find a listing of all the state's grant opportunities, call the governor's office and ask to be directed to the various agencies that give grants. Only track grant-funding opportunities from the agency that administers the federal programming for the type of funding that your organization is seeking. For example, a charter school will track state Department of Education grant alerts. A substance abuse prevention agency will track state Department of Health and/or Human Services grant alerts.

>> **Email or call each appropriate state agency.** Contact the agencies responsible for carrying out legislative funding mandates relevant to your own funding needs and be sure to get on their mailing lists for grant-funding opportunity alerts.

When you receive an alert about a state grant-funding opportunity you're interested in applying for, look for the website link that connects you to the grant application summary and download. Download the complete grant application (including guidelines) and look for the following information:

>> **Type of application:** Is it an electronic or a print application? For example, over 50 percent of grant applications are submitted electronically via online e-grant portals; some state agencies can still only accept hard copies.

>> **Due date:** Make sure the due date is manageable and gives you enough time to collect topic-related information and write the application. A reasonable amount of time is 30 days from the date the grant-funding announcement is published or issued via email and the actual due date of the application.

>> **Who's eligible to apply:** Every grant competition has a section listing the types of grant applicants eligible to apply for funds (Chapter 1 gives you a list of eligible grant applicants). If your organization's forming structure (local education agency, nonprofit, and so forth) isn't listed, consider partnering with an eligible applicant. (Head to Chapter 9 for more on finding the right grant-seeking partners.) You may also want to contact the funding agency to clarify any non-published eligible applicants because your organization may be eligible to apply after all.

>> **The number of grants to be awarded:** You may have to call the funding agency's contact person to find out the number of available grants; this information often isn't included in state grant application guidelines.

**TIP**

Unless you're the only organization delivering highly specialized services/programs and have no competitors, don't apply for competitive grant funds where fewer than three awards will be made statewide. The fewer the number of grant awards, the worse the odds are for winning an award.

All grant applicants have a fair chance of winning a state agency grant award if a sufficient number of awards are available. I always ask how many grants will be awarded so I know how many ways the money will be divided. This information helps me develop a more competitive project budget — staying conservative and on the low end of the average grant range. (Browse Chapter 17 for pointers on putting together a winning budget section in your grant or cooperative agreement proposal.)

## Looking for pass-through funding

At the local government level (county, town, village, township, hamlet, and city), look for public monies at the County Board of Commissioners, local Area Agencies on Aging, the Mayor's Office on Neighborhoods (or a similar Federal Community Development Block Grant administrator), regional housing authorities (they sub-grant for neighborhood-based services), your county-based department of social services, and more. All these agencies receive direct funding from state agencies and federal pass-through funding for re-granting purposes at the local level (more on pass-through funding in the following section).

TIP

Because not all funding opportunities are posted on websites that are easy to find, you want to develop connections with agency representatives to find out the inside scoop. Also, ask questions of local elected officials and track down these publicly available grant funds. Be aggressive in asking questions about what funds are available, who can apply, and who the contract person is for the agency re-granting the monies.

# Analyzing the Types of Federal Funding Available

Federal government grant monies come in two forms:

>> **Direct grants:** You apply directly to the federal government. There is no intermediary agency.

>> **Pass-through grants:** Your state applies to the federal government for a grant. After receiving the grant, the state then passes the federal monies on to applicants.

REMEMBER

Pass-through monies are still considered federal monies even though they're distributed by state agencies.

Whether in the form of direct or pass-through grants, federal monies are also classified as either *competitive* or *formula.*

In this section, I give you the scoop on the pros and cons of direct and pass-through grants, and I share the details you need to know about competitive and formula grants. *Note:* Some of the terms in this section may seem to overlap with the kinds of allocations listed earlier in the chapter, but that's just because the government ran out of unique names to use (that's my theory and I'm sticking to it). The grants in this section are different entities from those earlier terms.

## Discovering direct grants

The advantages to applying for a direct grant award or *cooperative agreement,* which comes straight from the federal government, include the following:

>> **Direct grants have no middlemen and none of the extra layers of red tape needed by intermediary grant-making agencies.** You apply directly to the federal government for a grant in response to an announcement of the availability of funds.

>> **When you compete for a direct grant, you communicate directly with a program officer in a division of a federal agency.** This interaction means one-on-one attention, so be sure to review the application guidelines thoroughly and then compile all your questions. You can email or call the grant-making agency's contact person for clarification and answers. Doing so upfront clears the way for the topic research and the grant-writing process.

REMEMBER

Avoid being a nuisance! Don't call and make small talk. Have your questions ready before approaching the agency contact, and ask if the individual prefers to have questions emailed. Be prepared to take copious notes. If you feel you still lack a clear answer about how to proceed, ask again.

Some federal agencies have a deadline for submitting questions via email or by phone; read the grant application guidelines to make sure you can still make the call or email contact. If the window has passed, look at the agency's website for a link to frequently asked questions (FAQs). Others have probably asked the same questions you have, and the agency may have posted the answer for the general public to review. Also, remember to check daily for modifications to the initially posted grant applications guidelines.

TIP

You can sign up for Grants.gov modification notifications via RSS to get these updates automatically. On Grants.gov, scroll to the bottom of the home page and click RSS to get instructions on how to add a feed add-in to your web browser and how to get updates on the funding program you're tracking. Everything you're writing in the application narrative can change with one modification posting.

**TIP**

Many federal agencies host a technical assistance call or webcast in which potential applicants can participate. In this forum, program staff members responsible for the grant application typically provide an overview of the application notice, highlighting key points of information, and then open the call to questions from potential applicants. These discussions provide a great opportunity to hear from program officers, ask questions, and learn from the questions of other applicants. You can find the date, time, and access information for any planned call/webcast in the Notice of Funding Availability (NOFA) announcement, Request for Proposal (RFP), Funding Opportunity Announcement (FOA), or Request for Application (RFA), as well as on the funding agency's program-specific website. It's important to participate in these webinars to hear the full scope of what's expected in a grant application recommended for funding.

**WARNING**

The one major disadvantage to applying for a direct grant award is that they're tough to win. You compete with other grant applicants from the 50 states and all the US territories. If the feds are only planning to award money to ten grant applicants, your chances are slim — even with a stellar funding request. You may even be competing with state agencies, which further narrows your chances. Urban and rural poverty pockets receive first priority for most social-services-related program funding (such as housing, education, and health and human services) and other grant-making areas earmarked for social-issue hot spots. If you aren't proposing services in one of these high-needs geographic funding areas, your chances of winning a federal grant from a competition that gives 5 to 25 extra review points to high-needs, census-data-supported geographic areas are reduced to almost nothing. Not all funding programs have these types of service priorities.

## Using the eligible applicant criteria to track the funding stream

Pass-through grants have two advantages:

>> **When you apply for pass-through grant funds at the state level, you compete against other grant applicants in your state only.** As a result, you encounter considerably less competition than at the federal, direct grant-seeking level.

>> **When you're making an appearance before the state agency program staff, you can get info on previously funded grants.** Under the Freedom of Information Act (FOIA), all government agencies must provide requested public information to the requestor (you, the public), so don't feel like you're being a bother. Make sure the list contains the grant recipients and award amounts.

And ask for a copy of a successful grant application from a previous competition. Knowing how winners write can boost your chances.

You can actually use the FOIA to obtain information about all types of grants funded by any government agency.

The only disadvantage to applying for pass-through grants is that the grant awards are often smaller than those for a direct grant. The legislation determines the award allocation. So, it's a trade-off: Pass-through awards are smaller, but they're also easier to win.

Pass-through grant awards can be significantly smaller than direct grant awards because the state takes money off the top of each federal grant to cover administrative costs. Then the amount that's left must be divided geographically and politically. For example, grants may go to certain areas of a state because those areas haven't won many grant awards recently. The money may go to other areas because that district's state senator or representative has a lot of power and influence with a state agency. Like it or not, politics can have a major influence over grant making.

## Knowing the difference between competitive and formula grants

To win a *competitive grant* or cooperative agreement, you must compete with other grant applicants for a limited amount of money. A team of *peer reviewers* (experts and laypeople who apply to read and score grant applications) looks at your application and decides how many points you receive for each narrative section in the body of the grant request. The applications with the highest scores are recommended for funding. (See Chapter 10 for details on the peer review process for grant applications.)

A *formula grant* (a fill-in-the-blanks, no-brainer form), on the other hand, is money disbursed by a state agency or municipality to a grant applicant based on a preset standard or formula.

A great example of formula monies is a grant program administered by the US Department of Justice. The Justice Assistance Grant (JAG) Program (not to be confused with the military's Judge Advocate General Program) is the leading source of federal justice funding to state and local jurisdictions. The program provides monies to states, tribes, and local governments, which they in turn use to support program areas including law enforcement, prosecution and courts, prevention and education, corrections and community corrections, drug treatment and enforcement, planning, evaluation, technology improvement, and crime victim and witness programs. All JAG allocations are calculated by the Bureau of Justice Statistics (BJS) based on the statutory JAG formula and displayed on the JAG website each fiscal year.

# Scanning the Catalog of Federal Domestic Assistance Correctly

You can find all sorts of information about where the money is and what it can be used for in the *Catalog of Federal Domestic Assistance* (CFDA). The CFDA, found at www.cfda.gov, provides a full listing of all federal programs available to state and local governments (including the District of Columbia); federally recognized Indian tribal governments; territories (and possessions) of the United States; US-based public, quasi-public, and private for-profit and nonprofit organizations and institutions; specialized groups; and individuals. The following sections get you acquainted with the information the CFDA does — and doesn't — supply.

REMEMBER

When you're looking for federal programs in the CFDA, zero in on programs that award project grants — the most plentiful category for local, regional, and national grant seekers. A *project grant* is funding for a specific period of time. These grant funds must be used to deliver the specific services outlined in the grant application narrative. Project grants include fellowships, scholarships, research grants, training grants, traineeships, service grants (to address needs of specific populations such as the homeless, adolescent parents, and so on), experimental and demonstration grants, evaluation grants, planning grants, technical assistance grants, survey grants, construction grants, and unsolicited contractual agreements.

Also, pay attention to the actual amount of dollars allocated for the most current fiscal year. If the current fiscal year's allocation is ($0), contact the program officer to find out if this grant will be available in the next fiscal year.

## Understanding static information and its use

The CFDA contains detailed program descriptions for 2,322 federal assistance programs administered by 69 federal agencies. Because not all the agencies are grant-making agencies, this section focuses only on the federal grant-making agencies:

**REMEMBER**

Federal agencies can have numerous grant-making offices within them. Start at each agency's website homepage to find lists or links to each of their grant-making divisions.

>> Agency for International Development

>> Corporation for National and Community Services

>> Delta Regional Authority

>> Department of Agriculture

>> Department of Commerce

>> Department of Defense

>> Department of Education

>> Department of Energy

>> Department of Health and Human Services

>> Department of Homeland Security

>> Department of Housing and Urban Development

>> Department of the Interior

>> Department of Justice

>> Department of Labor

>> Department of State

>> Department of Transportation

>> Department of Veteran Affairs

>> Environmental Protection Agency

>> Institute of Library and Museum Services

>> National Aeronautics and Space Administration

>> National Archives and Records Administration

>> National Endowment for the Arts

>> National Endowment for the Humanities

>> National Science Foundation

>> Small Business Administration

The entry for each federal program in the CFDA includes general information on the

>> Federal agency administering the program

>> Five-digit code that identifies the federal grant-making agency and subagency distributing the grant or cooperative agreement funds

>> Authorization upon which the program is based (the federal legislation that created the program)

>> Objectives and goals of the program

>> Types of assistance offered under a program

>> Uses and use restrictions placed upon a program

>> Eligibility requirements (explains applicant eligibility, beneficiary eligibility, and credentials/documentation required)

>> Application and award process (describes requirements for pre-application coordination, application procedures, award procedure, deadlines, range of approval/disapproval time, appeals, and renewals)

>> Assistance considerations (tells you whether there are formula or matching requirements and length/time phasing of assistance)

>> Post assistance requirements (gives you general expectations for grantee reports and audits, and for maintaining financial records)

>> Financial information (tells you the amount of *obligations* — how much money Congress allocated to this program — for the past, current, and future fiscal years; the federal fiscal year starts October 1 and ends September 30) and estimated average award sizes

>> Program accomplishments (generic history of what this federal program has done recently to fulfill its mission)

>> Regulations, guidelines, and literature relevant to a program

>> Information contacts at the headquarters and regional and local offices, and the federal website address for the grant-making agency

>> Related programs based upon program objectives and uses (helps you find other federal programs that award grants in your project's area)

>> Examples of funded projects (look for funded projects that sound like the project you're seeking grant monies for)

>> Criteria for selecting proposals

## Recognizing what's missing and where to find it

**REMEMBER**

The CFDA is static (published annually) and is not the go-to source for current grant-funding announcements. After you look through the CFDA to identify grants you're interested in applying for, you can subscribe to grant announcement alerts, by agency or keyword, published online at www.grants.gov or an online government grant research database. Grants.gov is where you can view the actual grant opportunity announcement, which lists the estimated number of awards and estimated average award size.

Also, note that the CDFA doesn't give specific deadlines for any grant-making agencies. All specific information, such as grant deadlines, is posted in the grant opportunity announcement.

# Orienting Yourself to Grants.gov

Every day you can receive a free email alert from Grants.gov announcing grant-funding opportunities from any of the federal grant-making agencies. Just log on and subscribe. Simply choose one or more agencies and wait 24 hours to start cruising through the daily list of federal grant announcements.

Here's how Grants.gov can help you find federal grant monies for your organization:

>> **You can search, on your own, for current and past grant-funding opportunities.** Log on daily and check for postings in your area of interest. A subject search (for example, "housing," "legal services," or "after-school programs") is the easiest way to narrow down specific grant competitions in your project or program area. I like to use the Newest Opportunities tab on the homepage. It allows you to double-check for federal funding availability alerts you may have missed.

>> **You can register for notification of grant opportunities.** Subscribe to a daily email alert. Look for the Manage Subscriptions link at the upper right of the homepage.

>> **You can browse through the APPLICANTS tab (at the top of the homepage) to look at all sorts of materials.** For example, you can apply for grants, track your application, or click one of the resource links for grant eligibility, individual and organization registrations, applicant tools and tips, applicant FAQs, Adobe software compatibility, submitting special characters in submissions, and encountering error messages.

You can also apply for grants directly through Grants.gov after you've reviewed the Apply for Grants link under the Applicants tab and completed the registration process. *Remember:* You must be registered in order to upload your grant application documents.

After registering, you can do the following:

>> **Prepare to apply for grants.** Click the link provided for a grant and read the full announcement. If it fits your organization, you can download the grant application package.

>> **Access active grant application packages.** In addition to the required forms, you can also access lists of FAQs regarding each grant. Usually, these questions originate at the funding agency's technical assistance call or webcast (see the earlier section "Discovering direct grants" for more on these discussions).

>> **Download, complete, and submit grant application packages online through the e-grant system portal.** Grants.gov gives you links to download the grant application forms or complete the forms online. You can also submit your entire grant application online, including uploading your narrative and attachments in the requested formats.

>> **Check the status of an application submitted via Grants.gov.** After you submit your grant application package, you can check back frequently to see whether your request has been accepted or rejected.

For more on federal grant application kits, turn to Chapter 5.

# Enlisting Political Advocates

Searching or applying for federal grant monies without emailing or calling staff at your elected legislators' offices doesn't make much sense. Getting to know these critical contacts on Capitol Hill and in your state capital can make the difference between finding out about funding opportunities before NOFAs are published and hearing about them with everyone else. Time is always of the essence, so why not get some strong-armed advocacy from your elected representatives?

TIP

After you've called your elected officials' office(s), ask their staff members to

>> **Keep you posted on future grant opportunities (no matter what your funding status is):** Get in the information loop for state and federal monies.

>> **Look for discretionary grant award opportunities near the end of the state or federal fiscal year:** Some states' fiscal years end June 30; others end September 30. The federal fiscal year ends on September 30. At these times, leftover monies are quickly dispensed before they have to be returned to the state legislatures or to Congress.

Representatives are elected to serve on your behalf in the national and state capitals, so use your leverage. Make a telephone call or send an email to the local or regional office for your state's congressional legislators. During your initial phone call or email, ask for a meeting or simply state your funding needs. Tell legislators that your organization critically needs their support in identifying federal funding.

Here are some pointers on when to make these critical contacts with elected officials:

>> **When you first realize that you're going to apply for a federal or state grant-funding opportunity:** It's critical to let your elected officials, both state and federal, know that you're submitting a grant application so that they can provide you with an introduction to the grant program's staff, giving you a direct dial-in number for queries. Your elected officials can also track the status of your grant application after it has been submitted to let you know when the application is under review by the program staff. Their processes for tracking your application will vary from state to state.

>> **When you need to request letters of commitment from elected officials:** For federal grant applications, ask representatives to send their letters directly to the federally appointed official who has jurisdiction over the funding agency (for example, the secretary of education, secretary of labor, and so forth). For state and local government agency grant applications, attach the letter to your grant application package.

>> **When you've uploaded or mailed the grant application:** Send a full copy of the application to your elected officials (national and state, depending on where you're submitting your application) along with a note that you'd like for them to work hard to get this request funded.

>> **When you find out that your application for funding was rejected:** Your elected officials can find out why the application was shot down — often faster than you can. And right or wrong, sometimes political clout counts enough to move a request from the rejection pile to the funding pile. (Note, though, that government funding agencies are required to provide written feedback to applicants rejected for funding.)

Also, work to engage elected officials in becoming oriented to your organization's needs. How? Host an annual legislative event (a breakfast, lunch, or dinner) where you present an overview of your organization and a wish list for programs and services. Make sure to use a slide-show presentation and give each attendee an information packet covering your presentation content. Your only agenda item is convincing elected officials or their staff members that your organization has the most need for government funding.

REMEMBER

Some elected officials have a policy of not providing letters of support, advocating, or communicating with nonprofits. While one elected official in your area may not be available, you should still go ahead and contact other elected officials.

Chapter 5

# Navigating the Grants.gov Gateway

E stablished in 2002, Grants.gov is the federal government's e-government initiative operating under the governance of the Office of Management and Budget. It provides a centralized location for grant seekers to find and apply for federal funding opportunities. Through it you can find information on the more than 1,000 grant programs available through the federal grant-making agencies.

In this chapter, I take you on a guided tour of the Grants.gov homepage and give you some pointers on getting your organization registered to apply for federal grants and cooperative agreements. I also lead you through those confusing grant application forms and the downloading and uploading processes for the entire grant application.

REMEMBER

Grants.gov has ongoing maintenance days that may coincide with the day you plan to submit your grant application. Monitor all alerts for maintenance starting ten days prior to your application's submission deadline. When you're ready to submit your application, follow the online directions, and don't procrastinate until the last minute to upload your application, you'll breeze through the once-stormy waters of federal e-grant applications.

# Navigating the Grants.gov Website

The Grants.gov homepage at www.grants.gov is your gateway to everything you need to know to find federal grants, apply for federal grants, and follow up on submitted federal grant applications. The page looks simple on first glance, but in reality it can be a bit confusing. So even though the information in this section may seem somewhat repetitive after you actually visit the Grants.gov website, I still want to take you on a guided tour.

Here's a breakdown of each key topic area tab on Grants.gov and what you can expect to find when you click them:

>> **HOME:** The big thing to pay attention to on the homepage is the Find Open Grant Opportunities section. It contains four tabs:

- NEWEST OPPORTUNITIES: This tab features a table that lists the *funding opportunity number* (an internal Grants.gov numbering system), the *opportunity title* (the name of the grant program), and the providing agency for roughly 25 of the newest opportunities available through Grants.gov.

- BROWSE CATEGORIES: Search through 23 different funding categories.

- BROWSE AGENCIES: Search through the federal grant-making agencies that offer funding opportunities through Grants.gov.

- BROWSE ELIGIBILITIES: This tab tells you who can apply for the various federal grants.

>> **LEARN GRANTS:** On this tab, you find the Grants Learning Center where you see links for Grants 101, Rules & Legislation, Are You Eligible, Grant Terminology, Who Gives Grants? Grant Community, Grant Systems, Find Funding, Reporting & Oversight, and Fraud & Abuse.

>> **SEARCH GRANTS:** This tab takes you to a new Grants.gov web page where you can not only view snippets of current grant-funding opportunities but also type in basic search criteria: keyword, funding opportunity number, or the Catalog of Federal Domestic Assistance (CFDA) number. (I introduce you to the CFDA in Chapter 4.) You can also search grant-funding opportunities that are posted (currently available to apply for), closed (no longer accepting grant applications), and archived (very old grant-funding announcements). The other search boxes are for the type of grant, by eligible applicant, by category, and by funding agency.

>> **APPLICANTS:** On this tab, there are eight categories of information: Check Your Eligibility, Get Registered, Apply for Grants, Track Your Application, Adobe Compatibility, Tools & Tips, Applicant FAQs, and Manage Subscriptions.

>> **GRANTORS:** This tab and its links allow staff at the federal grant-making agencies to register and post opportunities on Grants.gov, access training materials to assist the agencies in navigating Grants.gov, find FAQs, and get help.

>> **SYSTEM-TO-SYSTEM:** This tab provides applicants and agencies with the information necessary to link Grants.gov functionality with existing systems within their own organizations.

>> **FORMS:** Here you can access a variety of federal forms — including government-wide and agency-specific forms — currently used for creating grant application packages at Grants.gov. (For information about federal grant application forms, head to the related section later in this chapter.)

>> **OUTREACH:** On this tab, you find an overview of what's going on at Grants. gov. You can find out about system enhancements and maintenance.

>> **SUPPORT:** This tab takes you to Applicant Support, Grantor Support, Find Answers Online, and Report Fraud.

# Understanding Grant Applicant Eligibility

Many types of organizations are eligible to apply for government funding opportunities. Typically, most grant applicant organizations fall into the following categories:

>> **Government organizations:** State, local, city or township, special districts, Native American tribes (federally and nonfederally recognized).

>> **Education organizations:** Independent school districts, public and state-controlled institutions of higher education, and private institutions of higher education.

>> **Public housing organizations:** Public housing authorities and Native American housing authorities.

>> **Nonprofit organizations:** Nonprofit organizations with or without 501(c)(3) status.

>> **For-profit organizations:** Any for-profit group other than small businesses.

>> **Small businesses:** The US Small Business Administration (SBA) has established size standards for small businesses. Check out the standards at Grants. gov or the SBA's website, www.sba.gov. (For details on SBA grants, see Chapter 7.)

>> **Individuals:** An individual can submit grant applications on his own behalf, and not on behalf of a company, organization, institution, or government. If you're registered as an individual, you're allowed to apply only to funding opportunities that are open to individuals.

>> **Foreign applicants:** The authorizing legislation for each grant-making program determines if foreign applicants can apply for funding. Before applying, foreign applicants should thoroughly review the IRS website (www.irg.gov) and search for their most recent guidance for Aliens and International Taxpayers.

# Registering on Grants.gov

To apply for a grant, you and/or your organization have to register on Grants.gov. This registration process can take three to five business days, or as long as two weeks if you don't complete all the steps in a timely manner. The following sections explain how to register as an organization (which is most common) and as an individual.

## Registering as an organization

An *organization registration* is for an individual who is responsible for submitting a grant on behalf of a company; state, local, or tribal government; academic or research institution; nonprofit; or any other institution.

In order to get your organization registered to submit grant applications on the Grants.gov system, you need to follow these steps:

**1.** **Obtain a D-U-N-S number.**

D-U-N-S stands for Data Universal Number System; a *D-U-N-S number* is a common tracking number for doing business with the government (federal, state, and local). All D-U-N-S numbers are provided by Dun & Bradstreet. Call 866-705-5711 or access the Dun & Bradstreet website at http://fedgov.dnb.com/webform. (Refer to Chapter 3 for more on the D-U-N-S number.)

TIP

Before you apply for a D-U-N-S number, ask your grant administrator or CFO whether your organization already has one. You can also search online for an existing D-U-N-S number at http://fedgov.dnb.com/webform/CCRSearch.do. Select your country or territory from the pull-down menu, click Continue, then choose Continue to Government iUpdate to start your search.

2. **Register with the System for Award Management (SAM) at** www.sam.gov.

   If your organization already has an Employer Identification Number (EIN), your SAM registration will take seven to ten business days to process. If you're just applying for your EIN, you can get an EIN *immediately* by applying online at www.irs.gov/Businesses/Small-Businesses-&-Self-Employed/Apply-for-an-Employer-Identification-Number-(EIN)-Online.

   The information requested at SAM.gov is similar to what your organization submits in its annual IRS tax return, such as name of organization, address, contact person, and contact person's information. You also have to upload the organization's banking information (the bank's tracking number and the organization's bank account number) to facilitate electronic banking between the government and your organization. You didn't think they still sent the check in the mail, did you?

3. **Create a username and password with the Grants.gov credential provider.**

   You can create your own username and set a password on the Grants.gov and SAM.gov websites. After you complete all your SAM.gov information, you get directed back to Grants.gov to complete your registration with the access-point information. This is a same-day process.

TIP

   On SAM.gov, you'll find some new terms, namely MPIN and TPIN. An MPIN, or Marketing Partner ID Number, is a personal code consisting of nine characters; it's mandatory if you want to use SAM.gov. TPIN stands for Trading Partner Identification Number; it's a confidential number assigned to organizations that currently are or intend to become federal contractors.

4. **Obtain AOR Authorization.**

   If you're not the E-Business Point of Contact (E-Biz POC) at your organization, have that person log in to Grants.gov to confirm you as an Authorized Organization Representative (AOR). Only an AOR can log on and conduct business or grant-related transactions with the federal government. Your organization may have more than one AOR, or the AOR and E-Biz POC may be one and the same.

TIP

   An AOR can log in using the username and password obtained in Step 3 to track his AOR status and see whether he has been approved by the E-Biz POC.

   Logging in as an applicant is instantaneous, but you have to wait to become an AOR until your organization's E-Biz POC logs in and approves you as an AOR. Watch your email from SAM.gov and Grants.gov!

## Reviewing how to register as an individual

If you're submitting an application on your own behalf — not on behalf of an organization — the process is pretty simple. You don't have to mess with obtaining a D-U-N-S number or registering on SAM.gov. All you need to know is the Funding Opportunity Number (FON) for the grant you're interested in. I still walk you through the process, though:

1. **From the APPLICANTS tab on the Grants.gov homepage, click the Individual Registration link.**

2. **Click the Get Registered as an Individual link at the bottom of the web page (look for the red box).**

3. **Enter the FON of the grant you're applying for and click the Register button.**

   TIP

   You can find the FON on the Grants.gov homepage under the NEW OPPORTUNITIES tab or by searching using a keyword, CFDA number, or the agency name.

4. **Complete the registration form.**

   After you enter a valid FON, you need to complete a profile. Keep in mind that Grants.gov sends all correspondence to whatever email address you enter. For the secret question and answer, enter a question that only you can answer and that you'll be able to remember in the future. Then create a password and click the Continue button.

   On the next screen, you need to validate your information. If you need to change your information, click the Edit button; if your information is correct as entered, click Submit. If you've provided all the information correctly, you see a message at the top of the screen that reads "You are successfully registered." To continue to the applicant login page, click Continue at the bottom of the page. If you don't receive the successful message, a different message will appear stating what issue you need to address. Simply correct the error or reach out to the contact center for further assistance.

# Downloading and Uploading Application Packages

All the federal grant application forms you need are available through the Grants.gov website. These easy steps help you find and submit an application:

1. **Download your grant application package.**

   To download this package, log on to the Grants.gov homepage and click the APPLICANTS tab. At the Apply for Grants link, you need the FON or the Catalog of Federal Domestic Assistance (CFDA) number to download your grant application package. (Chapter 4 gives you the scoop on the CFDA.)

   **TIP**

   A lot of the documents uploaded for your grant application package must be in Adobe PDF format, so verify that your Adobe software version is compatible with Grants.gov. (The site offers a link to help you do just that.)

   Four sets of instructions are available to assist you when completing an application package:

   - **Agency instructions:** These agency-specific application package instructions must be downloaded separately from the application package.

   - **Application package cover sheet instructions:** These additional instructions provide information on how to complete application package forms. They're located on the cover sheet of the application package.

   - **Application package instructions:** These directions are located at the bottom of the application package and provide information about filling out the application.

   - **Field-level instructions:** These instructions are available by selecting the field-level help button, and they provide specific information about each field on the application.

2. **Complete the online application package forms.**

   Save changes to your application as you go; Grants.gov does *not* automatically save changes. Also, make sure you fill out the forms in their entirety. You can't submit your application package until all required fields are complete.

   **REMEMBER**

   The application package consists of front-and-back forms required by the grant-funding agency. This *package*, as Grants.gov labels it, doesn't refer to your grant application narrative or mandatory internal attachments or appendixes.

3. **Submit the completed grant application.**

   After you enter all the necessary information online *and* add all your mandatory and correctly formatted narrative and attachment documents, check the package for errors, save your package, and click the Save & Submit button on the cover page. Doing so automatically uploads your application package to Grants.gov. If you aren't already connected to the Internet, you'll be directed to do so and to log in to Grants.gov with your username and password.

After the submission is complete, a confirmation screen appears with a Grants. gov tracking number (at the bottom of the screen) as well as the official date and time of the submission. Record this tracking number so you can refer to it if you need to contact Grants.gov or give it to your congressional officials for tracking your grant application after submission.

4. **Track the status of your submitted grant application package.**

After submitting your grant application, you can check the status by clicking the Track My Application link under the APPLICANTS tab on the Grants.gov homepage. From there, enter your application's tracking number.

Your application status can be marked as any of the following:

- **Received:** Grants.gov has received the application but not yet validated it.

- **Validated:** Grants.gov has validated the application, which is now available for the agency to download.

- **Received by the agency:** The funding agency has confirmed receipt of the application package.

- **Agency tracking number assigned:** The funding agency has assigned the application an internal tracking number. (However, keep in mind that not all agencies assign tracking numbers.)

- **Rejected with errors:** Because of errors, Grants.gov can't process your application. You'll receive information by email on how to address the errors and resubmit the application.

You also get email updates from Grants.gov as the status of your application changes.

# Reviewing Some of the Mandatory Government Grant Application Forms

Each federal agency has its own standard grant application forms and its own guidelines for filling out the forms. Some agencies have fewer than 10 forms; others have more than 20. Underestimating the importance of the mandatory forms and the importance of filling them out properly may result in your grant application being disqualified on a technical error.

When filling in any form, always read the instructions that come with the online grant application guidelines first. Look for the checklist provided in every grant application announcement. This checklist tells you what to provide in your application, including mandatory forms, narrative sections, and attachments or appendixes.

TIP

Most federal grant-making agencies make exceptions to the standard Grants.gov application upload requirement and allow grant applicants to submit a paper application instead, although the agency may require that you request and receive approval to submit a paper application before the submission deadline. The checklist becomes even more important for hard-copy submissions, however, because you must assemble the forms, narrative, attachments, and appendixes in a specific order. Otherwise, your application may be rejected on receipt. If you can submit digitally, it is, by far, the best way to know it's over and done with. The paper submission process is cumbersome and a lot more stressful.

The *cover form* is the top page of all federal grant applications. It's what the feds see when they open your application package. For years, the application cover form has been known as the Application for Federal Assistance Cover Form. The current cover form — SF-424 — is five pages when printed out. It has 21 sections that cover the basic who, what, when, where, and why of your project and agency, with instructions for responding to each field, and ends with a federal debt delinquency explanation page. I tell you everything you need to know about filling out the SF-424 in Chapter 12.

The following sections provide an overview of the rest of the most common federal grant application forms: budget forms, assurance forms, and lobbying disclosure forms. Many state funding agencies use similar forms; the required forms are listed in the grant guidelines for each funding competition. These forms are listed in the order in which you're most likely to see them in grant application guidelines.

## Budget information forms: SF-424A and SF 424C

One form you have to fill out is a three-page, six-section set of federal budget forms often referred to as SF-424A (non-constructions programs) and SF-424C (constructions programs). You can download these forms at www.grants.gov/web/grants/forms.html. The six sections of this Non-Constructions Programs Budget Information form set are labeled Sections A through F:

>> **Section A** is where you lay out your budget summary (your federal grant request and your nonfederal matching monies).

TIP

Make sure the totals in your budget worksheet and budget narrative match the total in your SF-424A or C.

>> **Section B** is for detailing the budget categories line item by line item.

When you get to Section B, you especially want to have read the instructions for these forms, because each agency differs in how it wants you to fill in the columns for multiyear federal funding requests.

>> **Section C** is where you list the source of your nonfederal monies (called *nonfederal resources*).

>> **Section D** asks you to forecast your first-year grant-funding needs (referred to as *forecasted cash needs*).

>> **Section E** is where you tell the federal government the total amount of grant funds needed in the second through fifth years of your project. However, fill in this section only if the grant award is for multiple years.

>> **Section F** is where you explain any amounts requested in the federal portion of your budget that are unusual or unclear to someone (such as a federal grant reader/peer reviewer) outside your agency. In this section, you also explain your already-negotiated indirect cost rate (contact the Office of Management and Budget, www.whitehouse.gov/omb, to start this lengthy process well before you plan to apply for federal grant funding). Finally, Section F is where you can add any other explanations or comments to explain your rather large or mysterious budget.

Chapter 17 gives you greater insight into the budget line-item preparation process.

## Assurances form: SF-424B and SF-424D

The federal government wants assurances that your organization — the grant applicant — can meet all governmental funding expectations. And it gets these assurances from Standard Form 424B, or SF-424B (non-construction programs) and SF-424D (construction programs). This online form lets you add your electronic signature and submit.

If you have questions regarding this form, contact the awarding agency. Also, note that some federal awarding agencies may require you to certify to additional assurances; if that's the case, they'll let you know how to proceed.

The assurances cover your legal authority to (among other things)

>> Apply for grants

>> Address your commitment to record-keeping

>> Provide safeguards for conflict of interest

>> Protect the meeting time frame established in your grant application

>> Comply with multiple federal laws regarding fairness and equity for program staff and participants

**REMEMBER**

By signing the assurances and other required forms, you're conveying to the government funding agency that your organization will comply with all applicable requirements of all other federal laws, executive orders, regulations, and policies governing this program.

## Disclosure of lobbying activity form: SF-LLL

If you've hired a lobbyist to make sure more federal or state dollars come your way, you must fill out the Disclosure of Lobbying Activities form, or *SF-LLL*. (Read the funding agency's guidelines though, because often this form is optional.)

## CHECKING OUT OTHER E-GRANT PORTALS FOR FEDERAL GRANT-MAKING AGENCIES

Some federal agencies have their own e-grant upload portals separate from Grants.gov. The process varies from agency to agency, so read the grant application guidelines carefully to look for the submission process. Here are a few examples:

- **Department of Homeland Security:** The Federal Emergency Management Agency has created e-grant portals for its most popular competitive grant program: the Assistance to Firefighters Grant (AFG) program. When you click the application link for the funding opportunity notification on Grants.gov, you see specific directions for how to access the e-portal.

- **Department of Justice (DOJ):** Although you generally submit competitive/discretionary grant applications through Grants.gov, you must submit formula grants, congressional earmarks, and continuation grants through DOJ's Office of Justice Program's Grants Management System (GMS). For detailed instructions and tips on applying through GMS, refer to the GMS online training tool at www. ojp.usdoj.gov/gmscbt/.

- **National Science Foundation (NSF):** To apply for a grant from the NSF, you must register with FastLane, a portal that allows individuals and organizations to interact directly with the NSF regarding proposals, funding awards, and more. FastLane is available from the NSF homepage at www.nsf.gov or directly at www.fastlane.nsf.gov. FastLane can be tricky for new users. Make sure to spend time learning how to use the system before your grant application is due.

A *lobbyist* is an individual or a firm that spends a lot of time on Capitol Hill or at your state capitol schmoozing with elected officials. Lobbyists work for for-profit and nonprofit agencies. They're on a (paid) mission to convince legislators to vote one way or another to benefit their client agencies. Lobbyists apply a lot of pressure, and a lot of money flows as a result.

## Links for other federal grant application forms

If you're looking for any other federal grant application forms, this is the website to find them: `www.grants.gov/web/grants/forms/sf-424-mandatory-family.html`.

# Chapter 6

# Researching Potential Private-Sector Funders

The earlier chapters in this Part focus on grant-making agencies in the public sector. In this chapter, I take a look at the other segment of funding possibilities: private-sector grant makers. *Private-sector funding* comes from foundations and corporations. This philanthropic well represents corporate and foundation grant makers whose *endowments* (the funds that start each giving entity) came from individuals, families, and for-profit corporations or businesses.

These funders are plentiful at the local, state, national, and international levels. How do you find foundation and corporate funders and what they like to fund? In this chapter, I take you on a treasure hunt to find out.

# Finding Foundations and Corporations with Grant-Making Programs

**REMEMBER**

Conducting a thorough Internet search is the best way to find private-sector grant-funding opportunities. I can't shout loudly enough about the importance of reading grant research database funder profiles (which provide an overview of what they fund, how to make the initial contact, and whom to contact) and then searching the Internet for every bit of information you can find on each funder before you email, write, or call its office. If you don't do this homework, I guarantee you're never going to access the road that leads to building an initial and lasting relationship with potential funders. Don't be a time waster by trying to skip protocol — unless of course you actually *want* to commit grant-seeking suicide (this means never receiving a grant award)!

## Understanding the time and effort required

How do you set up your search? Start by writing down every possible descriptor of your project and its target population (who will benefit or be served). Then begin researching those keywords and fishing for clues in the resulting links. Sometimes the links returned by the search engine can be misleading, so you have to click through to see whether your hit is a relevant funding lead for your project. Time consuming? Yes! This is a daily process that can take upward from 10 to 30 days working with keywords and possible link leads for an hour or two at a time.

**TIP**

It's also a good idea to start flushing out your program description and objectives even before actually having a specific grant-funding opportunity available. This will also help you to further hone your keyword search skills when you've got a document that you can extract keywords from.

**TIP**

Not all potential funders become actual funders, and you don't want to spend 9 to 12 months counting on yeses from only one or two funders only to have them respond with a no. If you need up to $25,000, you must search for at least 5 potential funders. For up to $50,000, search for at least 10 possible funders, and for needs of up to $100,000, search for 20 potential funders. For amounts of more than $100,000, be sure to have at least 25 to 30 names on your list of possible funders.

## Subscribing to helpful funding alert resources

After doing Internet searches, the next best tactic is to subscribe to e-newsletters that contain private-sector funding alerts. These give you the inside scoop on what private-sector funders are currently funding. My favorite e-newsletters are the *Philanthropy News Digest* (http://philanthropynewsdigest.org) and the *RFP Bulletin* (http://philanthropynewsdigest.org/rfps), both of which are produced by the Foundation Center.

Here are some additional ways to set yourself apart from the grant-seeking bunch:

>> **Review each funder's online resource materials to help you tailor your grant application to the funder's current interest area.** I'm talking grant application guidelines and an annual report (which contains financial information on the funder and usually a section on previous grants funded).

>> **Look for lists of previous grantees on the funder's website.** This list can tell you how much the funder funds, whether grants have been awarded in your geographic area, and whom the funder has invested grant monies in (look for grantees similar to your own grant applicant organization).

>> **Email each funder to inquire about grant writing guideline updates that may not be posted on the funder's website yet.** It's always possible they exist; asking never hurts. Be sure to keep your email focused on guideline updates, though. Don't ask for money or write endless paragraphs about your organization.

>> **Follow to a T all the directions provided by the funding source on how to apply for grants.** If you get one item wrong, your proposal can be disqualified, even if everything else is golden.

**WARNING**

I'd be remiss if I didn't mention some pitfalls to avoid when grant seeking:

>> **Don't rely on outdated print (hard copy) funding publications or websites for current contact information.** Don't use anything older than one year (scroll down to the bottom of a website's homepage to see the date it was last updated). Current information is crucial because funders don't forward snail mail or email when a key contact person is no longer working for them. With snail mail, if you address your funding request to the wrong person, you simply get it back stamped *return to sender*. With email, you may get a message that this person is no longer with the funder, or you may not get any notice. So although you think you've initiated the first step to build a relationship with a program officer or foundation director, your mail is hanging out unread in some dormant email system.

Save embarrassment by calling for the current contact person, the correct spelling of the person's name, and the correct position title. Most importantly, ask how the person prefers to be addressed: Mr., Mrs., or Ms. Double-checking the email address doesn't hurt, either.

>> **Don't look for national funders before you start to contact local funders.** Look for money at home first. Check sources in your own community and county. You have a better chance of getting your first grant award from a funder that already knows about your organization.

>> **Don't call the funding source with a dozen questions before you read its grant application guidelines.** If you have new questions about instructions or information not found in the grant application guidelines, feel free to call. However, don't call repeatedly with questions that the guidelines answer.

If you decide to call, make sure to jot down some notes about the call and the person you speak with. Write down her name and title, the date and time of the call, and what you discussed. Having a contact at the funder's office can help if your grant application is rejected and you want the inside scoop on why.

>> **Don't write a grant application or proposal without having completed extensive research.** Know what your targeted funders fund — their grant-making priorities — and only submit requests that meet their current interests.

>> **Don't broadcast your funding sources to colleagues working for other nonprofits.** Keep in mind that you're competing for funding. Learn to treasure, or keep quiet about, your findings, lest others apply as well and lessen your chances of winning.

# Weighing the Usefulness of Free versus Paid Grant Research Websites

When you're seeking grants in the private-sector, you have tons of websites to screen. This section gives you my favorite websites. Using these resources is a must and saves lots of time.

## Using the Foundation Center's funding resources

In the United States, the most affordable nonprofit website with the largest database for corporate and foundation funding sources is that of the Foundation Center at www.foundationcenter.org. Headquartered in New York City, the Foundation Center has field offices in Atlanta, Cleveland, San Francisco, and Washington, DC.

If you're looking for freebies, the Foundation Center has *Cooperating Collections* across the United States and in Puerto Rico. These are free funding-information centers in libraries, community foundations, and other nonprofit resource centers. They provide a core collection of the Foundation Center's publications and a variety of supplemental materials and services in areas useful to grant seekers. If you have a Cooperating Collection near you, you don't have to pay for a subscription to access the Center's online materials.

Consider using a cloud-based file storage service so you can access your funding resources anyplace (at home, at work, on vacation, and just out of your work setting for a day or two).

## Paid online subscriptions

The Foundation Center's online directory, called the *Foundation Directory Online*, has three subscription levels ranging from Essential ( 100,000+ grant-maker profiles) to Professional (140,000+ expanded grant-maker profiles, key decision makers, keyword search including 990s and 990-PFs, their new online workspace, and a lot more). If you decide to pay for a subscription, you get access to detailed information on foundation and corporate funders at your fingertips when you need it — at home or at work. The pages of info you pull up on these funders are referred to as *grant maker profiles.*

Look under the Find Funders link for a bolded subsection labeled Identifying Funding Sources. Under this subsection, you can find links to Foundation Directory Online, Corporate Giving Online, and Foundation Grants to Individuals Online. Get out your credit card if you want to subscribe to these bountiful directories. The minimum Essential monthly subscription costs about $39.99 per month. There is also a Preferred subscription level with a few more amenities than Essential for $99.99 per month. And of course, the big enchilada, the Professional monthly subscription sets you back $149.99 per month.

After you become a paid subscriber to the *Foundation Directory Online*, you can start your funder research in four different ways, depending on your subscription level:

>> **Grant makers (available at all subscription levels):** This type of search, at a minimum, allows you to search by the following:

- Grant maker name

- Grant maker location (state, county, city, metro area, and zip code)

- Fields of interest

- Types of support

- Geographic focus

- Trustees, officers, and donors

- Type of grant maker

- Total giving

- Keyword

**TIP**

Searching by grant maker is easy and productive. With this search, I usually find at least 10 to 20 potential private-sector funding sources for each project I'm working on.

» **Companies (available at subscription levels higher than Essential):** This search option allows you to search *corporate grant makers* (businesses that have developed corporate giving programs). When you can't find funders in the Foundation-Only section, searching for grant opportunities in the Companies section is a good idea.

» **Grants (available at all subscription levels):** This option allows you to search by the following:

- Grant maker name

- Grant maker state

- Recipient name

- Recipient state/county

- Recipient city

- Recipient type

- Subjects

- Types of support

- Keyword

**TIP**

Searching with the Grants option is good when you want to know funders that have awarded grants in a specific county or region. However, this option doesn't give you a detailed profile of the funder.

» **Form 990s (available at subscription levels higher than Essential):** Why would you look at an organization's Form 990? Here is a link to learn more about the types of IRS 990 forms: www.irs.gov/Charities-&-Non-Profits/Form-990-Resources-and-Tools-for-the-General-Public.

To find out the total number of grants awarded in the grant maker's most recent *fiscal year* (the 12-month operating period determined by when the organization filed for IRS nonprofit status). Looking at the total number of grants awarded gives you an idea of the funder's financial capacity. If I find a funder awarding only ten grants per year, I see a red flag. That number usually means not too much philanthropy is going on there. However, when I see that a funder has awarded 100 grants, I'm ready to be a winner in next year's competition!

TIP

If you don't want to fork over the cash to subscribe at the professional level, remember that you can find most IRS Form 990s for nonprofit organizations, including grant makers, on the GuideStar website (www.guidestar.org).

## NAVIGATING IRS FORM 990

When I want to know everything about the financial picture of a specific private-sector funder, I look at the funder's IRS Form 990 (nonprofit tax return) to see all its assets, the major grants it awarded, and the contact information for its board members in the event that I need to ask one of them to be an advocate for my funding request.

When you view a funder's Form 990, pay attention to these key sections:

- **Part I: Summary:** This section includes the name, address, and telephone number of the funder (handy information to have if the funder doesn't have a website or contact information listed in a funding directory). Part I also notes the funder's mission or most significant activities, governance, revenues, expenses, and net assets or fund balances. (Here's a hint: If you don't see the mission on page 1, check page 2.)

- **Part VII: Compensation of Officers, Directors, Trustees, Key Employees, Highest Compensated Employees, and Independent Contractors:** This section includes the names and titles of the funder's officers, information that's helpful to have if you need to locate a specific officer or if the contact person listed on page 1 is actually a third party such as a bank trust officer, fiscal agent, CPA, or attorney. In the latter case, you can send your funding request to one of the funder's officers instead of sending it to the third-party contact.

- **Part IX: Statement of Functional Expenses:** This section lists the total grants awarded to governments, organizations, and individuals. Knowing this information gives you insight to the funder's overall giving ability. If the funder's total awards for the previous fiscal year were $100,000, you wouldn't want to ask for $90,000 in your request. Such a request isn't practical given the funder's funding capacity and would likely result in a rejection letter.

# Digital resources

The Foundation Center offers several digital resources that contain information on national, regional, and international funding sources. In addition to the *Foundation Directory Online* (described in the preceding section), the following digital resources are available:

>> **Corporate Giving Online:** This comprehensive database gives you access to more than 3,800 company profiles; more than 2,800 company-sponsored foundations; almost 1,400 direct corporate-giving programs; and more than 380,000 recently awarded grants.

>> **Grant Guides:** Available for order through the Foundation Center's website (www.foundationcenter.org), these guides contain profiles of grant makers and are available in the following funding areas:

- Grants for the Aging
- Grants for the Arts, Culture & the Humanities
- Grants for Cancer Research & Patient Care
- Grants for Capacity Building, Management & Technical Assistance
- Grants for Children & Youth
- Grants for Community and Economic Development
- Grants for Disaster Relief & Recovery: US & International
- Grants for Elementary & Secondary Education
- Grants for Environment Protection & Animal Welfare
- Grants for Foreign & International Programs
- Grants for Higher Education
- Grants for Hospitals & Health Organizations
- Grants for Mental Health, Addictions & Crisis Services
- Grants for People with Disabilities
- Grants for Religion, Religious Welfare & Religious Education
- Grants for Services for the Homeless
- Grants for Women & Girls

>> **Celebrity Foundation Directory:** Available as a downloadable PDF, this resource includes detailed descriptions of foundations created by well-known individuals in the worlds of business, entertainment, politics, and sports.

>> **Foundation Grants for Individuals Online:** As you might expect, this directory features entries geared toward individual grant seekers. The amount of information makes it a valuable resource.

>> **Guide to Funding for International and Foreign Programs:** This directory provides funding resources for international relief, disaster assistance, human rights, civil liberties, community development, conferences, and education.

TIP

You can access these digital resources for free at any library that's designated as a Cooperating Collections site. Most libraries have one or more computers dedicated to Foundation Center subscription resources.

## Free information

The following list highlights some online links through which you can access free information on the Foundation Center's website (www.foundationcenter.org):

>> **The Find Funders tab:** When you click this tab, you see these key subheadings: Fact Finder, Identify Funding Sources, Related Tools, and Check Statistics. Each of these subheadings has a bevy of click-through resources ranging from 990 Finder to the Common Grant Application Forms and Grant Stats.

>> **Newsletters link:** Click this link to find a list of email newsletters you can subscribe to free of charge. You don't even have to register for online access. You can use the free newsletters to find topic-specific Requests for Proposals (RFPs) released by foundation and corporate funders and to keep abreast of what's happening in the world of grant making. I have subscriptions for the following:

- *Philanthropy News Digest:* The *PND* is the Foundation Center's award-winning weekly news publication. It tells you what's happening in the world of philanthropy. Staying up to date on philanthropy is important if you want to know when foundation or corporate contact personnel are leaving or are hired. *PND* also fills you in on what each listed funder is doing that relates to its grant-making policies and trends.

- *RFP Bulletin:* This freebie is a weekly gathering of recently announced RFPs from private, corporate, and government sources.

- *Job Bulletin:* This newsletter provides a summary of recent job postings in *Philanthropy News Digest*.

- *Connections:* This newsletter provides philanthropy-related content.

# Using other online grant research databases

Although the nonprofit Foundation Center is one of my preferred databases because of the size of its grant maker and grant-making collection, I also use other online funding resources. Here's a brief list of the others I use, free and subscription-based:

>> www.ecivis.com/products-services/grants-network-research.html: The eCivis.com database, designed for units of municipal government, is the an all-in-one database with extensive profiles for federal, state, foundation, and corporate grant makers. Fees are quoted on requesting a demonstration via their online link.

>> www.fundsnetservices.com: Fundsnet Services is the blue-light special approach to online grant seeking. When you pull up the Fundsnet Services homepage, you find so many useful links that you may just have a dizzy spell. It's a virtual flea market with a plethora of information. Some of the links I find tremendously helpful are Arts & Culture Grants, Disability Grants, Education Grants, Environment & Conservation Grants, Foundation Directory, Community Foundations, Women Grants, and Computers & Technology. Each of the links on this website is topic-specific and includes click-through features to send you to a funder's website to read about grant opportunities firsthand.

**WARNING**

The downside of this site is that there are a lot of advertising links.

>> http://money.cnn.com/magazines/fortune/fortune500: This free website is full of news about the corporate world. I like to use the Fortune 500 lists to quickly find financially healthy potential corporate grant makers out of the top 500 US-based corporations. You can choose to view the entire list of Fortune 500 corporations and view financials and company information, including the name of the CEO. This is a two-step research process: (1) Find out about the financial health of the potential funders and (2) Research if they have a foundation.

**TIP**

If you're looking for multinational companies that may award grants, visit money.cnn.com/magazines/fortune/global500/index.html for *Fortune's* Global 500 list, which provides access to a full list of the global corporate rankings and the search options of the Fortune 500 list.

>> www.christianvolunteering.org: This website has a free online directory for churches, ministries, and other grant seekers looking for monies to start or expand religiously affiliated programs and projects. This site lists more than 10,000 church and ministry grant makers that fund a range of programs, including building projects, program support, equipment, renovations, youth programs, capital campaigns, outreach ministries, general operating support, mission trips, and seed money.

# Eyeballing the Funder's Criteria

After you locate information on a foundation or corporate funding source, you need to quickly scan its profile to determine whether you have a perfect match. A *perfect match* means that you fit the funder's organizational, geographic, and programming criteria and that the funder provides the kind of funding you need in an amount to make an approach worthwhile.

**REMEMBER**

You can't persuade a funder to change its award guidelines or funding priorities; you're the one who has to do the changing to fit the funder's funding criteria. If you can't change your program or project, that particular funding source isn't the best one for you. In that case, simply keep looking for a better match.

Every resource that lists funding sources presents the information on the funder in a generalized profile format. When you look at a funder's profile, you can scan some specific information fields to determine whether reading about this particular funding source is worth your time. Focus on the following fields:

>> **Limitations:** Look at the limitations field first. Your organization may be eliminated before it can even get to the starting gate. Does the wording in this section eliminate your program or project? If so, move on to the next funder's profile. If not, move on to the next critical information field.

Typical limitations you may see listed in the grant maker's online profile include

- Specific geographic giving area (countries, states, and counties)

- Restrictions on whom it funds and what it funds

**WARNING**

Most mainstream foundation funders don't award grants for religious purposes, to individuals, or for *capital projects* (building construction or renovation or major equipment purchases).

>> **Purpose and activities:** Every foundation and corporate giver has a purpose statement, located at the beginning of the funding profile. Does the funding source's purpose statement reflect your organization's values? Do any of the activities that the funder prefers to fund match activities that your organization is or will be undertaking? If not, read no further. Move on to another funder's information profile. If you can identify with this funder's purpose, move on to the next critical information field.

>> **Fields of interest:** Does the program area that you're seeking grant funds for match with any of the funding source's fields of interest?

Keep in mind that the language you use to describe your program may not be the language the funder uses to list its fields of interest. Think of your program area in broad terms and generic categories. For example, say you need grant funding for a program that will tutor and mentor at-risk elementary school students after school and on the weekends. You probably won't find terms/phrases such as *tutoring, mentoring, at-risk,* or *after-school* in the funder's fields of interest entry. Rather, you may find terms such as *education (K–12), elementary education, public education, private education,* and *youth programs and services.* The second list is broader than the first.

>> **Types of support:** What types of activities does this funder pay for? If you're trying to erect a new building and the funder lists only *general operating support, conferences,* and *seed money* under types of support, this funding source isn't the one you want to approach with a construction project.

Even if this funder isn't willing to support the type of activity you're currently seeking funds for, save the funder's information if you think it may be willing to support some other aspect of your organization.

>> **Previous grants or grantees:** Have any previous grants been funded in your state? Have any previous grants been for projects similar to yours or in your project area? Getting a funder to award grant monies in a state where it hasn't previously awarded grants is difficult. If a funder has a track record for previous grants in your state or previous grants for projects similar to yours, the door is open to receive your funding request. (You can search by location of foundation or geographic limitations to help narrow your search.) However, if these aren't the circumstances you face, you may have to email or call the funder to determine whether proceeding with a funding request is worth your time.

>> **Amounts of grants previously funded:** Does your guesstimated project budget fit into the range of prior grant awards? Use the funder's prior grant-making amounts to gauge where your request should fall.

You never want to request a grant amount that exceeds the top grant awarded by the funder — that strategy's a bit too risky. If you're looking for $100,000 and the largest grant awarded was $5,000, you need to find multiple funders for your project.

# Knowing Whom to Contact First

After you identify the potential private funders that are the best fit for your program, follow these steps:

1. **Contact each funding source (via email, letter, or phone call) and ask to be included in the funder's mailing list.**

   Doing so normally means that you get annual reports, grant-making guidelines, research, and other information that keeps you up-to-date. Armed with this information, you're ready to take the next step.

   You can also use this contact point to inquire whether the funding-request guidelines listed on the organization's website are current.

   **TIP**

2. **Organize your potential foundation and corporate sources by the application due dates.**

   This step is critical because some private-sector funders have only once-yearly competitions. You may be a few weeks or many months away from the annual date for grant submissions. After all your hard work, you don't want to miss an opportunity to get a grant funded because you submitted your application late.

   Sorting by due date helps you anticipate how much work you'll have in any given month. Be as organized as possible to maximize your chances of getting the grants you want. Grant-management software can be extremely helpful for organizing (see the nearby sidebar for advice on what to look for in this type of software).

   Subscribe to a cloud-based file storage service. You can create electronic folders for each funder. You should have massive amounts of information at this point, and keeping everything in order is crucial. If something that you want to keep is not in a downloadable file format, consider copying the information from web pages and pasting them into a word-processing program. This way, you can save them into the folder in readable and manageable formats.

   **TIP**

3. **When you're ready to write, focus first on the proposals and applications that have due dates in 60 days or less.**

   Get busy! Check out Part 4 for all the details on completing an outstanding application.

4. **Move on to the foundation and corporate funders who accept the Common Grant Application format anytime during the year.**

   The Common Grant Application (CGA) format is fairly easy to follow and is the best way to apply for grants from corporations and foundations that accept unsolicited proposals but don't have their own specific grant application formatting guidelines. You can access the CGA here: `http://chfs.ky.gov/nr/rdonlyres/635f46a0-8ef6-4ce7-a6ae-b33d3dbe35a6/0/nngcommongrantapplication.pdf`. (For more on the CGA, see Chapter 1.)

   I also include a CGA template at `www.dummies.com/go/grantwritingfd6e`.

## MAKING WRITING AND TRACKING EASIER WITH SOFTWARE

A grant-writing management software program allows you to keep track of the entire grant application process, including preplanning steps, partner information, funder information, due dates for fiscal and evaluation reports, and grant closeout. Commercial software programs are available to capture any and all segments of the grant-seeking process.

Search for "grant writing management software" with your favorite search engine to get links for everything on the current market. The best characteristics to look for in any grant-writing management software are the ability to

- Write grant proposals and track proposal submissions in the same software. Using one software or cloud-based grants management system (subscription-based) will help you keep track of the information you're collecting on potential funders, as well as set up alerts to grant application due dates and other critical to-do's.

- Set alerts for reports due or funding source decision-making dates so you can call or email the funder to see whether it has a decision on your request yet.

- Manage grant-related reports, including tracking financial expenditures.

# Chapter 7

# Finding What's Available for Individuals and Businesses

et me get this out of the way right off the bat: There are no grants for individuals or businesses to pay off old debts. If you're looking for a grant to fund your startup, it'll take you months and miracles to locate legitimate websites for these types of grants. One of my favorite websites that validates the no-free-money reality is `http://nofreemoney.com`. Check it out before you start chasing something that isn't there.

This chapter sets the record straight. Yes, selected types of grants are available for individuals and businesses. But they aren't as plentiful as you'd think, and you have to be able to hone and use your detective skills on the Internet to find legitimate grant-funding opportunities. I get you started in the following pages.

**REMEMBER**

As is the case with all types of grant monies — whether given by a foundation, corporation, or government grant-making agency — strings are attached. From eligibility strings to usage strings to default strings, you have to fill out paperwork from the start to the finish. And remember, if you receive a grant award as an individual, you'll owe Uncle Sam on April 15.

# Sorting Through Who Awards Grants to Individuals and for What Purposes

According to the website for the Foundation Center (`www.foundationcenter.org`), the nation's leading print and online authority on philanthropy, roughly 10,000 grant makers help with paying off education or artistic or research projects. To make this vast database work for you, you first need to get acquainted with the various types of grants available for individuals.

Commonly awarded grants for individuals include the following:

» **College scholarships and student loans:** The former category doesn't require repayment, but the latter does. Both college scholarships and student loans are awarded to specific financial institutions in the individual's name. Take a look at the College Board's Search for Scholarships website (`https://bigfuture.collegeboard.org/pay-for-college`) for resources. Take your time, take notes, and take advantage of this highly credible website with safe links.

» **Fellowships:** This grant type requires no repayment and may be taxable. However, fellowships are often restricted to specific institutions or fields of study. Some foundations award fellowships directly to individuals; others award them to specific colleges or universities. Type **fellowships directory** into your favorite Internet search engine to find industry-specific resources.

» **Specific funder-directed assistance grants:** These grants are available for patient-access programs, discount prescription medication programs, global humanitarian support, and more. For example, the Partnership for Prescription Assistance has an extensive list of assistance programs at `www.pparx.org/en/prescription_assistance_programs`; just click the Get Prescription Help button on the right-hand side of the page to access the list of participating programs.

» **Research grants:** This grant type is reserved for educational and scientific research projects. Research grants are awarded by both government and private sector funders. In the health arena, for example, the National Institutes of Health (NIH) is the foremost federal funder of research grants to individuals. For an example of a private sector funder, take a look at the website for the Foundation for the Future (www.foundationforfuture.org/en/WebPresence/Compendium.aspx).

>> **First-time homebuyer grants:** Just about every state offers these grants, which are earmarked to help eligible individuals and families purchase a first home with a reduced down payment. Most often, these monies originate from the US Department of Housing and Urban Development and are passed down through your state's housing authority or agency. That agency then subgrants these monies to regional and local housing assistance programs. To find a link to HUD-funding homebuyer grants and resources in your state, go to http://portal.hud.gov/hudportal/HUD?src=/program_offices/administration/grants/grantssrc and review the list of organizations and agencies to find the contacts in your state.

TIP

The easiest and fastest way to search for individual grants is to use the Internet because you can print out your search results and sort them from most likely matches to long shots. Then you can start the process of contacting each funder to obtain specific guidelines and due dates. Use this search string: Individuals can apply for this grant. You can also change the search string to something like this: Individual artists can apply. Either way, be prepared to read and screen all the results to find what you're looking for.

REMEMBER

Competition for individual grants is heavy, so start your search at least one year before you need the funds. This is especially true for fellowships and research grants. Contact the funders for qualification details that may not be posted on their websites. Then be sure to fill out all the required forms completely and accurately.

# Locating Credible Grants for Your Startup Business

I'd love to tell you that grants rain down on every square inch of the country to help you start your new business, but I can't, because they don't. Finding the monies to start a new business has always been an elusive and disappointing process. But don't let that get you down. In the following sections, I tell you where to look for private funding and how to apply for government funding.

## Competing against others for coveted startup funding

Some grants exist, both nationally and internationally, that can help you jump-start your new business. Where are they, and how the heck do you find them? Start by typing **business plan competitions** into your favorite search engine.

What is a *business plan competition*, you ask? It's when leading universities and other institutional-type funders put out a call for the best business plan models. (In other words, if you enter one of these competitions, you're competing against graduate and post-graduate students.) A panel of business experts reviews each plan and selects the winner(s). The prize can be up to $100,000 for some competitions.

A very reliable website that lists legitimate business plan competitions is www. bizplancompetitions.com. Click List from the pull-down menu under the Competitions tab. From there you can sort by state, prize year, and category.

TIP

Search the Internet weekly for reliable updated listings and emerging competitions. Be diligent because the early bird gets the worm — or the grand prize to start a new business!

## Reviewing research grants from Uncle Sam to fund your work

If you're in disbelief about the narrow field of grants for business startups, go to the US Small Business Administration's website at www.sba.gov. There you find this disclaimer under "What the SBA Doesn't Offer" when it comes to grants:

> SBA does NOT provide grants for starting and expanding a business.
>
> Government grants are funded by your tax dollars and, therefore, require very stringent compliance and reporting measures to ensure the money is well spent. As you can imagine, grants are not given away indiscriminately.
>
> Grants from the federal government are authorized and appropriated through bills passed by Congress and signed by the president. The grant authority varies widely among agencies. SBA has authority to make grants to nonprofit and educational organizations in many of its counseling and training programs, but does not have authority to make grants to small businesses. The announcements for the counseling and training grants will appear on Grants.gov. If Congress authorizes Specific Initiative Grants, organizations receiving such grants will receive individual notifications.

Some business grants are available through state and local programs, nonprofit organizations, and other groups. For example, some states provide grants for expanding childcare centers; creating energy-efficient technology; and developing marketing campaigns for tourism. These grants are not necessarily free money, and usually require the recipient to match funds or combine the grant with other forms of financing such as a loan. The amount of the grant money available varies with each business and each grantor.

If you aren't one of these specialized business, both federal and state government agencies provide financial assistance programs that help small business owners obtain loans and venture capital financing from commercial lenders.

Don't worry. The SBA doesn't drop you there like a hot potato. For businesses doing specific types of research, the homepage has a link on the bottom right-hand side: Research Grants for Small Business. When you see the list of federal grant-making agencies that award grants to businesses, click the agency name link to continue your research. You can also move over to Grants.gov to search for that specific agency's grant-funding opportunities, current and past. (See Chapter 5 for help navigating Grants.gov.)

## Small Business Technology Transfer Program

If your business is high-science/technology-related, you want to take a long look at the SBA's Small Business Technology Transfer Program (STTR). STTR is a highly competitive program that reserves a specific percentage of federal research and development (R&D) funding for small business and nonprofit research institution partners. The five federal agencies that award STTR research grants are the Departments of Defense, Energy, and Health and Human Services; the National Aeronautics and Space Administration (NASA); and the National Science Foundation.

STTR grant monies are awarded in three phases. Phase I is the start-up phase. Awards of up to $100,000 for approximately one year fund the exploration of the scientific, technical, and commercial feasibility of an idea or technology. (I cover phases II and III of these payouts in the later "Looking into research and development funding opportunities" section.)

Small businesses must meet certain eligibility criteria to participate in the STTR:

>> American owned and independently operated

>> For-profit

>> Principal researcher need not be employed by small business

>> Company size limited to 500 employees

Nonprofit research institutions must also meet the following eligibility criteria:

>> Located in the United States

>> Falls under one of three definitions:

- Nonprofit college or university

- Domestic nonprofit research organization

- Federally funded research and development center (FFRDC)

The SBA doesn't limit the number of employees a nonprofit research institution may have.

## Small Business Innovation Research

The Small Business Innovation Research (SBIR) Grant Program encourages small businesses to explore their technological potential and provides the incentives to profit from the grant applicant's ability to take its research or product to the commercialization phase.

Eleven federal agencies award SBIR research grants: the Departments of Agriculture, Commerce, Defense, Education, Energy, Health and Human Services, Homeland Security, and Transportation; the Environmental Protection Agency; NASA; and the National Science Foundation.

Like the STTR grants I describe in the preceding section, the SBIR grant monies are awarded in three phases, with phase I as the start-up phase. Awards of up to $150,000 for approximately six months support exploration of the technical merit or feasibility of an idea or technology. See the upcoming section "Looking into research and development funding opportunities" for more on phases II and III.

To participate in the SBIR program, small businesses have to match the following eligibility criteria:

>> American owned and independently operated

>> For-profit

>> Principal researcher employed by business

>> Company size limited to 500 employees

### Applying for SBA grants

**TIP**

If you want to apply for an SBA grant, monitor the SBA's website for announcements about technical assistance workshops and conferences around the country. I also recommend fine-tuning your email subscription on Grants.gov by typing "SBIR" and "STTR" in the keyword search for identifying grant-funding opportunity announcements. Doing so allows you to limit your daily email funding alert to only SBIR and STTR grant announcements.

Every state has an SBIR/STTR contact person appointed by the governor's office. After you find an SBIR/STTR grant-funding opportunity on Grants.gov, you must take two steps immediately, because the deadline for researching and writing your grant application will be less than 60 days. Here's what to do:

1.  **Download and print out the application announcement.**

    This announcement provides information on what will be funded and how to apply.

2.  **Call your governor's office to locate the state's SBIR/STTR contact person.**

    This individual can connect you with experts in your research and development field who can help strategize your approach for federal funding. He can't write your application for you (that's your job), but he can tell you what the government is interested in funding and the best way to present your specific information in a competitive research and development grant application.

# Digging for Business Expansion Monies

Foundations and corporations don't provide grants to help you expand your business (or to help you start your business or pay off existing bills). You may want to consider a loan from your bank as an alternative source of funding. Or you may prefer to check out the business-expansion funding available through both federal and state governments. The following sections delve into these opportunities in more detail.

## Looking into research and development funding opportunities

Good news: The Small Business Technology Transfer Program (STTR) and Small Business Innovation Research (SBIR) Grant Program I introduce you to earlier in the chapter also offer business research expansion grants.

Basically, if you're award an STTR or SBIR grant, you may be eligible for a phase II award of up to $1,000,000 for as long as two years to expand phase I results. (Phase I is the initial start-up payout, which I cover earlier in this chapter.) During this period, the research and development work is performed, and the developer begins to consider commercial potential. Only phase I award winners get phase II consideration.

Phase III is the period during which phase II innovation moves from the laboratory into the marketplace. No STTR or SBIR funds support this phase. The small business must find funding in the private sector or other non-STTR/SBIR federal agency funding.

## Tracking down other business expansion funding opportunities

Every state has some type of economic stimulus fund to help with business and industry expansions. Turn to your state's department of commerce as a starting point in your grant-information search. (Some states have changed this historical agency's name to something different, so use this easy interactive map web page to locate your state's commerce agency: www.commerce.gov/about-commerce/services.)

REMEMBER

When you call or email your state agency to discuss your business's expansion needs, make sure to include the name of your business, its products or services, the county in which you're located, and why you need to expand (what's the driving force behind growing larger?). Don't waste time with long-winded statements meant to impress. Even if you hit a dead end (meaning you find no funding), thank the recipient of your call or email for his time. After all, you can always use a friend in state government!

IN THIS CHAPTER

**Knowing who can apply for international funds**

**Searching the Internet for international grant-funding opportunities**

**Tailoring your request based on the location of the grant maker**

# Chapter 8

# Identifying Funds for Nongovernmental Organizations

This chapter is for you if your organization plans to provide programs or services in a country other than the United States. It helps you figure out how to ensure you can qualify for international grants, points you to where you can find international funding opportunities, and gives you some inside scoop on how to improve your odds of getting funded.

WARNING

Read no further if you're writing grants for a US-based nonprofit organization with no programs or activities in other countries. You shouldn't approach funders outside the United States, because funding agencies in other countries have specific funding priorities related to programs in their countries of interest.

# Acquiring NGO Status

Nonprofit organizations that provide programs and services in an international arena rather than a US arena are considered to be *nongovernmental organizations* (NGOs). If you have (or will have) nonprofit programs or activities outside the United States, you must either file for NGO status in every country your organization currently operates in (or plans to operate in) or register with each individual country's national taxation authority, or whatever such an agency is called in the country in which you're providing services. After you receive approvals, you can use your NGO approval letter when seeking grant funding in each specific country.

**TIP**

Get your organizational information together in advance to speed up the NGO approval process. Each country will likely want to see a written description of your organization's purpose and programs, and maybe even multiyear financial data. Visit www.icnl.org/research/monitor to find information on the legal documents required in several countries and how to file them.

**WARNING**

After you have your NGO approval letters in hand from each country, make multiple copies or scan them into an electronic file. If you lose this letter or mistakenly attach your only copy to a grant proposal, it may take months or years to obtain another official copy.

# Finding Funding Sources for NGOs

If your organization provides services in another country, you may be wondering where to look for grant opportunities to keep those programs running. One place to look is the US government. You can also find out about opportunities from formal networks of grant makers outside the United States, such as the European Foundation Centre and Imagine Canada. I tell you more about these international funding source resources in the following sections.

## The US government

Perhaps the first place to look for grant money to fund an international project is the US Agency for International Development (www.usaid.gov). This federal grant-making agency awards grants and contracts to organizations providing international programming in the following areas:

>> Agriculture and food security

>> Democracy, human rights, and governance

>> Economic growth and trade

>> Education

>> Environment and global climate change

>> Gender equality and women's empowerment

>> Global health

>> Science, technology, and innovation

>> Water and sanitation

>> Working in crises and conflict

Other federal agencies that fund internationally include, but are not limited to, the following:

>> Centers for Disease Control and Prevention

>> Department of Commerce

>> Department of State

>> Fish and Wildlife Service

>> National Institutes of Health

>> National Science Foundation

TIP

To find grant-funding opportunities available from federal agencies for international projects, head to www.grants.gov, click the SEARCH GRANTS button at the top of the page, and type **international** into the Keyword(s) search box.

## The Foundation Center Online

The Foundation Center (www.foundationcenter.org) provides a resource page with several informational links related to finding foundation in the US that will fund international projects. Of course, you'll need to subscribe to access full profile information because your search options without a subscription are limited to the foundation's name, state, and *zip code*. I have more information on the Foundation Center's resources in Chapter 6. Here is a link to its Topical Resource Lists web page: http://foundationcenter.org/getstarted/topical/international.html.

# The European Foundation Centre

The European Foundation Centre (EFC) is an association of foundations and corporate funders with members from across Europe and around the world. Founded in 1989, the EFC represents more than 200 foundations. The EFC doesn't give out grants, but it does provide some valuable information for organizations seeking international funding.

To find funders through the EFC, visit its website, www.efc.be. There you can find links to members via the Membership tab. When you click a country, you're taken to a list of grant makers in that country. Then you can see individual names of foundations. Click one of these links to review more about the foundation's grant-making processes and to find contact information. All this information is available for free.

**TIP**

Always email each funder to determine how to approach it with a funding request. Ask if the funder wants a letter of inquiry (see Chapter 2) and/or a short hard-copy proposal (Part 4 covers all you need to know about writing a grant proposal). Also ask whether the funder has an electronic (e-grant) application process. Most importantly, ask what language is preferred for submitting grant documents.

**REMEMBER**

International grant makers have much stricter protocol for contacting their offices, getting grant application information, and submitting grant requests. Also, not all their websites or materials will be printed in English. Make sure you can read and speak their native language; if you can't, you might be able to get away with installing a web browser add-on tool for translation of web pages to English.

## Imagine Canada

Imagine Canada is a national charitable organization whose cause is Canada's charities and nonprofits. It operates Grant Connect (grantconnect.ca), the new name for the organization's *Canadian Directory to Foundations and Corporations*. Grant Connect is a subscription-based online database with information on every Canadian grant-making foundation and hundreds of corporate community-investment programs, plus government funding programs and American foundations willing to fund Canadian charities. A subscription ranges in price from $745 (one year) to $1,245 (two years).

# Knowing What Non-US Funders Expect

Most international funders (independent foundations and corporations) insist that you contact them via email or telephone to request their grant application guidelines and forms. Some may query you about your project, asking about location, population served, and what you intend to request from them.

REMEMBER

Because the foundation landscape in Europe and the rest of the world is varied, the grant eligibility requirements and monetary differences from one country to the next also differ, making adherence to the procedures laid out by each foundation crucial. If you don't follow the rules, you don't get the grant — it's that simple! In the following sections, I cover some of the basic differences.

## Adapting to submission differences

Do your homework before approaching a funder for support. Being prepared is the key to successful grant seeking. A few of the most important steps to take in advance:

1. **Find out the funder's preferred language before you start writing.**

   A Spanish funder may prefer to see applications in English as opposed to Spanish, for example.

TIP

   If the preferred language isn't English, you may want to consider using a translating service after you've written your letter of inquiry or grant application in English. The quickest way to find a translating service is to conduct a general Internet search. Just type in **Spanish translator** or whatever language you need. This type of search finds translators for any language. Asking for references from the translators you find is always a good idea; that way, you get an idea of their work.

2. **Follow the recommended method of initial approach, which should be spelled out in the foundation summary you find during your research.**

   Unless you're directed otherwise, your first contact should be a well-written letter of inquiry (see Chapter 2 for instructions).

REMEMBER

   Keep in mind that spelling is one of the adjustments you have to make when approaching Europe- and Canada-based funding sources. *Program* may become *programme, organization* may become *organisation,* and *center* may become *centre,* just to name a few of the most common spelling quirks.

3. **Understand your lack of a competitive grant application advantage if your organization lacks fee-for-service revenues.**

Your organization will be in competition with organizations that have some form of fee-for-service income and an understanding of the accountability measurements adherent in social impact investing approaches that have been adopted by most international funders.

## Preparing a non–US dollar budget

When you're preparing the budget section of your international funding request, write it first (in draft form, of course) using US currency for all the monetary figures. Then prepare a budget page and budget narrative detail using the currency for the grant maker's country. (For more about preparing budgets, see Chapter 17.)

Following are just a few of the various monetary conversion websites out there, so let your fingers do the typing to convert US dollars (USD) to British pounds or any other type of currency desired:

>> http://finance.yahoo.com/currency-converter

>> www.oanda.com/converter/classic

>> www.x-rates.com/calculator.html

**WARNING**

Make sure your conversion is accurate, or you may be shortchanged if you win the grant.

# 3

# Maximizing Your Chances of Winning a Grant Award

Identify the best-fit and no-go public-sector grant-making agencies for your funding needs. Establish partnerships with organizations willing to commit in writing to help your organization better deliver the services funded by the grant.

Take a journey into the minds of government grant peer reviewers to get a firm understanding of how they read and score your grant applications.

Embrace the fact that telling your story is the best way to win grant monies and discover three simple ways to add life to your statement of need.

Figure out how to draw and keep a reader's attention by using tactics that keep the reader focused.

Find out how to rack up peer-review points with government funding agencies.

Chapter 9

# Finding Federal Grant Opportunities That Fit Your Needs

**M**ost grant writers start out their grant writing endeavors by writing proposals for foundation and corporate grants. This is definitely the easier route for most grant writers, new or veteran. However, sooner or later you'll need to start exploring bigger pots of money. These bigger pots are typically found in grant-funding opportunities at the federal level, which means you need to get comfortable reading a Notice of Funding Availability (NOFA), searching for and highlighting the technical requirements for your grant application, and rounding up the right crew of potential partners to support your grant application's submission.

All federal funding agencies publish guidelines that spell out the type of grant or cooperative agreement application that they expect grant applicants to submit (the NOFA language). The guidelines and the review points assigned to each section of the grant or cooperative agreement narrative and the budget set the stage for what you must write and score to be considered for a grant award. The higher your score, the higher your chances of actually winning.

**REMEMBER**

You must read and reread every sentence of a NOFA *before* you start researching the topic and writing your federal grant application. Then you need to mark up the entire document with highlighting to note the mandatory requirements in order to be considered for a grant award.

In this chapter, I cover everything you need to know to decide whether your organization should apply for a federal grant-funding opportunity once you scrutinize the NOFA details and your organization's capability to manage a grant-funded program.

# Reading the Notice of Funding Availability (Over and Over Again)

Suppose you receive an email alert on a grant or cooperative agreement opportunity from a federal grant-funding agency, and you think that you have a chance to win the grant. But you don't know where to start or whether the grant's really worth going for. In this section, I walk you through the essentials of determining whether this competition is right for your organization. I also give you a quick lesson in what I call *Grantlish* — the art of talking about grants — so you have a better understanding of the review criteria language and terms.

**REMEMBER**

Winning a coveted government grant award means you must understand the importance of reading and following directions with no deviation from the funding agency's guidelines. When I open a NOFA from Grants.gov, I read the entire notice four times:

1.  **The first time, you look for the list of eligible applicants that can apply for the funding.**

2.  **On the second pass, you skim the basics, such as the name of the funding agency, the deadlines, the number of grants to be awarded, and the range of the grant awards.**

3.  **The third time, you zero in on the application formatting requirements, such as page limits, margins, and font types and sizes.**

4.  **On the fourth and final pass, you seek out the peer review criteria.**

    The *peer review criteria* is the point-based rating system a government agency uses to decide — section by section — whether your grant or cooperative agreement application cuts the mustard and is recommended for funding.

# Figuring out who can apply

Before you look at the details of the funding announcement to see what's being offered, you must determine whether your organization is eligible for the competition and, if so, whether it's ready to start competing. The following sections help you do both of these things.

## Verifying your eligibility

Are you eligible for that NOFA you just came across? Before you conclude that the grant or cooperative agreement matches your needs, check out the eligibility paragraph in the funding synopsis or full announcement to make sure your organization is eligible to apply for these federal funds. Otherwise, you'll waste a lot of time working on an application that will no doubt be rejected.

Here's a sampling of what you see when you look under the Eligible Applicants section of the synopsis or full announcement:

» Nonprofits having a 501(c)(3) status with the IRS, other than institutions of higher education

» Nonprofits that don't have a 501(c)(3) status with the IRS, other than institutions of higher education

» For-profit organizations other than small businesses

» Small businesses

» Native American tribal governments (federally recognized)

» Native American tribal organizations (other than federally recognized tribal governments)

» Public housing authorities/Native American housing authorities

» Independent school districts

» Private institutions of higher education

» Public and state-controlled institutions of higher education

» State governments

» County governments

» Special district governments

» City or township governments

**TIP**

If your organization's structure is listed under the eligible applicant section, great! If not, don't give up; look for a potential partnering organization that's eligible to apply, and then contact that organization as soon as possible to see whether it's interested in being the grant applicant and fiscal agent. What's your role in this situation? You're considered a subcontracted and funded partner agency. Remember, you don't have to be the grant applicant to secure a portion of the grant funds. Partnering with another organization as a subcontractor can be an excellent strategy for building financial sustainability for your organization.

**WARNING**

If your organization has not won previous federal grant awards and has no experience in managing large amounts of electronic reporting processes, the applying for Uncle Sam's money — at this time — may not be the best move on your part. Why? It takes all staff onboard and willing to assist with any new programs. In addition, you may have to hire new staff on Day 1 of the proposed program start date; however, the feds won't be transferring any money from the big bank account in Washington, DC, to your local bank account upfront. If your organization's finances are limited, you'll need money in the bank to support early-on program startup expenses until your reimbursement or other type of payment arrangement comes in.

## Making sure you're ready to take the plunge

After you're sure of your eligibility, you have to ask yourself whether your organization is ready to start competing for a specific grant award opportunity. You also need to decide whether you're willing to fulfill the grant program's purpose after the organization is funded. When you click the full grant-funding announcement link (found in the synopsis), look for the *purpose of funding* or *description of funding* statement (usually a paragraph in length), which tells you exactly what the funding agency plans to fund.

Here are some examples of purpose of funding statements:

>> **National Institutes of Health, Department of Health and Human Services, Applied Research Toward Zero Suicide Healthcare Systems:** This funding opportunity announcement (FOA) is intended to support applied research that advances the National Action Alliance for Suicide Prevention's "Zero Suicide" goal of preventing suicide events (attempts and deaths) among individuals receiving treatment within healthcare systems. Zero suicide is a commitment to the prevention of suicide among individuals served by healthcare systems and is also a specific set of healthcare strategies and tools intended to eliminate suicide events. Research is needed to implement effective and comprehensive suicide prevention strategies in a variety of settings, including behavioral health and substance abuse outpatient clinics, emergency departments, and crisis care programs and centers, hospitals, and integrated primary care programs. To achieve the aspirational goal of zero

suicide events within healthcare settings, research is needed to improve healthcare approaches for the following: systematic approaches to suicide risk detection (acute or long term); appropriate risk documentation and follow-up care that is practical and effective; interventions earlier in the course of suicide risk trajectories that reduce incident suicide events in care systems; identification of effective service delivery components that work as safety nets to prevent suicidal events; and identification of service delivery policies and practices that support and maintain "Zero Suicide" goals and reduce suicide events.

>> **National Endowment for the Humanities, Museums, Libraries, and Cultural Organizations: Planning Grants:** This grant program supports projects for general audiences that encourage active engagement with humanities ideas in creative and appealing ways. Many different formats are supported, including permanent and traveling exhibitions, book or film discussion programs, historic site or district interpretations, living history presentations, and other face-to-face programs in public venues.

>> **Department of Transportation — Federal Transit Administration:** The Commercial Motor Vehicle Operator Safety Training (CMVOST) grant is a nationwide federal financial assistance program intended to reduce the severity and number of crashes on US roads involving commercial motor vehicles (CMV) by training operators and future operators in the safe use of such vehicles.

>> **Department of Labor, Summer Jobs and Beyond: Career Pathways for Youth (CPY):** The CPY grants are designed to provide resources to local workforce development boards (LWDBs) to expand and enhance existing summer employment programs and work experiences throughout the year for eligible youth and to implement innovative practices.

If, after reading through your selected federal funding opportunity's purpose of funding statement, you find that one or more fits your organization's long-range plan for program development or expansion, you have a green go flag. (Head to the next section for more on identifying go and no-go points.)

**WARNING**

If your organization has no experience in any of these programming areas and you just want to apply for easy money, be aware that your capacity to fulfill the purpose on receipt of funding may be limited. This situation definitely signals a red flag.

## Using a checklist to determine whether you should apply for a grant

Grants.gov is the go-to resource for finding the most current federal grant-funding opportunities. (Refer to Chapter 5 for more information on Grants.gov.)

To start receiving free email alerts, simply enter your email address under the Manage Subscriptions link at the top of the Grants.gov homepage (`www.grants.gov`). If you think you have a lot of email now, just wait until you start receiving the Grants.gov daily "here's the money" list. It's detailed and filled with clickable web addresses where you can go to read full funding announcements — not just a few lines of detail. This site is the beginning of your journey to read about each grant program's application guidelines and the peer review criteria that determine whether you win or lose.

When you receive the email from Grants.gov, you see a listing of potential grant-funding announcements. Here's an example of an entry:

> FY2016 Commercial Motor Vehicle Operator Safety Training Grant Program
> Department of Transportation
> DOT/Federal Motor Carrier Safety Administration

The listing also includes a link to the web address where you can click through to read the synopsis (summary) of the NOFA and click through again to read the full application document. In the synopsis, you can quickly cruise through the summary of the announcement to look for information that can best be called *red stop flags* and *green go flags.* A red flag means "Warning, do not apply!" Take these steps when you're cruising through the summary:

1. **Look for the number of grants to be awarded.**

   The number of awards is one of the first flags. You literally have no chance at winning a highly competitive grant award when the number of grants awarded is in the single digits (meaning only one to nine awards will be made). How can you stand a chance of winning one of these limited awards when you're competing with grant applicants from 50 states, several US territories, and possibly any one of nearly 600 federally recognized tribal organizations?

   What number of awards can you consider to be a green "get ready to apply" flag? If the funder is awarding at least ten grants for general competitions (open to a very large list of potential grant applicants) and at least five grants for a limited competition (open to a small number of industry-specific grant applicants, such as museums or libraries), then you're good to go.

   Here's an example of how this information will look in an industry-specific NOFA:

   > Expected Number of Awards: 10

2. **Determine the grant application deadline.**

   For example, you may see application deadline information that looks like this:

   > Original Closing Date for Applications: April 5, 2017

   > Current Closing Date for Applications: April 15, 2017

The reason this announcement has an original closing date and a current closing date is because some aspects of this NOFA have likely been changed based on funding agency updates. This is a red flag because it means you need to read the updated set of grant application guidelines to see the specific changes. Any change may affect your grant application narrative, due date, required attachments, or state agency sign-offs. (Sometimes a federal funding agency requires you to submit your grant application package to a state agency for review and sign-off before it'll accept your application.)

Most competitive NOFAs give the grant writer at least 30 days — often more — from the date of publication on Grants.gov. For example, if this announcement were published on February 1 and marked as due February 5, that's a sign the feds already know whom they want to award this grant to, which is why the turnaround time for the grant application due date is so short.

The following NOFA example is a luxury timeline for any grant writer because there are more than 60 days between the NOFA's first publication and the closing (due) date. If your organization is eligible and you're planning to apply for these grant monies, such a timeline is a definite green flag.

Posted Date: January 5, 2017

Creation Date: January 5, 2017

Original Closing Date for Applications: April 3, 2017

Current Closing Date for Applications: April 22, 2017

**WARNING**

Many times, funding agency staff find errors in the first publication of the NOFA or interested grant applicants start emailing and calling the funding agency's program officer with questions because there is a bit of confusion or lack of clarity in the first NOFA release. When this happens, the funding agency publishes modifications or addendums. This is labeled as an update in the synopsis and usually all the changes within the guidelines document are highlighted to reduce confusion. If you miss modifications made midway through the grant-writing process, your application will not score high peer review points because it won't fit what the most recent updates require. Check Grants.gov daily for these unexpected changes and be ready to redirect your writing or modify your project budget well before the grant application deadline. You can also sign up to be alerted for modification updates.

**TIP**

If you're going to research and write a winning government grant application, you need time on your side. Any deadline that's 30 or more days from the date of the grant-funding opportunity announcement is definitely appealing. Less than 30 days is not so appealing.

**REMEMBER**

If you're making your first attempt at applying for a government grant, look for a closing date that allows you at least 30 days for researching and writing. Having less than three weeks to write your first federal grant may be over-whelming unless you can devote 100 percent of your work time to the grant.

Normal writing time for a federal grant is 40 to 100 hours, and research can add another 20 to 40 hours. So give yourself ample time — even if you're a veteran grant writer.

**3.** **Find out the total estimated funding available for grant awards.**

Say the estimated total program funding noted in a funding announcement is $20 million. The NOFA further states the *award ceiling* (maximum grant award for one grant applicant) and *award floor* (minimum grant award for one grant applicant). Here's a green-flag example:

Estimated Total Program Funding: $20 million

Award Ceiling: $200,000

Award Floor: $100,000

Ready to put the preceding steps into practice? Take a look at Figure 9-1, which shows a Grants.gov NOFA for a special funding initiative (not published annually; could be a one-time grant program). Look for the red flags. If you follow Step 1, you notice that there will be ten grant awards. So far, this NOFA is a go! There is a red flag rising up from the posted date and the date of the most recent update in this example:

Posted Date: December 17, 2016
Last Updated Date: February 25, 2017
Current Closing Date for Application: March 16, 2017 no later than 4:00 p.m.
Eastern Time

**WARNING**

Everyone who started working on his grant application narrative in December and continued writing in January and most of February now has to go back and review every section of his narrative(s) and budget(s) and make changes based on the most recent update. Having to rework a grant application at this late date is a huge unexpected red flag for the grant writer or grant-writing team. The updates could make this a no-go (you won't be applying for this grant).

**REMEMBER**

When you have no obvious red flags and several green flags (meaning you have at least 30 days to research and write your federal grant application and at least ten grants will be awarded), you can start eyeballing the full application document.

## Scanning for standard terms

All federal grant and cooperative agreement announcements use two types of terms: general and program-specific. *General terms* are words or phrases that appear in all funding announcements. *Program-specific terms* are words or phrases used in connection with a particular program. Knowing both types of terms and using them correctly throughout your grant application increases your review criteria points and therefore the likelihood that your application will be recommended for funding.

**FIGURE 9-1:**
A sample
of a NOFA.

Source: www.grants.gov/view-opportunity.html?oppId=283700

## Getting the gist of general terms

Knowing general terms can help you understand what any funding agency is talking about in the grant or cooperative agreement announcement. If you've only been schooled in oranges, and the funding agency writes its entire announcement in apples, you'll be lost if you don't understand the key terms used.

Some key general terms you may encounter in grant announcements include the following:

>> **Budget period:** The interval of time by which a grant program defines its funding cycle. The cycle can range from one year to multiple years. For example, a large percentage of federal grants start on the first day of the federal fiscal year, October 1; the budget period for grants awarded on October 1 ends on September 30 of the following year.

- >> **Nonprofit organization:** Typically defined according to what the tax code classifies as a "charitable" or 501(c)(3) organization.

- >> **Project period:** The total time a project is approved for support, including any extensions. This time period can range from 12 months to 60 months (or longer).

- >> **Third party:** Any individual, organization, or business entity (different from your partners) that isn't the direct recipient of grant funds but will subcontract with the grantee to act as its fiscal agent and carry out specified activities in the plan of operation.

- >> **Third-party arrangement:** An arrangement in which the fiscal agent is the third party in the grant or cooperative agreement application. (See the nearby sidebar titled "Understanding how third-party arrangements work.")

## Seeking out program-specific terms

Every government program, both federal and state, has its own terms and definitions. These program-specific terms appear in the full grant application guidelines.

## UNDERSTANDING HOW THIRD-PARTY ARRANGEMENTS WORK

Check out this example of a third-party arrangement: Say you find a competition that fits your organization, which is a zoological society located in an urban area. However, under the eligibility section of this grant opportunity, only zoological society consortiums that jointly cover more than three states can apply for these funds.

Using your regional and national zoological society networking list (or your favorite search engine), you contact several similar organizations in your region to ask whether they're aware of the available funding and whether they want to form a consortium with your society. Depending on which society has the strongest credentials (years in operation, size of property, annual visitor count, number of exotic animals, and so on), your society or another society with more impressive credentials may take the lead as the grant applicant.

When you have a working Memorandum of Understanding (MOU) or Memorandum of Agreement (MOA), you're ready to start negotiating your piece of the financial pie — a place in the contractual section of the budget summary and detail. In other words, your society is on its way to becoming a third-party contractor.

**TIP**

Each government agency provides its own definitions of the terms in the grant-funding opportunity announcement (see the earlier section "Figuring out who can apply"). Use the same terms as those published in the announcement when you write your grant application. By using each agency's terms and its definitions, you meet the basic requirement of the review criteria — showing that you understand the feds' language.

## Embracing the Review Criteria

When you click the link to access the full announcement in a grant-funding opportunity announcement (the synopsis), you see the full-blown grant application guidelines document, usually as a PDF file. Scroll down in the document to look for the *review criteria* section. (This section is also often called the *evaluation criteria* section.)

Understanding the review criteria can help you determine whether the grant-funding opportunity is one you should invest time and effort in pursuing. After all, if you can't fully meet key criteria, you have no reason to go after the grant or cooperative agreement. Likewise, if you can meet all the criteria, following the guidelines closely gives you a much better chance of receiving the points needed for recommendation.

**REMEMBER**

The review criteria section of the document cuts to the chase by showing you how each section of the grant application narrative will be rated. This section tells you — to the letter — exactly what the peer reviewers expect to read in a winning grant application. It also tells you the total number of possible points a winning narrative section can earn during the peer review process. (For more details about peer reviews and the points they award, see Chapter 10.)

## Finding the Right Partners

The right partners can be essential in a winning government grant application. Some funding guidelines give favorable consideration (and thus more review criteria points) to applicants who can get cash or in-kind contributions from partner organizations. Moreover, partnering with another organization may open the door to government funding for which your organization isn't directly eligible to apply.

# Identifying the right implementation partners

The old method of grant seeking was to identify a ton of community partners (any agency with letterhead) who would agree to write a generic — and somewhat weak — letter of support. The new and improved way to create partnerships is with collaborative partners who agree to provide letters of commitment to support your grant application.

*Collaborative partners* are government, health, education, faith-based, business and industry, social, and human services agencies at local, regional, and state levels that commit in writing (via *letters of commitment*) to use their resources to help your organization better deliver the services funded by a grant. These organizations are signing on for the long haul to help your organization implement the grant-funded activities. Collaborative partners also help draft and then sign detailed *Memoranda of Understanding* (MOU) or *Memoranda of Agreement* (MOA) — working agreements that spell out the scope of services that both parties (you and the partner agency) will perform.

TIP

Federal funding agencies prefer that partnerships are documented in letters of commitment, MOU, or MOA rather than their weaker cousin — letters of support.

As you can imagine, involving your organization in a partnership has pros and cons. On the pros side, partnerships have the potential to do all of the following:

>> Create new opportunities

>> Initiate trust at the local level

>> Expand your organization's marketing/target-population area

>> Expand your public image (via links to your organization or services on the partner's website and mentions in the partner's press releases related to the grant-funded program)

>> Help maximize your financial assets to a grant maker by adding external leveraging and/or matching resources

>> Increase your competitive advantage in the grant-seeking arena

>> Provide access to broader financial and human resources

The cons of partnerships are mostly related to what the partners expect. They expect all of the following:

>> A piece of the grant pie

>> An equal voice and vote in group decisions

>> Reciprocal benefits from your organization — letters of commitment, expeditious signing of future MOU for upcoming grant submissions, grant alert sharing, and more

TIP

When looking for a collaborative partner, look for an agency that already serves all or part of your target population. For example, a faith-based group may not be a good partner if you're trying to secure funding for a sex-education program for adolescents. A better match may be an agency that focuses on sexual and repro-ductive health, such as Planned Parenthood. Also, make sure to select partners that have a history and background in your specific grant application area for each grant or cooperative agreement you plan to pursue.

As a successful grant writer having brought in more than $430 million in awards, I'm often asked "How many partners do we need?" I have a solid rule that I apply to that question: I believe the magic number is ten or more partners. Because the partners you select must fit the project topic/funding area, your list of ten will change with each grant application. Partners will tire of writing letters of com-mitment multiple times per year, so try to switch out partners from time to time to invite some new players to your grant-seeking game. Types of partners include (but are not limited to) the following:

>> Referral partners (agencies that refer clients to your organization and agencies that your organization refers its clients to as well)

>> Public sector partners (state, county, city, and other government agencies that have representatives assigned to your governing body or any advisory boards or committees)

>> Business partners (any type of business that has a vested interest in your clientele, such as banks, potential client employers, retail establishments, and for-profit employment agencies)

>> Professional sector partners (for example, law firms, accounting firms, and professional associations that can provide adult mentors)

It's okay to have multiple partners from any one of the categories. Of course, the number of partners for each grant application depends on the project and the organizations needed to provide complimentary services or funding.

WARNING

Not having any partners can be detrimental to your grant application during the peer review process. I'm a federal peer reviewer, and when I come across a grant or cooperative agreement application with fewer than ten partners listed — or even worse, no partners listed — I deduct at least five review points from the program design section. A loss of five or more points in any section can result in your application not making the cut for funding. The typical make-or-break score is 95 points — that is, if you fail to score 95 out of 100 possible points on your funding request, you won't be recommended for federal funding support.

## Getting commitments from partners

Before you meet with a prospective partner, prepare a fact sheet on the grant program's purpose and goals. Email or fax a copy to each agency you plan to invite onto your team. This way, before you meet face to face, the other agency can start thinking of ways to collaborate with your organization.

At your first meeting, ask for at least one of the following contributions:

>> **Cash-match monies:** A commitment of actual cash in the form of a contribution toward your proposed program's expenses

>> **In-kind contributions:** Donated personnel, office space, training space, transportation assistance, supplies, materials, printing services for classroom training use, and other needed items

TIP

If you receive a commitment for cash or in-kind contributions before you even write your grant application, you've already chalked up points with reviewers. In the eyes of those who hand out the grant money, having one or more partners gives you a huge advantage over any grant-seeking organization without partners because partners mean that community resources will be maximized to benefit the target population.

After you have a committed partner, you're ready for the official MOU or MOA. Some funding agencies request that you attach MOU or MOA as an appendix to the funding request. Other funding agencies simply require that the documents be on file with your organization and that they be accessible by the funding agency if monies are awarded. Remember to reference the MOU partnership in your grant application narrative when it isn't a required document in the funder's guidelines.

WARNING

An MOU or MOA should be treated like a legal document and should *not* be developed by a grant writer. Assign this task to your organization's executive director or legal staff; don't take it on yourself.

Chapter 10

# Winning with Peer Reviews

onsider the grant writing process: You open your email to find the daily alert from Grants.gov or another funding alert subscription database. As you scroll through the alerts, you find a notice that looks perfect for your organization. You quickly click the handy link to read the Notice of Funding Availability (NOFA) synopsis. Wow, you may be on to something here. Now you click through again to read the full grant application announcement. Yes, your organization qualifies to apply for this funding. Yes, your organization is ready (capable) to take on this challenge with an intent of finishing first. And finally, you see that 40 grants will be awarded. Jackpot! Go! Green flag! The competition will be stiff, but at least your organization has a chance at winning the bucks. You even have all your collaborative partners onboard, and a third-party evaluator has stepped up to write the evaluation plan section of the grant application's narrative. (Chapter 9 explains partnerships and "Considering the Use of Third-Party Evaluators for Help" is included later in this chapter.) The stars are aligning for this grant application to really happen.

Now that everything's falling into place, you're ready to start writing your grant application narrative. This chapter provides an overview of what's required based on standard government agency review criteria (I get into specifics for each part of the application in Part 4). Remember that writing to meet a grant application's review criteria is as important as identifying the right funding source and preparing your response.

REMEMBER

In general, the basics of review criteria apply to all types of grant guidelines. Because government guidelines are the most rigid, I use them as my example throughout this chapter. Trust me: You can write *anything* if you can write government grant applications.

# Complying with the Technical Review Requirements

When you first submit a grant application to a federal agency for funding consideration, your application goes through a *technical review process* (or simply *pre-review*). This pre-review includes checking to see whether you've completed and signed all the required forms. The pre-review process also verifies your compliance with formatting instructions and checks the page length of your narrative and all other documents. Many government grant and cooperative agreement applications have narrative length restrictions, such as no more than 20 double-spaced pages.

REMEMBER

The *narrative* is the body or main event in your grant application. It's where you write about your organization's history and capability as a grant applicant, the statement of need for grant funding, and the program design (plan of action) for planning and implementing the grant-funded program. In addition, the narrative of a grant application also contains writing sections for the program's management plan (key personnel responsibilities, and task descriptions), the evaluation plan, the sustainability statement, and the budget details and summary.

WARNING

If you fail to pass one of the pre-review mandatory checks, your application doesn't move from the pre-review phase to the peer review phase.

When you first read a grant or cooperative agreement opportunity announcement (refer to Chapter 9 for more on these announcements), some basic information points can give you clues about how to set up your word-processing software to correctly format the narrative. As you read through the formatting instructions, pay attention to the following information. The quicker you find this often buried information in the Notice of Funding Availability (NOFA), the sooner you can get started with the writing process.

>> **The line spacing required:** This can be single or double. Either way, it matters. Press Ctrl+F (⌘+F) to open the Find window. Type **single** to find any references to single spacing. If you don't find single, type **double**. This approach is the easiest way to find and note line-spacing requirements.

>> **The font type and size you must use:** Press Ctrl+F (⌘+F) and type **font** to quickly locate the mandatory or strongly suggested font you have to use to type the documents. Not all grants require a specified font, but many do.

>> **How page limits and page numbers are handled:** Most grant application narratives have page limits. The limitations may apply only to the narrative or they may apply to the narrative plus all the mandatory or required attachments. Typically, extra narrative-supporting charts, résumés, letters of commitment, and other documents are considered a part of the attachments. When they're included in the page count, it can be stressful for the grant writer. Page numbering can also present due diligence moments. The pagination requirements can begin with the first form and end with the last page in the appendixes or can apply only to the narrative section of the request. Some funding agencies also require that you write an abstract (read more about how to create an abstract in Chapter 12). Press Ctrl+F (⌘+F) to open the Find box; type **page** to find all references for page limits, page numbering requirements, and page formatting. Keep in mind that e-grant applications (where the entire grant application is filled out online) have character limits as opposed to pagination requirements found in a hard-copy grant application.

**REMEMBER**

In addition to the formatting requirements, the instructions may include specific program requirements. To be sure of the requirements, check the actual funding announcement before preparing your application.

**REMEMBER**

Always read the grant application guidelines and then be sure to follow the instructions for forms and formatting to the letter.

# FORMATTING WHEN YOU AREN'T GIVEN SPECS

For the roughly 10 percent of government funding agency announcements that *don't* specify font type and size requirements for writing the grant application's narrative, I recommend you call the program officer and ask what the preferred formatting is by the agency. This way, you can't go wrong and you eliminate guessing and stressing.

# Mapping Out the Peer Review Process

After you pass the technical review process (and I know you will!), your application goes to a peer review panel to begin the peer review process.

A *peer review panel* usually includes at least three experts from around the country who work in the field that the grant competition is directed to. It's called *peer review* because you're accepted or rejected by your peers, not by a government program officer. Each reviewer gives a numerical score to each application reviewed. In most instances, the scoring of your entire grant application package is based on a total of 100 points, and typically your grant application needs to score in the high 90s in order to be recommended for the grant award. Explanatory statements on a formal rating form support the numerical score; for each section of the application's review criteria (criteria that was published in the Grants.gov announcement), reviewers describe your application's major strengths and weaknesses.

TIP

Peer reviewers can be fickle about what they like and dislike. Be careful not to deviate from any of the grant application guideline's headings, subheadings, bullets, or specific word-for-word narrative section headings. Read and retype to guide the peer reviewers through their part of the application's evaluation process.

You may wonder what happens when two peer reviewers rate you highly (95 points or higher) and the third reviewer rates you below the cutoff score for an award. After each reviewer independently scores your application, all three get together (over the telephone or in person) and discuss and defend their scores. The general rule is that all three reviewers must come within ten points of each other in order for an application to go one way or the other; often, after discussion, application scores change, sometimes in your favor and sometimes not.

## Knowing how much to write in your narrative sections

Most government grant application narratives are weighted for a total of 100 possible points. The most comprehensive writing section of any grant application narrative is usually the program design section because this is where you write your goals, measurable objectives, implementation strategies, and timelines; create a Logic Model; develop the management plan; and comply with any additional information requested by the funding agency. (See the later section "Presenting your program implementation strategies" and Chapter 15 for more on this important section.)

**WARNING**

Some government agencies assign more than 100 points to the narrative sections of grant applications. Read every word in the guidelines so you know what to shoot for. You may need to write extra response sections to be considered eligible for the additional review points (see the next section for more details).

In the example that follows in this section, note that the largest point section is the program design, management plan, and evaluation methodologies section, which weighs in at 50 points. Because program design is worth 50 percent of the entire grant application's scoring schematic of 100 points, you want to take more time to research and write this section of your grant application narrative. If the funding agency's formatting instructions tell you that the grant application narrative can't exceed 20 single-spaced pages, you want to earmark 50 percent of the 20 pages (so 10 pages) for the program design and methodologies section.

**TIP**

When you know the maximum number of pages that you're allowed to write for the entire grant application narrative, you can take the total points (100 points) and divide them by the points for each section. Translate this number into a percentage, and you know how many pages you need to write in each narrative section to fulfill the peer reviewers' expectations.

In the following list, I note the maximum number of pages you should write in each narrative section based on a 20-page limit. I also provide you with some of the questions that peer reviewers keep in mind when reading your application. Remember, the total possible peer review score for your grant application is 100 points. (*Note:* The point values I include are fairly typical, but the values vary from application to application, as do the section headings.) Here's how it breaks down:

>> **Statement of Need — 20 points (20 percent of 20 pages equals 4 pages for this section):** Does the application specify those issues that this project will address from the list of issues facing the target population? Overall, is this project likely to successfully address the issues identified? Will the target population be involved in the design and implementation of the project? Does the project meet the objectives of the funding and provide sufficient justification for funding the proposal? (See Chapter 14 for more about the statement of need.)

>> **Program Design, Management Plan, and Evaluation Methodologies — 50 points (50 percent of 20 pages equals 10 pages for this section):** What are the goals and measurable objectives for the project? Are they aligned with the purpose of the funding as it's articulated in the grant announcement? Are the proposed program activities likely to achieve the stated goals and objectives? Is the scope and duration of the program adequate to achieve the proposed outcomes? Have collaborative partners been included in the planning of the program design, and will they remain involved in the project's implementation? Is the appropriate research base used to support the proposed

interventions? Is the Logic Model comprehensive? Does the applicant provide an impact statement? Are the evaluation designs and methodologies adequate to measure the extent to which program indicators and outcomes are being met? Is there evidence of strong and adequate project management, including key staff and their functions, timelines, accounting procedures, reporting, and collaborative efforts with the partner organizations? (See Chapters 15 and 16 for more on these specific details.)

>> **Applicant Capability — 20 points (20 percent of 20 pages equals 4 pages for this section):** How long has the grant applicant been in operation? Does the grant applicant have sufficient human and financial resources to implement the project successfully? Does the grant applicant have previous experience and expertise in working with the proposed target population and/or delivering similar services? Has the grant applicant managed federal grants previously? What were the outcomes of these previously funded programs (number served, measurable benchmarks achieved, and other statistical indicators demonstrating implementation success)? What is the grant applicant's organizational structure? Is the board of directors hands-on and involved in providing management and financial oversight to administrative staff? Are there clear lines of accountability in the organizational chart?

>> **Budget and Sustainability — 10 points (10 percent of 20 pages equals 2 pages for this section):** Is there an appropriate amount of money allocated to each key activity/task? Is the total budget allocation adequate to reach project goals? Can the applicant sustain the grant-funded program after the funding period has ended? What percent of the applicant's total project cost is in-kind (non-cash) from the applicant? In-kind from collaborative partners? Cash match from the applicant? Cash match from collaborative partners? (See Chapter 17 for more on presenting your budget.)

## Jumping high to meet the scoring process

TIP

You can get an edge on the competition by meeting the funding agency's *funding priority* for a specific grant competition. Funders often identify one or more priority target populations, geographic areas, or performance criteria and award a funding preference to applications that document that they meet that preference.

For example, when NASA issues a NOFA for classroom-based space exploration education and summer camps, it may include an opportunity for grant applicants to earn an extra five or ten funding priority (read: bonus) points if their program will be located in the Alaska and Pacific Rim regions. If NASA receives 400 applications and plans to award only 20 grants, the grant applicants who write the best-of-the-best narratives and also meet the funding priority will be at the top of the point list for funding recommendation. Because of funding priority, a normal 100-point application (the best peer review rating possible without the funding opportunity) may be given an extra 10 points, for a total of 110 peer review points — a huge advantage over not-so-competitive grant applications.

# Writing to the Peer Review Requirements

Before you start writing, read *all* guidelines for government grant applications and cooperative agreements. Then read them again. In fact, I suggest you read them four times, focusing on different aspects with each review:

1. **The first time through the guidelines, concentrate on the list of applicants eligible for funding.**

2. **During your second read, check for due dates, number of awards, and average size of grants.**

3. **The third time, look at the technical requirements.**

   By *technical requirements,* I mean whether the grant competition requires that you submit your grant application to a state agency for preapproval before the final submission due date or that you use a specific font or adhere to line spacing and margin formatting requirements. Also, pay attention to the maximum pages allowed for the grant narrative sections.

4. **During the fourth review, read for narrative content requirements.**

   The following sections walk you through the narrative content requirements for government funding applications (grants and cooperative agreements) so you can understand what you should look for in content requirements.

**REMEMBER**

Your government funding request should contain a lot of words and phrases that you cull from the grant application guidelines in the section detailing the *purpose of the grant funding.* Plan to use these terms in almost every section of your grant narrative; doing so shows that you're familiar with the guidelines and that your program is in line with the grant.

## Writing and validating a compelling statement of need

One of the major sections in government grant narratives is the *statement of need,* which is usually an explanation of the problem you hope to address if you receive the grant. Normally, when you're writing a grant or cooperative agreement application, this section is worth about 20 of the possible 100 points a review committee can grant.

**TIP**

The statement of need is the place to write about not only your own research findings on the target population but also facts and figures garnered from regional and national research. (See the "Researching Needs and Best Practices" section later in this chapter for details on how to gather all the information you need before you start writing this part of your application.) To win all the points allocated to this section, follow these tips:

>> **Try to be as comprehensive as possible in describing the needs you want to address.** Be sure to address what the problem is, when it started, and how you know it's a problem.

>> **Always include results from recent community needs assessments.** Doing so shows the funder that you're basing your statement of need on valid findings about your target population or community.

>> **Describe service gaps in the current service delivery system, particularly those that will be addressed with additional funding support.** If your organization has a waiting list of clients who can't be served because of its limited capacity, this is a service gap.

>> **Don't talk in generalities.** Use current facts, statistics, quotes, and citations.

>> **Cite all your sources and stay current.** Don't use anything older than five years.

>> **Show that you know what you're talking about.** You can do so by comparing your problems to similar problems in other communities of your size.

In your statement of need, weave a story about the large black hole of gloom and doom if that's what you see based on the facts. You're not exaggerating with the information you include in this section; you're simply writing to meet the review criteria, and you're addressing each point covered in the program's or agency's goals. (For more on communicating your needs, see Chapter 14.)

## Presenting your program implementation strategies

Another major section in a funding request narrative is what's often referred to as the *program design*. In this section, you lay out your strategy (or your program) for addressing the problem(s) presented in your statement of need. In grant applications and cooperative agreement narratives, this section is usually weighted more heavily than any other section of the narrative (anywhere from 25 to 60 points).

In order to receive the most points possible, the program design must be sound and must contain program elements directly linked to the achievement of project objectives. Therefore, you need to write in a way that uses the language of the government agency's own objectives.

In other words, the program design section includes your proposed project's goals and objectives, which should reflect those of the funder's purpose. Always give back to the reviewers the same language used in the application for grant review criteria.

REMEMBER

Also, always write measurable objectives that state who will be affected (at-risk students), what the change will be (an increase of at least 20 percent), and by when (at the end of one year). Language concerning a time frame is optional in the objectives only when the grant application guidelines ask for a separate timeline section.

The objectives or measurements stated in a grant announcement are like a big finger pointing in the direction you need to write in order to win a grant. The objectives shout out, "Write me, write me!" For more about goals and objectives, head to Chapter 15.

## Demonstrating accountability with an evaluation plan

A sound *evaluation plan,* the next major part of your program design narrative, is essential to winning big review points. In some grant applications, the evaluation section is included as a component of the program design section; in others, it's a stand-alone section. Regardless of where it's placed, this section is usually weighted between 5 and 20 points.

Typically, an evaluation plan focuses on two main questions:

>> Was the program implemented effectively? (This is the *process evaluation.*)

>> Did the program achieve its intended objectives and outcomes? (This is the *outcome evaluation.*)

The evaluation plan should answer the following questions:

>> What qualitative and quantitative measures will you collect data on?

>> What data collection tools will you use to measure qualitative and quantitative data?

>> How frequently will you measure the data?

>> How will you use the data collected?

>> How often will you implement corrective actions when the data shows that you're falling short of your measurable objectives in any area?

>> Who will conduct the evaluation?

>> How will the results of your evaluation be shared with stakeholders?

TIP

If you brought in a third-party evaluator during the planning stages of your project or service, she's automatically a member of the narrative writing team. The evaluator can write the entire evaluation plan section because she should be an expert in gleaning a program design and quickly developing research-driven evaluation plans. Head to the later "Considering the Use of Third-Party Evaluators" section for more details on working with these folks.

## Proving your organization's ability to manage a grant-funded project

The project management and overall organizational capability section of your grant application or cooperative agreement narrative typically carries double-digit peer review points (usually 10 to 20). If you're not capable of carrying out and managing a federal grant award, that inability will show up in this section in one way or another. In a well-constructed *project management statement,* you cite your organization's capability and relevant experience in developing and operating programs that deal with problems similar to those addressed by the proposed project or service. You should also cite the organization's experience in operating programs in cooperation with other community organizations, including collaborative partners.

Also remember to identify your program's executive leaders in the project management section. Briefly describe their involvement in the proposed project or service and provide assurance of their commitment to the successful implementation of that project or service.

TIP

Keep in mind that all key personnel (the people responsible for the project's implementation) should have extensive experience in programs and services like the one you're proposing. You score more points during the review process if you can name actual staff members and show their titles and credentials instead of relying on the standard "yet to be hired" statement. *Note:* Don't forget to identify your third-party evaluator upfront; be prepared to include a copy of her full résumé in your appendixes, if requested.

To advance your claims regarding project management, include documentation that briefly summarizes similar projects undertaken by your organization and note the extent to which your objectives were achieved. Also, record and justify the priority this project or service will have within your organization, including the facilities and resources available to carry out your plans. If you have volunteers, mentioning them (how many, what they do, and the value of their contribution to your organization) in this section is helpful. You can determine the value of a volunteer hour on the website www.independentsector.org.

REMEMBER

Losing even one or two points in the project management section can hurt you when the total score is tallied.

## Developing an expense-drive budget

Your budget forms and detailed narrative must show the grant reviewer that your costs are reasonable, allowable, and worth the result you seek. The budget section is usually worth the remaining review criteria points (five to ten), although not all funders score the budget as part of the review process.

With your budget narrative, most government grants and cooperative agreements ask you to provide a detailed budget worksheet for each year of the project period. You also need to include an explanation of the basis for computation of all costs. (See Chapter 17 for more about budget presentation.)

REMEMBER

Add up your budget, and then add it up again. Make sure each expense is directly related to an activity necessary to reach the project's objectives. Don't introduce any costs here that you haven't addressed in your main application narrative.

When you read the guidelines for preparing the budget, look closely for any language about construction costs. Most government grants don't cover new construction, but they do allow program-related renovations.

TIP

When in doubt about the guidelines and how they relate to your budget, call and ask the government agency's grants management officer. Then follow up with an email to create a paper trail for future reference. This contact — even if it seems trivial — can establish a relationship that may be beneficial in getting your grant funded.

# Researching Needs and Best Practices

You probably know a lot about the population you want to serve with your hoped-for grant monies. And if you're at the grant-writing stage for a program, you're probably pretty well versed in what you want to accomplish and how you plan to go about putting the program in place. But to write an award-winning application, you need to beef up your facts with even more facts.

Knowing the grant or cooperative agreement's intent or focus sets the direction for the type of research you must do in order to write a high-scoring, competitive grant application. For example, if the monies are intended to fund a new economic development initiative for small businesses for the City of Phoenix, you need to research demographics on the needs of small businesses in the county and city. You can get information about small business demographics by state by typing keywords into your favorite Internet search engine or by using some of the resources available on Small Business Development Center website for the state. When I typed **statistics on Arizona small businesses**, links came back for multiple websites with recent reports on small businesses located in Arizona.

TIP

I always create an online electronic folder for my research data so I have it at my fingertips when I'm not at my home office's computer, and I recommend that you do the same. Having access to critically needed information from all forms of mobile technology is the best plan when you may take your work home from the office and you need access to files. I use Dropbox (www.dropbox.com) and have the mobile application downloaded on my smartphone, tablet, and laptops. Remember, when you're on a grant application deadline, all your work may not be done during traditional work hours.

TIP

Google Scholar (http://scholar.google.com) is a great resource for finding publications if you're affiliated with any college. In addition, you'll also have access to enormous publication databases.

Publications produced by the government agencies that award grants are another good source for facts and figures. You can obtain these valuable resources from each government agency's information clearinghouse. Check out agency websites for links labeled Resources or Publications. You may encounter any of the following publications, which can be of great help:

>> **Bulletins:** These documents summarize recent findings from government program initiatives. Designed for use as references, they may contain graphics such as tables, charts, graphs, and photographs. You can re-create some of the most current and relevant graphics in your statement of need or program design.

>> **Fact sheets:** Fact sheets highlight, in one to two pages, key points and sources of further information on government programs and initiatives. You can cite the most recent facts (never more than five years old) in your statement of need.

>> **Journals:** These publications highlight innovative programs or contain articles on critical issues and trends. You can cite some of the model programs at the beginning of your program design section to show how you're modeling your project on a successful program. You can also use any critical issues or trends covered in journals in your statement of need.

>> **Reports:** These documents contain comprehensive research and evaluation findings; provide detailed descriptions of innovative programs implemented at the national, state, and local levels; and present statistical analysis, trends, or other data on selected topics. Reports may include explanations of case studies, field studies, and other strategies used for assessing program success and replication. Some reports provide training curricula and lesson plans as well.

>> **Summaries:** Summaries describe key research and evaluation findings that may affect future policies and practices. Summaries highlight funded programs implemented at the national, state, or local level that may serve as models for other jurisdictions. These publications usually include appendixes and lists of resources and additional readings.

**TIP**

You can cite research on evaluation findings in your statement of need. Cite innovative programs considered models in your program design section to build the basis for proposing your own program model.

**TIP**

I save every research-oriented publication I can get my hands on to my Dropbox by subject category. As new reports are published, I replace the older reports so that I'm working on my grant applications with the most current research findings. Grant writing is so much easier when you have the information you need (and the information you didn't even know you needed) at your fingertips. The Internet has also made it easy to bookmark a favorite website.

# Considering the Use of Third-Party Evaluators

Writing an application for a federal grant or cooperative agreement requires making new friends in your community — not only collaborative partners (see Chapter 9) but also community specialists such as evaluators. You can always score more review points by using a *third-party evaluator* — basically a person or organization that can operate in an objective mode and give you factual, third-party feedback on your grant-funded goals and objectives.

As a frequent federal grant reviewer, I'm more likely to award more review points for the evaluation plan when a third-party evaluator is proposed. Even though evaluators are typically paid from grant funds, I know that they will call the situations as they see them when helping grant applicants develop data collection tools, collect and interpret data, and compile comprehensive evaluation reports for funders and other stakeholders. (I cover the evaluation process in depth in Chapter 15.)

TIP

The following folks make excellent third-party evaluators:

>> **Evaluation consultants:** These people normally have years of experience in the field of evaluation. You can often find evaluation consultants by calling your local community foundation. Community foundations often use evaluation consultants to assist in evaluating their own programs.

>> **Retired college or university faculty:** Often, these individuals have participated in the grant writing process and have even helped their college or university development offices design evaluations for government grant applications.

>> **Retired government personnel who worked in an administrative capacity in a finance department:** These individuals usually have years' worth of work experience in internal reporting requirements for major organizations or government agencies.

As far as timing's concerned, the best time to bring in an evaluator is when you're sitting down with your staff and your collaborative partners to plan what you'll propose in the grant or cooperative agreement application.

REMEMBER

Running an online search for third-party evaluators is also helpful, but you may not locate an evaluator close to home. Using an evaluator who doesn't live in your city or town is okay as long as she is familiar with the area, but keep in mind that hiring an evaluator from outside your region may increase the cost of the evaluation if site visits are necessary to plan and conduct the evaluation.

# Getting Invited to Join a Peer Review Team

Before you start writing your grant application narrative, I want to share an insider secret with you about how to connect mentally and skill-wise to the peer review process: You can search for and sign up to become a government peer reviewer, also known as a *grant reader*. Yes, you! Simply type **call for peer reviewer** into your favorite search engine or look directly on the federal funding agency's website.

Desirable peer reviewer characteristics include the following:

>> Formal education in the grant-funding topic area

>> Volunteer experience in the grant-funding topic area

>> Work experience in the grant-funding topic area

Here are the benefits of participating in the government peer review process:

>> **You gain valuable insight into the peer review process.** You experience firsthand how applications for a particular funder are evaluated and scored. Plus, you get to see how other grant writers state their cases, incorporate compelling graphics, and present research-based evidence of their need for the grant funding and how that funding will impact their target populations.

>> **You have the opportunity to network with other peer reviewers from throughout the United States and its territories.** Today, most peer reviews are done online via a password-protected portal managed by the grant-funding agency. My typical peer review assignments have required that I review 10 to 12 grant applications online and enter the strengths and weaknesses of each narrative section into the online text box windows. After I've completed my set of assigned grant applications, I notify the peer review manager. This person checks on the progress of the other peer reviewers assigned to the same set of grant applications as I reviewed. When the entire team is ready, the peer review manager schedules a conference call (lasting from two to four hours) for the consensus discussion. This team peer review process (where you must come to a consensus on the final scoring for each application) is when you are acquainted with many types of connected individuals.

By *connected individuals,* I mean people who are experts in the grant-funding field. These same people can become your best friends when you need a third-party evaluator (or a referral for one) or when you need a copy of a successful grant application they've written for a particular funding agency.

>> **You get paid!** At the federal government level, compensation is about $125 per grant application reviewed, or more depending on the agency's budget for the peer review process. At the state government agency level, the compensation is typically not as much as Uncle Sam's lucrative offer. Most often, state grant-making agencies set a flat rate for reviewing 10 to 15 grant applications.

If you don't have a full-time day job working as a grant writer for an employer, taking on state agency grant reviews may or may not be financially worth the effort required by grant-writing consultants. I've been paid as low as $750 for reviewing 15 applications to as high as $2,500 for reviewing 20 applications and spending six hours in multiple "change in the peer review process" types of calls. At best, it's not always the smoothest process for the reviewer, but the experience you can gain is worth a pot of gold!

REMEMBER

Sometimes, if the peer review database is already full, you may not be contacted for months — even a year or longer. But don't give up! Continue to email the agency's peer reviewer database contact person and indicate your enthusiasm about being invited to participate in the peer review process. You may have to update your résumé and the peer review application every year, so make a note on your annual calendar now.

TIP

A federal agency constantly looking for peer reviewers is the US Department of Justice Bureau of Justice Assistance.

# Chapter 11

# Resuscitating Your Writing

The old-school style of grant writing was cut and dried; actually, it was boring! Page after page of term-paper paragraphs with few injections of case statements (stories about the target population in need) and not many eye-catching, easy-to-read sentences. However, when it comes to writing competitive grant applications today, most funders want brevity, real-life examples, and alignment between what they fund and your project in need of funding. There are a lot of easy writing spin tips that can help you breeze through writing online e-grant applications. as well as paper funding submissions.

So, do you need an advanced degree in creative writing? No! Do you need to hire a spin master? Well, it might help to reduce your stress, but what you really need to shift your writing style is this book and, most importantly, this chapter. In it I share with you some vivid words and phrases that are sure to jump-start your creative side. This chapter is where I share the best of the best from Bev with my faithful readers. I think you'll find yourself returning to these pages over and over — every time you write. Sit back and get ready to discover the real definition of *wordsmithing* or *grantspeak.*

# Putting a Heartbeat in Your Writing

If you've read other chapters in this book, you know that I give you tons of action steps for every point in the grant-seeking and grant writing processes. But for this chapter, I want you to throw out those "get to the point" ideas about writing. Reprogram your brain with passion, creativity, and emotion — the qualities that really equate to the art of storytelling, which is the new way to present your organization's case (needs) to funders and win grant funding. Make every sentence one that contributes to the big picture for needing funding and implementing solutions.

**REMEMBER**

Even with today's grant makers, shifting grant submissions from paper copies to online e-grant copy and paste templates, you can still add life or put a heartbeat in your writing. You won't be wasting spaces or characters. You will be writing within the parameters for characters and spaces. However, your words can and will come to life by following the tips in this chapter!

At first, being creative and pulling words from the sky seems difficult and awkward. But you did it as a child, and you can do it again. Give yourself some time to practice this storytelling (giving it life) approach, and in no time you'll be writing like the pros! To help you settle into the writing process, the next sections offer you three easy-to-follow steps.

## Step 1: Describe who, what, and where

Some grant seekers spend pages writing about what they need but then include only one paragraph to take the reader on a virtual tour of the community where the grant funds will have an impact. A better strategy is to present a basic "this is who we are" paragraph to explain to the funder's decision-making staff the who, what, and where about your organization.

**REMEMBER**

Be brief, but make every paragraph of your grant application count. Remember that money comes, in part, from the heart of funding decision makers and, in part, from the logical thinking process. Foundations and corporations are more receptive to this type of writing than government agencies. In Chapter 6, I give you the definition of private sector funders. In Chapters 4 and 5, I write about government agencies that award grants.

Here's a compelling example that describes the who, what, and where of a nonprofit organization. Use it to kick-start your journey of exploring creative writing and using words that work.

**Applicant Organization:** Founded in 2010 by Sisters of Mercy, Mary's Kitchen is an IRS-approved 501(c)(3) nonprofit life-saving agency that provides hot eat-in and brown-bag takeout nutritional meals to 10,000 homeless veterans annually. Mary's Kitchen has a 2,000-square-foot communal kitchen in the City of Phoenix's (AZ) downtown Human Services Campus located in the heart of the business district.

TIP

Typing a very brief paragraph for an online e-grant application copy and paste field will require creative writing and brevity. Remember, there may not a sizeable space and character allowance. However, if you're going to submit a paper copy for uploading in Microsoft Word or Adobe PDF format, you can certainly add volumes of paragraphs about your organization. Chapter 13 covers how to write lengthier replies to describe your organization to funders.

REMEMBER

Ultimately, you want to write to meet the funder's guidelines while spinning a story about the applicant organization, where it's located, and whom it serves.

## Step 2: Present the need

If the sun is shining and everything is fine inside and outside your organization, you really don't need any grant monies, right? That's how the grant readers view what you write. If you write only about the good things happening, you don't really have a justification or need for outside funding. I know it may be difficult if you're a really positive person by nature, but when writing an application, you need to do the following:

>> Focus on the gaps in existing programs and services within your organization.

>> Research and write about the community's gaps or needs to amplify what's missing in the targeted area.

>> Be prepared to tell and support with recent statistics just how dire the situation is for your target population.

Head to Chapter 14 for a tour of how to write your statement of need with doom, gloom, drama, and trauma.

Here is an example of a brief statement of need:

Mary's Kitchen's capacity has breached the city's fire codes 50 times in 2016 (COP Fire Department) in the first six months, so we've had to shift our focus of feeding homeless veterans to taking constant head counts to avoid any further over-occupancy citations and fines. With more than 58,000 (Arizona Coalition to End Homelessness, 2014) former service members without homes, jobs, transportation, and more, our kitchen has become a daytime refuge for early-morning and late-evening survival stops. More than 20,000 (annual report, 2015) meals are prepared and served in-house or bagged for the veterans who cannot sit still or who do not feel safe in a communal eating environment. Mary's Kitchen is the largest homeless veterans food-serving agency in the southwest United States. Our facility needs to expand by 100 percent to 4,000 square feet. There is also a critical need to upgrade kitchen equipment, dining tables, and chairs, and create a larger food distribution area. There is limited available space on the Human Services Campus; however, a local business owner is going to allow us to lease an insulated 6,000-square-foot warehouse (built in 2010) for $1 per year on a ten-year renewable lease. Your support is urgently needed to help us with the rest of the items needed. Volunteer members of the National Guard will move our existing equipment and furnishings free of charge. Men and women who have served our country and lost their limbs, houses, and families should not be digging through commercial garbage bins for meal. Compassion toward this population in need has dissipated for many unjustified reasons.

**TIP**

The example for Mary's Kitchen is less than 300 words and 1,700 characters with spaces. This can be trimmed to meet more stringent e-grant application requirements.

When you write about your unfortunate situation, I don't want you to go overboard. To be safe, select a dozen or so terms from the following lists to build the "justification for why your organization needs grant funding" sentences:

Alienate, abandon, abashment, abbreviated, abortive, adjudicate, aghast, aimless

Backbone, backfire, barren, baseless, benign, besiege, betray, beyond, bland, blast, blatant, bottom, boundary

Capitulate, categorical, ceaseless, censor, challenge, cheapen, choke, clash, close-minded, collateral, commonplace, compound, concealed

Danger, deadly, decadence, decay, decline, defection, demoralize, depressive, despairing

Economical, eject, elongated, emaciated, emergency, endless, endure, entangle

The next group of words calls out to grant readers consciously and subconsciously. Use these words to grab and keep the attention of grant readers:

Fade, fallacy, fallible, faltering, fault, feckless, fend, feverish, fictitious, final

Germane, glaring, gloom, glum, gradual, grasping, grave, gulf, gut

Habitually, hallow, halfhearted, hamper, haphazard, harbor, harden, hardly, harrowing, harshly

Icy, idleness, immoral, impassible, immutable, impenetrable, imperfect, impractical

Jagged, jolt, judicious, jurisdiction, justification, juxtaposed

Keen, kick, kill, knifelike, knock-down-and-drag-out

Lacerated, lackadaisical, lambaste, lapse, lash, latitude, levity

Your words must come to life and create a story that is worthy of a competitive grant award. The following strong words can give you the winning edge every time:

Madness, maggot, makeshift, malign, mandate, matchless, migratory

Nameless, near-at-hand, neglectful, never-ending, nonetheless

Object, oftentimes, ominous, once and again, one-sidedness, outcry

Painful, pallid, paradigm, parallel, paralyze, paramount, pariah, partiality, precarious, propensity

Quagmire, queasy, quit, quizzical

Rabid, ration, rattle, ravage, recluse, reevaluate, relinquish, remedy, remiss

Writing with words that bring life and attention means you have to start and keep thinking outside of the box. Granted, this strategy isn't the way you usually load up your paragraphs with words, but you're ready to start winning all your grant requests:

Sacrifice, safety, sanction, scant, scatter, search, seedy, seemingly, separation, seriously, shallow

Tacit, tantamount, tarnish, temperate, thwart, tight-fisted, timeworn

Unaccompanied, unadvisable, unbiased, indescribable, unthinkable

Vacancy, vacillating, vague, value, vanish, variance, vegetate

Waive, wallop, waning, watchful, weakling, weary

Yearning, yielding, yet, yonder

Zealous, zenith

**REMEMBER**

Don't underestimate the power of the written word. Using powerful words to paint a picture of where the problem is geographically located is especially important when you're approaching potential funders who aren't located in or near your community. However, when you use new words in a grant application, make sure you know the meanings and connotations of them so you don't end up using them incorrectly.

## Step 3: Validate the need

Don't be shy about using an online thesaurus to bring your thoughts to life in a way that conveys true and serious need. You can also find synonyms and antonyms online. Just type **thesaurus** into your favorite search engine. Most word processing programs come with a thesaurus as well.

**WARNING**

A thesaurus is a wonderful tool to help you expand your vocabulary and ultimately become a better writer, but if you're new to vocabulary expansion, be careful to avoid words that most people aren't familiar with. In an attempt to sound smart, your writing style may be viewed as confusing and convoluted by potential funders.

# Racking Up Peer Review Points in the Program Design

In some foundation and government grant-writing formats, the program design requests a *purpose of this request* statement. This is one sentence that precedes your goals, objectives, implementations strategies, and the rest of the program design narrative. (You can read specifics about the program design in Chapter 15.)

One sentence may not seem to be enough, but remember that this sentence is the bridge between the statement of need and the full program design text. The following example will work great in either an online e-grant template or a full-fledged Word or PDF upload document.

## Starting with the purpose of this request statement

In most grant-writing application formats, the program design must be written after one or two first-priority narrative sections. These sections are the organizational capability component and the statement of need. By now, the grant readers need a mental regrouping to remind them of the purpose of your grant request. This applies to foundation and government grant applications. A one-sentence purpose statement looks like this:

> **Government requesting language:** The purpose of this grant application is to request federal funding support for the Mary's Kitchen Expansion Project (located in downtown Phoenix, Arizona).

**Foundation requesting language:** The purpose of this proposal is to invite the ABC Foundation to become a financial stakeholder in the Mary's Kitchen Expansion Project.

**REMEMBER**

In these examples, can you see how just changing a few of the words softens the request to foundations? The government purpose statement is straightforward. The foundation purpose statement is worded like an invitation for a funder to come onboard to help Mary's Kitchen.

## Aligning your goals and objectives with the purpose of the funding

Remember, you want to win grants from Day 1 as a grant writer. To do so, carefully review the funder's mission and funding priorities. Look at funding program-specific information on their websites. Bookmark these pages because you'll be looking at them multiple times when you create your grant application's goals and objectives. Everything you write in your grant application must align with the purpose of the funding (government and foundation).

Here is a purpose statement from a US Department of Justice Notice of Funding Availability (NOFA):

**Second Chance Act Technology-Based Career Training Program for Incarcerated Adults and Juveniles**

**Overview** (found on page 4 of the NOFA)

The Second Chance Act of 2007 (Pub. L. 110-199) provides a comprehensive response to the increasing number of incarcerated adults and juveniles who are released from prison, jail, and juvenile residential facilities and returning to communities. There are currently over 2.2 million individuals serving time in our federal and state prisons, and millions of people cycling through local jails every year. Ninety-five percent of all people incarcerated today will eventually be released and will return to communities. Programs funded under the Second Chance Act help ensure that the transition individuals make from prison and jail to the community is successful and promotes public safety. Securing employment can facilitate successful reentry for people leaving correctional facilities. However, there are many barriers people with criminal records encounter as they attempt to reenter both the community and the workforce. Improving employment outcomes for this population can contribute to recidivism reduction and increased public safety. Section 115 of the Second Chance Act authorizes federal awards to states, units of local government, territories, and federally recognized Indian tribes to provide technology-based career training to persons confined in state prisons, local jails, tribal jails, and juvenile residential facilities. This program supports training for technology-related jobs and the continuum of reentry transition planning, including education, training, support services, and building connections to local employers that will enable participants to secure employment prerelease.

Goals, Objectives, and Deliverables (found on page 4 of the NOFA)

The goal of this program is **to increase the post-release employability of the incarcerated population in technology-based jobs.**

The objective of the program is to establish and provide career training programs for incarcerated adults and juveniles during the 6- to 36-month period before release from a prison, jail, or juvenile facility with connections to follow-up services after release in the community.

Training components should be relevant to specific technology-related needs of in-demand jobs within the geographic area to which the individuals will be returning. Each participant should receive an individualized reentry plan that addresses post-release transition services, including employment support services.

When you're writing your goal for this grant application, extract Uncle Sam's language and keep the goal statement down to one sentence. Remember, label your sentence *Goal.*

> **Goal:** Provide post-release technology-based job training in five southern Mississippi confinement facilities for formerly incarcerated adults and juveniles released and returning to the targeted communities.

Next, look in the NOFA for clues about objectives or measurements. This is what I found in the NOFA that I'm using for this example:

> **For the objective:** The objective of the program is to establish and provide career training programs for incarcerated adults and juveniles during the 6- to 36-month period before release from a prison, jail, or juvenile facility with connections to follow-up services after release in the community.

> **For the measurements:** I clicked a *performance tools* link in the NOFA on page 13 (yes, you have to view the NOFA with an eagle eye!) and found a link to a document with the performance measures for this grant program:

> The performance measures for this SCA program were established to indicate to what extent grant activities meet the following objectives:

> 1. Partner and work with a technology career partner to provide evidence-based reentry services to offenders.
>
> 2. Develop a technology career–specific curriculum for offenders.
>
> 3. Train instructors to teach curriculum in technology career fields.
>
> 4. Reduce recidivism.

**TIP**

Write your objectives using the SMART structure, which means that your objectives are **s**pecific, **m**easurable, **a**ttainable, **r**ealistic, and **t**ime-bound. A winning-minded grant writer will look at the initial objective and the performance measures and create the following objectives in her grant application:

> **SMART objective 1:** By the end of Year 1, increase career partners engaged in the project by 50 percent or more as demonstrated by the number of partners involved in southern Mississippi workforce development programs targeting ex-offenders currently (baseline) and the number of new partnerships created during the planning year.

> **SMART objective 2:** By the end of Year 1, increase the content and competencies of the region's current state-designed technology curriculum by 80 percent as demonstrated by the number of national technology training standards added to the community college and trade school curricula in southern Mississippi.

> **SMART objective 3:** By the end of Year 1, increase the number of instructors trained to teach the new rigorous curriculum in technology career fields by 90 percent as demonstrated by comparisons of the number of teachers currently certified to teach the outdated technology curriculum in the region and the number completing the 12-week, 20-hours-per-week training program and recertified by the Mississippi Department of Education.

> **SMART objective 4:** By the end of Year 3, decrease recidivism among the targeted population enrolled in the Second Change Act Technology Careers Program in southern Mississippi by 20 percent as demonstrated by tracking incarceration reentry rates for the experimental group compared to the control group in the same region.

## Closing the deal by focusing on the lasting impact of the funder's investment

Use words and phrases such as *external, internal, local fundraising, creating future funding partners, inviting more external funding sources to the organization's table of partners, seeking to identify more investors in our stakeholders,* and *continuing grant-funded activities after the funding is gone.* These words and phrases don't just point to something; they rocket off the page and say, "We're planning for the future of this organization and asking for your help, and we have a plan for keeping this program alive after we spend your money."

**REMEMBER**

All types of funders want assurances that when you finish spending their money, the show or program will go on. No funder wants the efforts supported by its investment to suddenly shut down at the end of the funding period.

In your program design and evaluation section, you must write a paragraph to address the funder's concerns about continuity, which arise during the funding request review stage. In fact, most grant applications include a question or a section on the sustainability of the project, where you must outline your plan for maintaining the project after grant funding ends. If this information isn't explicitly requested, be sure to include it anyway.

This paragraph from the Project Live grant request lays out the organization's financial plan for its project's future:

> The City of Hopeful has been successful in securing grants and contracts to support Project Live. In 2016, Project Live was awarded $3 million from the US Department of Housing and Urban Renewal for a transitional housing facility and supportive services. This grant will cover five years of construction and operating support. This grant application seeks funding for three years of entrepreneurial training which will immensely benefit the clients served by Project Live. On completion of this anticipated grant award, the City of Hopeful will have formed a Grants Advisory Committee and identified ongoing funding support for all aspects of Project Live, including the proposed entrepreneurial program. In addition, several local philanthropists have requested one-on-one presentations from City Council members. One of our sustainability goals includes starting an endowment fund to perpetuate Project Live for this community.

# 4

# Following the Funder's Guidelines

Pull together all the critical support documents — cover letters, abstracts, tables of contents, forms, and more — to ensure you don't forget any of the smaller yet still relevant pieces of your grant application.

Write about your organization's background and capabilities in a way that presents your target population and programs or services offered in a clear, straightforward, and statistically framed manner.

Make grant reviewers grasp the dire need of your organization by using statistics, case studies, and visuals to craft a compelling statement of need.

Build a solid program design with goals and objectives that meet (and exceed!) the peer reviewer's and program officer's expectations. This section is the heart and soul of your grant application, so make it sing!

Clarify who's going to implement the project if it receives funding and how your organization plans to demonstrate accountability.

Calculate the budget, making sure it matches the monies requested, dollar for dollar. Remember that every action requires an expenditure.

Chapter 12

# Preparing Preliminary Documents

over letters are no longer a standard requirement in a grant application, but some private sector funders (that is, foundations and corporations) still require that a formal cover letter accompany a paper grant proposal. What do you write in these cover letters? How long should they be, and should they be formal or informal? What do you do if you have to fill out a cover form (something many private sector and all public sector grant makers require)? I answer all these questions in this chapter.

I also introduce you to some of the standard information-gathering forms and other pre-narrative sections you can expect to see. Remember that every type of funding source has different grant proposal formatting and submission requirements. With so many types of funding applications floating around, determining what goes where can be confusing. That's why I explain it all for you in this chapter.

# Complying with Mandatory Document Requirements

Not sure what to include in your application? Don't stress. I break down the standard ingredients for you right here by order of typical appearance. I also clarify when each preliminary document is required.

**WARNING**

Always read each funding agency's guidelines and give the funder exactly what it asks for in the instructions. Never, ever deviate. Also, try not to alter any PDF-formatted forms if at all possible. Changing the forms because you need more space on a typing line or changing the font in a form can result in automatic rejection. Make sure that all PDF forms are filled in accurately and uploaded in the funder's required PDF version.

These upfront components (the items that come before the grant application narrative), when asked for, should be in this order — although, remember, not every piece applies in every case:

>> **Cover letter:** Only for foundation and corporate requests that ask you to include a cover letter.

>> **Common grant application form:** Only for foundation and corporate requests when the funder doesn't have its own specific application form or format and instructs you to submit a common grant application form.

>> **Application for Federal Assistance:** Always for federal grant applications and sometimes requested by state agencies. Most often referred to as *SF-424* (*SF* stands for Standard Form).

>> **Abstract or executive summary:** Appropriate for all types of funders and typically required.

>> **Table of contents:** Most often requested in federal and state grant applications. Not every government agency requires a table of contents.

# Drafting a Cover Letter (If Requested)

Thanks to the increasing number of funders that now require e-grants (electronic online submissions in the funder's template) , I only type cover letters for foundation and corporate funders that request one in their published guidelines. (Government funders rarely, if ever, ask for a cover letter anymore.) Read more about e-grants in Chapter 11.

If you have to supply a cover letter, make sure it's brief and to the point. When a funder opens your request for assistance, the cover letter should provide the first inkling of how well you understand the person you addressed the letter to — the funder. Also, avoid merely regurgitating the information in your grant request.

TIP

Write the cover letter last, after you've completed the entire funding request and are in a reflective mood. As you consider your great achievement (the finished funding request), let the creative, right side of your brain kick in and connect your feelings of accomplishment to the person who will help make your plans come true.

Follow these handy tips when you write your own cover letters (and check out the cover letter example in Figure 12-1):

>> **Use the same date that you'll send the complete grant application to the funding source.** You want to create documents that are consistent, so the dates on cover letters and accompanying cover forms should be the same.

>> **Open with the contact person's name and title, followed by the funding source name, address, city, state, and zip code.** Remember to double-check the contact information with a telephone call or email to the funder. You can also search via the Internet for the correct information.

>> **Greet the contact person with "Dear" plus the personal title (as in Mr., Ms., Mrs., or Messrs.), followed by the last name.** This greeting is your first point of introduction to a potential funder, so you need to use a personal title. Call to make sure the personal title you're using is correct. I once used "Ms." for a female program director who preferred to be addressed with "Miss." The request was denied because I didn't do my homework on her correct personal title.

>> **Keep the first paragraph short and focused.** Start by introducing your organization (use its legal name). Then introduce yourself and give your job title (executive director, development officer, and so forth). Finally, get to the point. Tell the funder how much money you're requesting and why your organization needs it. Write a sentence or two about what your organization does. Validate your existence by adding at least one sentence that includes research-based evidence that there's a need for what your organization does.

>> **Write a second paragraph that's brief and to the point.** Include no more than three sentences stating your organization's corporate structure status and the date it was founded. Then tell the funder your organization's purpose and how it aligns with the funder's mission or funding priority.

>> **Wrap up your cover letter with a summarizing paragraph.** Share a closing thought or reflection about what this funding partnership can mean for the future of your project's target audience.

Rule
of Thumb

**Small Business Book Series**

428 Joslyn Castle Drive
Omaha, NE 92203

December 1, 2016

Mrs. Jennifer S. Randall
Trust Administrator
The John B. and Beverly A. Browning Trust
123456 W. Social Security Lane
Medicare, IA 45678

Dear Mrs. Randall:

I am writing on behalf of the Rule Of Thumb for Business (ROTB) based in Omaha, Nebraska. As the Secretary of the Board of Directors, our Executive Committee has authorized me to submit a grant proposal to the Trust requesting $5,000. This generous gift from the Trust will allow us to purchase additional online marketing services to promote our Small Business Book Series. A 2014 report published by the American Small Print Books Association showed that marketing small print books rigorously online (our books are 125 pages or less) can generate 10 times the sales as other non-social media venues. With over one million small businesses (under 500 employees), there is a high demand for our book topics.

Founded in 2012, ROTB is an IRS-recognized 501(c)(3) nonprofit corporation. Our mission is to provide topics of interest and relevance to small businesses to help them to get started and stay in business. When Mrs. Browning started her family's trust, she had already published 39 books. Her 40th book was titled *A Guide to Sustainability for Small Business,* and it targets the same market as ROTB.

In summary, an ongoing partnership with the Trust would indirectly benefit small businesses nationwide. With limited market presence, ROTB has the ability to promote Mrs. Browning's book as well to generate additional income for the Trust.

Awaiting your response,

*Bev*

Beverly A. Browning
Secretary, ROTB Board of Directors

ATTACHMENTS

**FIGURE 12-1:**
A fully developed cover letter leaves the funder feeling connected to the applicant.

*Illustration by Ryan Sneed*

>> **Use a creative closing, such as "Awaiting your response," "With great hope," or something else that fits your project's theme/topic area.** Sounding both thankful and optimistic as you close your request for funds is important.

>> **Sign your first name only; doing so invites an informal, long-term relationship.** Below your signature, type your first name, middle initial, last

name, and job title. **Remember:** The executive director or board president is the appropriate signatory.

>> **At the bottom of the letter, include the note "ATTACHMENTS" or "ENCLOSURES."** This note indicates that a grant proposal is included in the same packet. The capital letters signal that the grant proposal is important.

TIP

You can access an easy-to-use grant cover letter template at www.dummies.com/go/grantwritingfd6e.

# Shuffling through Common Application Forms

Many groups of grant makers, from foundations to corporations, have created their own customized common grant application forms and formats. These types of commonly developed and used forms and formats can be found on the Foundation Center's website, www.foundationcenter.org. (See Chapter 6 for more on the Foundation Center.)

No one group of funders is using the exact same formatting or forms. So, in the following list, I give you the most commonly requested information fields you can expect to see with any of the state-level applications and the Regional Association of Grantmakers common grant applications:

>> **Organization name, tax-exempt status, year organization was founded, date of application, address, telephone number, fax number, director, and contact person and title:** These items give the funding source straight information about your eligibility to apply for funds.

>> **Grant request:** The funding source wants to know how much money you're asking for before it even reads the full proposal. The amount listed here is the first clue to the funder that you're counting on it to provide a specific percentage of your project support.

REMEMBER

This figure doesn't mean that you're requesting the total amount needed from just one funder; you still send your customized common grant application proposal package to other funders willing to accept this format. Having more than one potential funder lined up increases your chances of receiving the full amount needed.

>> **Period grant will cover:** Most foundation and corporate funders award grant monies for only one year. Some fund you for multiple years, but they don't represent the norm among private sector funders.

>> **Type of request:** Typically, the funders want to know whether you're request-ing general support (money to pay the day-to-day bills), start-up funds (you're just beginning operations), technical assistance (training, accounting aid, or some other type of specialized consulting), and so on. See Chapter 1 for your grant language choices when it comes to the type of funds requested.

>> **Project title:** I personally like every funding request to have a project or program title. A title gives your request personality. Remember to be consis-tent in the use of your title. It should be the same from the cover letter to the cover form to the grant proposal.

>> **Total project budget:** The amount you enter here is the total cost to imple-ment your program. Include the value of your in-kind and cash contributions in addition to the amount needed from the funder. (Go to Chapter 17 for budget terms and definitions.)

>> **Start date of fiscal year:** The date your organization's financial year begins. For example, your fiscal year may begin on January 1, July 1, September 1, or in any month. Check with your financial staff to determine your start date.

>> **Total organizational budget:** This amount is your organization's total operating budget for the current fiscal year.

>> **Summarize the organization's mission:** The word *summarize* is key here. If you have a long mission statement, give the abbreviated version. Remember that the entire cover form usually fits on one page.

TIP

>> **Summary of project or grant request:** Don't fill out this field until you've written the grant application narrative. Then cut and paste into this section the sentences that most effectively summarize your project. This field typically includes one sentence that provides a brief overview of your project. For example, "The purpose of this project is to provide 5,000 Puerto Rican families displaced by Hurricane Beverly with temporary housing, food, and medical care."

# Knowing What the Feds Want in a Form (SF-424)

The electronic Application for Federal Assistance Form (also known as SF-424 and available at www.grants.gov/web/grants/forms.html) asks for four pages of information. Here, I walk you through the sections you can expect to see when you're filling in the SF-424 online. Better yet, I tell you exactly what the govern-ment wants you to include. (Note that mandatory fields are outlined in red in the digital version of this form.)

**REMEMBER**

Each federal grant-making agency may use a variation of SF-424. Always use the funding agency's link for the specific form to use.

You can read the full instructions for filling in the Application for Federal Assistance (SF-424) on the grants.gov website on this webpage: `www.grants.gov/view-opportunity.html?oppId=283700`.

**TIP**

If any of the SF-424 instructions use the term *require*, you must enter the requested information. Leaving this section blank will disqualify your grant application from funding consideration.

Here's a brief glimpse of the forms information fields on the SF-424:

>> **Item 1 – Type of Submission:** Your options are Pre-application or Application or Changed/Corrected Application.

>> **Item 2 – Type of Application:** Your options are New or Continuation or Revision. If you choose the Revision option, there are five fields (A–E) to review and select from. They all relate to increasing or decreasing the award amount or the duration of your grant cycle. There is also an Other option.

>> **Item 3 – Date Received:** You're instructed to leave this field blank.

>> **Item 4 – Applicant Identifier:** Here you enter the entity identifier assigned by the federal agency, if any, or the applicant's control number if applicable.

>> **Item 5a – Federal Entity Number:** In this field, you enter the number assigned to your organization by the federal agency, if any.

>> **Item 5b – Federal Award Identifier:** You're instructed to leave this field blank if this is a new application. For a continuation or revision to an existing award, enter the previously assigned federal award identifier number. If you're submitting a changed/corrected application, enter the federal identifier in accordance with agency instructions.

>> **Item 6 – Date Received by State:** Leave this field blank. This date will be assigned by your applicable state agency, if required.

>> **Item 7 – State Application Identifier:** Leave this field blank. This identifier will be assigned by your applicable state agency, if required.

>> **Item 8 – Applicant Information:** Here, you must enter, at a minimum, the *Required* information requested for subsections A through F:

   A. **Legal Name:** Here, you're required to enter the legal name of the applicant that will undertake the assistance activity. This is the organization that has registered with the Central Contractor Registry (CCR). You can get information on registering with CCR from Grants.gov.

**B. Employer/Taxpayer Number (EIN/TIN):** Here you're required to enter the employer identification number (EIN) or taxpayer identification number (TIN) as assigned by the Internal Revenue Service (IRS). If your organization is not in the United States, enter 44-4444444.

**C. Organizational DUNS:** Here, you're required to enter the organization's DUNS or DUNS+4 number received from Dun & Bradstreet. You can get information on obtaining a DUNS number from Grants.gov.

**D. Address:** Enter your complete address. You're required to include your county/parish, state (required if you're located in the United States), province, and country. You're also required to enter your nine-digit zip code if you're located in the United States.

**E. Organizational Unit:** Here you enter the name of the primary organizational unit, department, or division that will undertake the assistance activity.

**F. Name and Contact Information of Person to Be Contacted on Matters Involving This Grant Application:** Here, you enter the first and last name (required), prefix, middle name, suffix, and title of the contact person, as well as the phone number, email (required), and fax number. Also, enter organizational affiliation if you're affiliated with an organization other than that in 7a.

» **Item 9 – Type of Applicant:** Here you're required to select up to three applicant type(s) in accordance with agency instructions. In this information field, you select your type of organization. The choices are A through W. Check with your finance staff or executive director to determine your organization's legal structure.

» **Item 10 – Name of Federal Agency:** Here you enter the name of the federal agency from which assistance is being requested with this application.

» **Item 11 – Catalog of Federal Domestic Assistance Number/Title:** Here you enter the Catalog of Federal Domestic Assistance number and title of the program under which assistance is requested, as found in the program announcement, if applicable.

» **Item 12 – Funding Opportunity Number/Title:** Here you're required to enter the Funding Opportunity Number and title of the opportunity under which assistance is requested, as found in the program announcement.

» **Item 13 – Competition Identification Number/Title:** Here you enter the competition identification number and title of the competition under which assistance is requested, if applicable.

» **Item 14 – Areas Affected by Project:** This data element is intended for use only by programs for which the area(s) affected are likely to be different from the place(s) of performance reported on the SF-424 Project/Performance Site Location(s) Form. Add an attachment to enter additional areas, if needed.

>> **Item 15 – Descriptive Title of Applicant's Project:** Here you're required to enter a brief descriptive title of the project. If appropriate, attach a map showing project location (for example, construction or real property projects). For pre-applications, you're required to attach a summary description of the project.

>> **Item 16 – Congressional Districts Office:** The actual form abbreviates Office as "Of." Here you're required to enter all district(s) affected by the program or project. Enter this in the following format: two-character state abbreviation, a hyphen, and the three-character district number. For example, CA-005 for the California 5th District, CA-012 for the California 12th District, or NC-103 for the North Carolina 103rd District. If all congressional districts in a state are affected, enter "all" for the district number (for example, MD-all for all congressional districts in Maryland). If nationwide — all districts within all states are affected — enter "US-all." If the program/project is outside the United States, enter 00-000.

This optional data element is intended for use only by programs for which the area(s) affected are likely to be different than place(s) of performance reported on the SF-424 Project/Performance Site Location(s) Form. Attach an additional list of program/project congressional districts, if needed.

>> **Item 17 – Proposed Project Start and End Dates:** Here you're required to enter the proposed start date and end date of the project.

>> **Item 18 – Estimated Funding:** Here you're required to enter the amount requested or to be contributed during the first funding/budget period by each contributor. The value of in-kind contributions should be included on appropriate lines, as applicable. If the action will result in a dollar change to an existing award, indicate only the amount of the change. For decreases, enclose the amounts in parentheses.

>> **Item 19 – Is Application Subject to Review by State Under Executive Order 12372 Process:** Here, you're required to contact the State Single Point of Contact (SPOC) for Federal Executive Order 12372 to determine whether the application is subject to the state intergovernmental review process. Select the appropriate box. If "a." is selected, enter the date the application was submitted to the state.

>> **Item 20 – Is the Applicant Delinquent on Any Federal Debit:** Here, you're required to select the appropriate box. This question applies to the applicant organization, not the person who signs as the authorized representative. Categories of federal debt include, but may not be limited to, delinquent audit disallowances, loans, and taxes. If yes, include an explanation in an attachment.

>> **Item 21 – Authorized Representative:** This final section is where the authorized representative of your organization must sign and date. You're required to enter the first and last name, prefix, middle name, and suffix. Also,

enter the contact person's title, telephone number, email, and fax number. **Note:** A copy of the governing body's authorization for you to sign this application as the official representative must be on file in the applicant's office. (Certain federal agencies may require that this authorization be submitted as part of the application.)

# Saving the Abstract or Executive Summary for Last

The *abstract* or *executive summary* is a brief, page-limited overview of what the grant reviewer will find in the full grant application. Brevity is important (this section should be no longer than one page unless the guidelines indicate the need for a two-page summary). I recommend writing (or assembling) your abstract or summary *after* you've written the entire grant application narrative because by then you should have all the wordy explanations out of your system. (*Note:* Federal applications often specify a word or line limit for abstracts.)

**REMEMBER**

Always follow the funder's guidelines regarding word or line limits and the structure of the abstract or executive summary.

If no specific structure is requested, you can create an abstract or executive summary like the one in Figure 12-2 by pulling the most significant sentences from each key writing section in the grant narrative and doing a quick cut-and-paste. Take key sentences from the following areas, and keep them in the same order in the abstract or executive summary as they appear in the narrative:

>> **Proposed initiative:** Here you enter the name of your project or program and the full name of the funding competition you're applying to for grant consideration.

>> **Introduction of target population:** Copy and paste a sentence or two about whom you're planning to target and serve with grant monies.

>> **Goals:** Copy and paste your goals from the project design section of your proposal narrative.

>> **Program measurements and performance targets (also known as objectives):** Copy and paste your objectives and performance targets from the program design section of your proposal narrative.

>> **Plan of action:** Copy and paste the key activities that comprise the program's implementation process.

**Abstract**

**OJJDP FY 2016 Comprehensive Anti-Gang Strategies and Programs**
**Grant Application – CFDA 16.544**
**Submitted by: Leadership Training Institute – Hempstead, New York**

**Proposed Initiative:** Long Island Comprehensive Gang Model

**Target Population:** Comprehensive anti-gang strategies are critically needed in Nassau (pop. 1,357,429)[1] and Suffolk (pop. 1,518,475)[2] Counties (a.k.a. Long Island), New York. The communities of Hempstead, Roosevelt, Freeport, and Westbury/New Castle in Nassau County, and Huntington Station, Wyandanch, Central Islip, and Brentwood in Suffolk Counties are under violent and continuous attack by 5,000 members that reside on Long Island.[3]

**Goals:** Goal 1 - Provide opportunities to youth at high-risk of gang involvement. Goal 2 - Involve key stakeholders in connecting high-risk youth to community-based social interventions. Goal 3 - Catalyze cross-agency organizational change and development.

Leadership Training Institute (LTI) is adopting OJJDP's Comprehensive Gang Model.

**Program Measurements and Performance Targets:**
**SMART Objective 1a:** By the end of the model's implementation period, the number of enrolled youth completing program requirements will increase by 70% or more.
**Resulting OJJDP Performance Target**
&#x21B6; Percent completed.
**SMART Objective 1b:** By the end of the model's implementation period, the number of enrolled youth who will have completed an evidence-based program/practice will increase by 70% or more.
**Resulting OJJDP Performance Target**
&#x21B6; Percent exposed to evidence-based model.
**SMART Objective 2a:** By the end of the model's implementation period, the number of stakeholders engaged in the Steering Committee/Policy Group (currently known as the Building For Success Partnership) will increase by 60% or more.
**Resulting OJJDP Performance Targets**
&#x21B6; Number of planning or training events held.
&#x21B6; Percentage of program policies changed and/or rescinded.
**SMART Objective 3a:** By the end of the model's implementation period, the number of policies changed or rescinded to address local gang problems will increase by 25% or more.
**Resulting OJJDP Performance Target**
&#x21B6; Number of program policies changed and/or rescinded.
**SMART Objective 3b:** By the end of the model's implementation period, the number of OJJDP-involved (training and technical assistance recipients) agencies reporting improvements in operations will increase by 25% or more.
**Resulting OJJDP Performance Target**
&#x21B6; Percentage of organizations reporting improvements in operations based on training and technical assistance.

**Plan of Action:** The **Long Island Comprehensive Gang Model** will have three strategies. They include:
1. *Opportunities Provision*
2. *Social Intervention*
3. *Organizational Change and Development*

---

[1] http://quickfacts.census.gov/qfd/states/36/36059.html
[2] http://quickfacts.census.gov/qfd/states/36/36103.html
[3] National Drug Intelligence Center to 2016

**FIGURE 12-2:**
The abstract or executive summary draws critical details from different parts of the narrative.

*Illustration by Ryan Sneed*

**TIP**

You can find a template version of the abstract or executive summary at `www.dummies.com/go/grantwritingfd6e`.

# Crafting the Table of Contents

Whether you include a table of contents depends on the grant application guidelines. Rigidly structured guidelines typically call for a table of contents, particularly if the narrative is long (more than ten pages) or if you're asked to provide several attachments or appendixes.

**REMEMBER**

The table of contents shouldn't include the abstract or executive summary because those parts almost always precede the table of contents. Exceptions to this rule are applications from state or federal agencies that stipulate a format in which the table of contents comes before the abstract or executive summary. Grant guidelines and writing formats vary from one agency to another and even within departments in an agency, so be sure to read the grant application guidelines and follow the format listed in the reviewer's criteria (see Chapters 9 and 10 for details on review criteria).

Figure 12-3 provides you with an example of a federal grant application table of contents.

---

**U.S. Department of Justice**
**Law Enforcement Training – Discretionary Funds – CFDA 12.345**

**Table of Contents**
**Submitted by: Grant Writing Training Foundation – Goodyear.**

| Grant Application Narrative Sections | Page |
|---|---|
| Need for the Project | 1–3 |
| Foundation for Implementation | 4–8 |
| Quality of the Project Design | 9–19 |
| Quality of the Management Plan | 20–22 |
| Quality of the SLC Project Evaluation | 23–24 |
| Appendices | 25–44 |
|    Appendix 1: Letters of Commitment | |
|    Appendix 2: Organizational Chart | |
|    Appendix 3: Resumes of Key Personnel | |
|    Appendix 4: Copy of IRS Nonprofit Status | |
|    Appendix 5: Nonprofit Survey | |
| Mandatory Assurances and Certifications | 45–50 |

---

**FIGURE 12-3:**
A sample table of contents for a federal grant application.

*Illustration by Ryan Sneed*

Keep the following points in mind regarding your application's table of contents:

>> The reader expects to see sections and subsections of the grant application listed.

>> Appendixes must be listed and numbered.

>> Federally mandated or state-mandated forms and attachments or appendixes must be listed as well. (Including mandated forms in your table of contents lets the government know that you included them in the application. If a form disappears during the review process, at least the grant reviewer can affirm that it was included in the original application.)

Visit www.dummies.com/go/grantwritingfd6e for a helpful table of contents template.

Chapter 13

# Developing the Organizational Capability Boilerplate Narrative

Whether your organization is a first-time grant applicant or a veteran, you must write current and relevant boilerplate information about the organization in the organization background/history section of the narrative. (A *boilerplate* is information that has minimal changes from year to year.) The section of the grant application narrative that houses this information, whether upfront, in the middle, or at the end, communicates who the grant applicant organization is, where it's located, and what services and programs it provides. This section also includes information on your organization's primary community partners — agencies that support your mission, programs, and services by collaborating with you to strengthen your financial, physical, and program-related assets. How much you write for this section depends on each funder and its specific guidelines (content and page or character limitations) for what and how much it wants to see.

In this chapter, you find out how to build your organization's background, programs, and affiliations into compelling introductory paragraphs. These opening sections convince the grant reader that you're financially and operationally capable to receive and manage grant monies.

**REMEMBER**

A little trivia and a lot of facts create the kind of reader interest every successful grant writer shoots for. The longer you can keep readers' attention, the better your chances are of getting recommended for a grant award.

**TIP**

I include a full-length grant application at `www.dummies.com/go/grant writingfd6e`; be sure to check it out before you write.

# Adhering to the Funder's Guidelines

In most cases, the funding source's narrative-writing instructions point you in the right direction for what to include in the capability section of the application. Some funders title this section *organizational background* or *history*. Others label it *grant applicant capability* or *organizational capability.* Regardless of what the funder calls this section, when introducing your organization, be sure to divide the information into different parts for easy digestion by the grant reviewer.

For example, you may include these different parts: background (history and accomplishments), programs and activities (current services), constituency demographics (information about your service population), and community affiliations (local, regional, and state partners).

Remember, federal grant application guidelines require extensive, detailed responses; therefore, the writing guidelines are very long as well. Here are some examples of the types of narrative section writing instructions you may see in your application guidelines:

>> **Community foundation example:** Organization Background: Please provide the history of the organization, its broader purposes, and services to the community.

>> **Federal example:** US Department of Labor — Veteran's Employment and Training Service Grant Program: Organizational Capability and Experience — You must describe in your application your organization's ability to manage the operational, administrative, programmatic, and financial reporting requirements specified within this funding announcement. You must describe key staff skills, experience, history, knowledge, qualifications, capabilities, and office locations, and provide an organizational chart.

You must also address your capacity for timely implementation of the program, programmatic reporting, and participant tracking. You must fully describe how the proposed program can or will outlast the federal funding being provided under this grant. You must describe in your application a diverse funding base or illustrate an organizational strategic plan that will lead to the attainment of financial resources beyond those secured through the grant. If you have previously operated a veterans' employment and training program, then you must include the performance outcomes from your last, or most recent (if the grant is active), fourth quarter Technical Performance Report (TPR) and the planned goals for that grant. If you lack prior experience with implementing these types of grants, you are required to provide program outcomes from other similar programs you have operated. You must describe specific outcomes previously achieved against set targets within these related programs, such as number of enrollments, number of participants who entered employment, cost per placement into employment, benefits secured, and coalitions.

For new grantees that may not have past experience operating an employment and training program, it is important to have detailed information on the specific ability to manage these types of programs.

# Creating Organizational Credibility as a Grant Applicant

When writing the organizational capability section of your application, you need to clearly and concisely give the grant reader just enough information about your organization's experience and accomplishments to pique his interest and keep him reading word for word. Remember that you're just introducing yourself — jabbering about the money you need or the problems you have isn't polite. In a federal grant application, you'll lose peer review points if you don't respond to every mandatory requirement for each section of the narrative and budget. Chapter 10 explains the federal peer review process and how to write to the requirements for what peer reviewers want to read.

**TIP**

Although you're shooting for clarity and precision, in order to get your grant application funded, you must be able to make the mundane interesting to the grant reader. Your narrative must be magnetizing to all who read it, from your community partners to potential funders. After years of experimenting, I'm thoroughly convinced that telling and *selling* your organization's story is critical when funders are at the point of making a decision to fund or not to fund. You must write to hit them where their hearts and their minds are!

The first two sections that follow describe how to write the organizational capability section for private sector funders. The last section explains how to write the same section for public sector funders.

## Stating the history, mission, and logistics

The grant reader wants to see the following in the first few sentences:

**TIP**

>> The full legal name of your organization.

>> The year the organization was founded, by whom, and for what purpose.

If you don't know the appropriate answers, ask a long-term employee or a longtime board member. Sometimes, you can also find the history of an organization in its annual report or in an anniversary issue of its newsletter. Keep researching and asking others until you strike gold.

>> The location of the organization's headquarters and any other operating sites (name, city, county, state).

>> The mission statement.

In the example that follows, I make the text inviting by putting a face on the organization's history. (See Chapter 11 for pointers on using colorful language in your writing.)

> The Grant Writing Training Foundation was founded in 2007 by Dr. Beverly A. Browning in Buckeye (Maricopa County), Arizona. Dr. Browning's vision for this 501(c)(3) foundation emerged when she was managing a for-profit consulting business that wanted to offer more affordable training for nonprofits and units of government. Her vision unfolded in the mission statement of the Foundation: Provide affordable and relevant training in grant seeking and proposal writing. Dr. Browning has 43 years of experience in grant writing and creating training curriculum across industry topics. The most important achievements for the Grant Writing Training Foundation include the following:
>
> ● Donated 10% or more of annual proceeds to training-site hosts and other charitable causes.
>
> ● Provided new computers or grant-related textbooks at venues to at least one of the attendees annually since 2007.
>
> ● Facilitated low-cost training to over 400 nonprofit site hosts since its founding.

# Presenting key milestones

Complete the organizational capability section by writing about important milestones in the organization's history that relate to the activities covered in the grant application. Write a brief introductory paragraph before you begin listing the milestones.

**WARNING**

Even though your organization may have dozens of milestones, don't include every last miscellaneous award and achievement. If you're seeking grant funds for a new after-school program, for example, don't mention unrelated accomplishments, such as the school football team's winning record or the cabinet full of medals from the swim team. Taking the grant reader down a dead-end road with unrelated information is a fatal flaw, and it can result in your application not being read or funded.

**TIP**

Use bulleted, abbreviated statements to share the top milestones. And use a casual voice to make the list more inviting. Your organization's milestones narrative may look something like this:

> The Grant Writing Training Foundation currently offers a full menu of grant-related and small business capacity-building training programs to nonprofits throughout the United States, including foundations, community service organizations, colleges and universities, and government agencies. Current training programs include but are not limited to:
>
> • Grant Writing Boot Camp
>
> • Grant Writing Boot Camp Express
>
> • Nonprofit Board of Directors Boot Camp
>
> • Small Biz Boot Camp

When writing the organizational capabilities section, I like to use customized bullets to draw attention to the grant applicant's attributes. For example, you can use a dollar sign or a red heart to point to the Grant Writing Training Foundation's accomplishments.

**REMEMBER**

If your organization is new (just starting up), list the background of the founders and your governing board members along with the planned milestones from your strategic plan. Chapter 2 gives you more information on the strategic plan.

# Shifting gears for government grants

Strong, emotional writing works best with foundation and corporate grant applications, but you need to adopt a different writing style for government applications. When you describe your organization's history in a government grant application, follow these tips to rack up the review points (see Chapters 9 and 10 for more on review points):

>> Use a compelling writing style; remember to only write what's asked for — no more, no less.

>> Stick with the cold, hard facts.

>> Don't write the history and accomplishments section in the first person (using pronouns such as *I*, *our*, and *my*). Instead, use the third-person writing approach. When you write in third person, you're writing as if you're on the outside of the grant applicant organization and looking in with a third-party perspective. Your reference to your organization must be from a formal and straightforward approach. Here are two examples that allow you to compare first- and third-person writing styles:

- **First person:** Our organization was founded in 1989 and is located in Phoenix (Maricopa County), Arizona. Last year, we provided more than 15,000 water bottles, blankets, and T-shirts to homeless veterans.

- **Third person:** Mary's Kitchen was founded in 1989 and is located in Phoenix (Maricopa County), Arizona. Last year, its staff provided over 15,000 water bottles, blankets, and T-shirts to homeless veterans.

# Sorting Out Relevant Programs and Activities

Use the program section of your opening narrative to write about the day-to-day happenings at your organization. Describe the programs that you currently provide to your constituency (also called the *target population*), not what you plan to provide when your grant request is funded. (You can read more about target populations in the next section.)

If you work for a smaller organization, you probably have only one or two programs. However, keep in mind that having fewer programs doesn't decrease your chances of winning a grant award. Grants are available for organizations of all sizes and shapes. Remember, it's all in the writing.

REMEMBER

In the program section, the grant reader is looking for you to briefly

>> Give the name of the program and state how long it has existed (focus on long-lasting and successful programs).

>> Tell whom the program serves (youth, adults, women, seniors, veterans, people with physical or cognitive disabilities, or whomever).

>> Describe how the target population benefits from the program.

Following is a comprehensive list of current programs from an actual grant application that was funded:

>> Behavioral Heath Outreach Program:

  - Family violence services

  - Family support services

  - Therapeutic visitation services

  - Children currently in state custody

  - Children transitioning home from foster care and their families

  - Youth with juvenile court involvement

  - Parents who are seeking reunification with their children

  - Parents in need of parenting assessment, parent education, and marriage and/or couples

  - Counseling

  - Children and parents in need of signs of abuse education or anger management/conflict resolution skills

  - Sex abuse education, child abuse education

  - Youth needing positive role models through mentoring services

>> Mid-Cumberland Relative Caregiver Program:

  - Grandparents and relatives caring for minor children

  - Children and teen social skills groups

  - Youth needing positive role models through mentoring services

  - Parenting education groups

>> Community Prevention Initiative Program:

  - Youth needing positive role models through mentoring services

  - Youth with juvenile court involvement

- Children and teen social skills groups
- Tennessee Commission on Children and Youth
- Social skills groups for high-risk youth

>> Lottery for Education and after-school programs:

- Middle-school students in need of academic enrichment and tutoring
- 21st-Century Community Learning Center Program
- Adult and youth therapeutic groups

>> Metro Government of Nashville Juvenile Court Program:

- High-risk youth with juvenile court involvement
- Therapeutic groups for youth suspected of alcohol, drug, and tobacco use

**WARNING**

Don't make the mistake of pulling the language for this section from a previously written grant (such as last year's failed attempt). Always use fresh, up-to-date programs and activities information. Grant readers are very intuitive and can pick up on outdated, out-of-place information.

# Presenting and Validating Your Target Population

The target population section is the place to write about the people you serve. If you're serving certain organizations, you write about the organizations. If you're writing a grant for an animal shelter, you write about the animals.

Give just enough detail to aid the reader in understanding whom your operating dollars benefit — community members who are poor, adults who are unemployed, youths who have dropped out of high school, people who are homeless, or those with a terminal illness, for instance. To make this section as accurate as possible, do your homework. Pull old evaluation reports from previously funded grants, and review reports given to your board members — both types of documents should detail exactly who benefits from your organization's services.

**REMEMBER**

In the target population section, the grant reader wants to see

>> Characteristics of your target population (age range, gender, ethnicity, education level, and income level). Clearly define your target population. You must convey to funders that you're serving a constituency that falls within

their funding parameters. Also, be sure to cite the source of your demographics.

>> Numbers served by each program (make a table that covers the past five years).

>> Changes in the target population that may relate to why you're asking for grant funds.

**TIP**

When you write the target population section, use words describing the population that tell your story with accuracy and emotion for the grant reader. (Chapter 11 has tips on how to resuscitate your writing to win grants.)

In the following example from a Federal Mentoring Children of Prisoners' grant application, I introduce the grant reviewer to a faith-based nonprofit organization serving inner-city residents. Because I want the reader to understand the importance of the funding request, I use a lot of boldface to make phrases stick in the reviewer's mind.

**TIP**

Usually, I advise grant writers to refrain from putting any language from the statement of need in the section of the proposal narrative that contains a description of the organization. However, I break this rule when I'm writing about projects serving children — specifically, a target population under the age of 18. For children's services programs, I drop hints of need every chance I can. This strategy helps reach out and touch the hearts of the grant readers, whether foundation, corporate, state, or federal.

**Conditions and Characteristics of Youth and Families Affected:** According to a 2016 needs assessment conducted by Prison Families of New York, Inc., children of prisoners:

- **Blame themselves for their parent's incarceration** (one in five children witnessed his mother's arrest)

- **Are embarrassed about their peers finding out about their parent's incarceration**

- **Have difficulty dealing with the loss of a parent** to the prison system

- **Fail to address their emotional hurt** and **often act out**

- **Lack anyone who encourages them to achieve life success**

- Are **deeply negatively impacted by the separation** (demonstrated in lower self-esteem and loss of personal and cultural identity)

- Are **in critical need of an adult mentor who can help them express their feelings** about the incarcerated parent

Almost 58% of mothers and almost 59% of fathers in state prisons report never having a visit with their children since they entered prison. African American children are 7.5 times more likely to have a parent in prison than white children. Latino children are 2.5 times more likely than white children to have an incarcerated parent. The incarceration of a primary caretaker is traumatic and disruptive for children. Children of incarcerated mothers often move at least once and live with at least two different caretakers while their mothers are in prison. When a parent is incarcerated, children may face dramatically changed family conditions, particularly if the incarcerated parent was the sole or primary caregiver.

# Including High Stakes Partners to Boost Your Credibility

Your grant guidelines may call for your partnership information to appear at the beginning of the narrative, before the history and accomplishments. However, the partnerships can just as easily be placed after the statement of needs or as an attachment. Read your grant application directions carefully before you start writing. The great thing about modern technology, however, is that little tool called *cut and paste.* You can move anything anywhere after it's written.

**REMEMBER**

If your application guidelines require a separate partnership section, you can and should still have a one- or two-line boilerplate about how many partners your organization has in the organizational capacity narrative section.

In the partnerships section of your organization description narrative, write about your organization's local, regional, and national collaborative partnerships. What organizations do you team with to provide your program's services? What organizations have asked you to write letters of commitment for their grant applications? What groups have historically supported you? If you find that this section of your narrative is a bit slim, Chapter 9 gives you more information about establishing community partners to give your grant application the competitive edge.

Partners are like friends: You get to know them inside and out, and you complement each other in the delivery of like or unlike services. For example, say you operate a group home for adults with cognitive and physical disabilities. In that case, you need to depend on the Get 'Em There Transportation Service to take your clients to and from medical appointments.

When writing about your partnerships, list the partner's full name and its role in relation to your organization. Whether you're writing a corporate or foundation funding request or a government funding request, the information you provide in your narrative on partnerships is the same: who and where the partner is and what role the partner plays.

As you write about your partnerships, don't include an organization that you're considering partnering with without first talking to a representative about what you're doing and asking permission to include the organization in your proposal. It doesn't reflect well on you if the funder calls your "partner" and that organization has no clue who you are and no knowledge of a partnership.

When reviewing the partnership section of your funding application, the grant reader looks for evidence of

>> Collaborative efforts with multiple partners to maximize the use of grant funds by coordinating services to the target population (see the preceding section for the lowdown on target populations)

>> Partners that commit cash to reduce the amount of grant funding you need (known as *cash contributors*)

>> Partners that contribute personnel, space, equipment, supplies, and other valuable items to reduce the amount of grant funding needed (known as *in-kind contributors*)

>> Evidence that your partners are committed in writing courtesy of signed Memoranda of Understanding (MOU) and/or letters of commitment

In the following example, I briefly introduce a grant applicant's partners and their roles in helping the applicant organization coordinate its services. *Note:* Mention partners who contribute cash simply as *cash contributors* in your narrative. (See Chapter 17 for how to incorporate matching funds from your organization and its partners into the project budget summary and narrative detail.)

> The Northern Arizona Association for the Blind formed the Building Your Vision Partnership in 2013. Current cash contributors include: Sunrise Village Triathlons, Coconino County Center for the Visually Impaired, and Peak Performance. Each of these partners contributed $5,000 towards general operating expenses. Partners that have contributed in-kind (non-cash gifts) include: March for More ($10,000 in technical assistance) and Sight Right ($5,000 in donated assistive technology equipment).

If you prefer, you can present your partner organizations, their partnership roles, and the values of their contributions in a table rather than a paragraph, as shown in Table 13-1. After all, sprinkling graphics and tables throughout your narrative gives the grant reader a break from reading straight text. Remember that grant readers may have to read dozens of grant requests each week. You can give them a much-needed respite from standard sentences and win them over by using a table effectively.

**TABLE 13-1**     ## Sample Partnership Table

| Partner | Role |
| --- | --- |
| Arizona State University Cooperative Extension | Life-skills classes for current and former gang members |
| Six Towns Community Center | Training and employment services for current and former gang members |
| Girl Scouts of Coconino County, Inc. | Gender-based programs for female children of current and former gang members |
| Coconino County Housing Authority | Affordable and safe housing, parole violation alert system, as well as family in crisis alert system |
| Coconino County Hispanic Civic Association | Cultural programs to instill a sense of heritage and pride in Hispanic participants |
| City of Flagstaff Police Department | Parole violation alert system; coordination with Project IMPACT, and participant crisis alert system |
| Coconino County Public Schools | Educational and vocational programs for current and former gang members |
| Impact University, Department of Psychology | Interns to mentor and to support project goals for participants |
| Incorporated Village of Kayenta | Technical assistance with linkages |
| Leadership Training Innovations | Grant applicant and lead agency |
| Coconino County Department of Public Health | Health care services and coordinated case management systems for participants with health issues or wishing to have tattoos removed |
| Coconino County Youth Board | Technical assistance throughout project funding period |
| Coconino County Council on the Aging | Volunteers for mentoring current and former gang members |

TIP

When I'm writing a short (five pages or less) proposal for corporation or foundation funding sources, I don't create a table to spotlight the grant applicant organization's partnerships unless I have sufficient room on the second page to accommodate the entire table. Remember, you have four subsections to squeeze into five pages. Revert to using a narrative to describe your partnerships when a table format puts you over the page limit.

# Chapter 14

# Validating Your Needs with a Compelling Narrative

Your *statement of need* (also referred to as a *problem statement* or *needs statement*) tells the grant reviewer that you know what you're talking about. It oozes gloom, doom, drama, and trauma (my four favorite words). You use your statement of need to get your point across in the most effective, attention-drawing, memorable way you can. How do you do that? By writing from your heart (where your emotional center lies) and by telling the story of how bad things really are for your target population. Transport the grant reviewer into the setting of the problem so she can make positive decisions about funding your grant proposal or application.

**REMEMBER**

Gather the facts, read them, feel them in your heart, and formulate them in your mind. Then think about how you'd feel if you were reading those compelling or startling statistics, events, life stories, situations, and so forth about yourself, your family, or your close friends. Keep those feelings fresh, and you're ready to write a compelling statement of need!

This chapter explains how to fill your statement of need with engaging information and visuals that help drive the point home in a way that makes your grant application stand out from the pack.

**TIP**

You may find this chapter particularly helpful if you've been casting your line into the grant writing competition pool and receiving multiple rejection notices. Odds are your grant requests have been flat, to the point, and significantly lacking in tables and charts. Even if you're submitting mostly e-grant applications (which I cover in Chapter 5), you can still beef up your content with a compelling format for your statement of need. The magic is in the storytelling and the visuals. Trust me. I use a storytelling approach, and 90 percent of everything I write for my clients gets funded.

# Convincing Funders of Your Need

When you're writing your statement of need for grant funding, remember this: Grant writing has progressed from rote and boring to individual/personality-packed/engrossing/exciting. Like all great stories, your presentation of what's wrong with this picture must be compelling, magnetizing, tear-jerking, and believable. But it must also be supported with facts. In the next sections, I tell you how to build your case and then how to tug on the grant reviewer's heartstrings — because she's the one deciding whether your request gets approved or rejected for funding.

## Researching recent and relevant information

**REMEMBER**

Every good statement of need is like a well-written story. And every well-written story is filled with compelling details that bring the narrative to life in the reader's mind. To write your story, you need to gather all the available data from your organization's previous grant evaluations, which may show gaps that still existed when the grant funds were expended.

You may have to play detective to find copies of old grant applications. Whether these applications were funded or not, they still contain critical statistics and other statement of need information. *Remember:* Only look at applications written in the last two to three years; anything older is too outdated for your current funding request.

Start off by looking for current demographics (numbers to support your statement of need) on your services, programs, and *target population* (the folks or animals that your grant, when funded, will impact). Get permission to look at case management files; these files can provide rich details and even quotations regarding clients' needs and service barriers when they came to you for help. Also, look at minutes from board of directors meetings and annual reports (usually gathered by the program staff and presented to the board in the first quarter of your organization's fiscal year).

After you review your organization's materials, conduct an Internet search in hopes of finding the following problem-related information:

>> Local and state-level data on the scope (size, demographics, and so on) of the problem. The websites of city-, county-, and state-level human service; public health; police and corrections departments; area universities; research and policy think tanks; and advocacy coalitions are excellent sources for this type of information. Look for congressional testimonies related to your subject area, research findings by experts and graduate students, and newly issued press releases from government agencies or government watchdogs.

>> Similar problem area trends in other communities with characteristics like yours (rural or urban, increases or declines in population).

>> Solutions to the issue (even though you don't present solutions in the statement of need section of your proposal).

TIP

To find up-to-date and relevant information, I recommend running a general search on a major search engine. A general search results in hundreds of local, regional, and national government website links. This approach is much easier than trying to find the Internet address for a specific information site. For example, if your organization works with local businesses to help them expand their facilities and relocate to your new state-of-the-art industrial park, you can enter the phrase **economic development statistics for [your state or county]** in your favorite search engine.

When I'm visualizing and writing my statements of need, I like to have a Dropbox folder with files of current problem-related information in front of me for review. I look at information provided by the grant application organization and study my own Internet research findings. I sort all this information by topic (for example, rural development, community development, economic development, trends in industrial parks, business growth trends, and more). To expedite locating or validating the information used after the grant application has been submitted, I store all website addresses in my Favorites folder under the project's or client's name in addition to Dropbox.

**REMEMBER**

The more information you have on your topic, the more easily you can write a winning statement of need. With the right preparation, you aren't grasping for straws or generalizing; instead, you're able to give the grant reader true, hard, grant-getting facts. And by including recent (no more than five years old) citations for data sources and names of noteworthy researchers, you show the grant reader that your information is accurate and reputable. Finally, I recommend that you establish a six-month project timeline to gather all the data. Your process must be systematic and seriously undertaken — and certainly not left until the applications are nearing their due dates.

## Incorporating real-life information about your target population

The grant reviewer reads your statement of need with the following questions in mind:

>> How and when did you identify the problem?

>> Do you have a thorough understanding of the problem at the local, regional, and national levels?

>> Do you cite statistics and research conducted by your organization and others that support the statement of need? Is this information current? (See the preceding section for guidance on finding up-to-date data.)

In a foundation or corporate funding request, your statement of need should be one typed, single-spaced page unless the funder requests a specific page count/limit or has character/space limitations for each section of the grant proposal narrative. In a government grant or cooperative request, the statement of need can be anywhere from two to ten typed single-spaced or double-spaced pages depending on the number of pages allowed for this section of the grant application narrative.

For government grant applications, I use a pages-to-points formula. Here's an example using a 20-page maximum page-limit scenario: If the total pages you can write in the narrative is 20 pages (100 percent of the total point or percentage value for the peer reviewers) and the peer review points for the statement of need is 15 points (or 15 percent), you multiply 15 percent × 20 pages and your result is 3 pages. This means that your statement of need should be exactly — on point — three pages. Some grant applications will have more than 100 percent for a total weight; adjust your calculations accordingly.

**REMEMBER**

Write each paragraph in your statement of need so that it builds on the paragraph before it. Making your ideas connect and flow is important because each new paragraph is a step forward. Each new paragraph adds excitement and urgency, just like a good fiction or nonfiction storyline. If these steps sound like those used to write a bestselling story, you're right on target. You write your winning grant proposal the same way you would a bestseller!

In my statements of need, I love to use words and phrases that carry a lot of weight, such as *economically distressed, orphaned, abandoned, socially isolated, politically disenfranchised, disconnected from the community, underemployed or unemployed, chronically homeless, taken for granted, throwaways,* and *disrespected.* Are you getting a picture of the problem? Do you have your tissue out because your eyes are full of tears? This type of writing works well in both public and private sector grant narratives.

**TIP**

Don't hide key words or phrases in ordinary text. Elevate your grant writing by using bold type and italics (minimally but effective, when allowed by the funder's format) to make a word or phrase stand out. Personally, I like to call attention to important text with italics. When you use italics in the right places to emphasize the right words, it's as if you're talking one-on-one with the grant reader. Using this approach to tug one's heartstrings may result in your application landing in the funded pile.

## Building a strong case study

If you're lucky enough to have access to actual client files or case management staff, you can survey them for information about a specific client or member of the target population that sought services from your organization. Being able to incorporate a compelling story about a real client who was in need and came to your agency or organization can really put the icing on the storytelling cake. Here's an example of how to kick off your statement of needs with a case study:

> Sara Jones walked into the doors of the Avondale Area Agency on Aging office on a Friday several months ago. She was wearing bloody clothing and had dark circles around her eyes. Sara was carrying a large suitcase and a paper bag with greasy food-type stains seeping through it. She walked up to the counter and politely whispered, "May I please speak with someone in charge of old people?" The receptionist was speechless but recovered quickly to ask this potential client how we could help her.

> Sara answered using proper English and being very careful not to mix what had happened with her emotions. All the case workers in the front office sat still and gave Sara their full attention. As the workers strained to hear Sara, her story began to unfold.

**TIP**

Opening your statement of need with an engaging story is guaranteed to keep the grant reader on the edge of her seat and interested in reading more.

Your case study should include information that addresses the following topics:

» Details of the applicant and the problem's background

» Information about the people being served and how those services are rendered

» The environment in which the organization operates, the number of people served, and who they are

» How dire the problem is

What follows is a grant-winning statement of need that shows how to make this section walk, talk, tell, and sell the case for grant funding. Compare the preceding list of topics to the narrative:

> **Detail of the applicant and the problem's background:** Sara's story is not unique, and it's not the first one we've heard that highlights an elderly person's courage, fear, and innate will to survive. These are Sara's exact words: "I am 79 years old and I lived in my own house, which was paid for 10 years ago, with my husband Bill until two years ago when he died. Of course, we had our struggles having been married for 57 years. Bill did not have much of an education, you know. I met him when I was tutoring adults who could not read. Bill had dropped out of school after sixth grade to help support his six younger brothers and sisters after his father was run over by the train and killed. Oh, they had a tough time! Please don't think that I'm rambling. I just want you to know the type of people we were before I tell you about what happened."

> Sara went on to talk more about Bill and their life together. "Even though Bill only earned minimum wage and I worked as a school teacher, we made a good life for ourselves and our son. We even managed to set aside a few dollars a week so we could send Bill Junior to college. You know, he went for six years and graduated with his masters degree in nonprofit philanthropy. Yes, our boy was a smart one until he met Leah. After Bill Senior died, Bill Junior sent Leah over to take care of me. First, she asked me to sign everything over to her name so she could manage my bills. I didn't see anything wrong with that at the time. Next, she took away my car keys, saying it was in my best interest. The telephone service was turned off too. At first, I thought how lucky I was to have someone looking out for my finances and saving me money. Leah was a smart woman. Did I tell you that Bill Junior met Leah when he was working at the county jail? She had been mistaken for a real criminal and was locked up waiting for a hearing. Bill Junior was doing his internship for college and chose the jail for his project. I seem to be rambling; it must be the concussion I suffered when I escaped out of the bedroom window when Leah had one of her crazy spells."

Sara said, "Let me get to the end of what seems to be a never-ending story. Leah locked me in my bedroom for three days. There was no food and only small amounts of water. I was hungry and desperate. As soon as I heard Leah drive away in my car this morning, I used a chair leg to break the glass in the first floor bedroom window! I was able to make it to the dry cleaners on the corner. They called the police, but the police never came. So the owner called a cab and gave me your address to come for help. I need a lawyer, a place to live, food, clean clothing, and a telephone. Can you help me?"

Sara's story is not unique. Last year there were 125,000 reported cases of elder abuse in the United States (National Elder Abuse Association, 2016). Ten percent, or 4,500, of those cases resulted in criminal charges. Why so few? Legal services for the elderly are not as plentiful as one would think. Seventy-five percent of communities (remote and rural) where elder abuse was reported had no free or low-cost legal services available within 100 miles. The National Area Agency on Aging reports that more than 50 percent of victims never report the crimes that a family member or caregiver commits against them.

**Information about the people being serviced and how those services are rendered:** The Avondale Area Agency on Aging contracts with local and regional eldercare agencies to deliver home health care, home housekeeping care, transportation to senior community centers and medical appointments, congregate meals (meals served in a communal setting of large groups of people), and emergency social services. Services are rendered on a first-come, first-serve basis.

**The environment in which the organization operates, the number of people served, and who they are:** The Avondale Area Agency on Aging operates in Coconino County located in northern Arizona. Most of our staff is over the age of 55 and can easily identify with the clients. This is a community where everyone knows everyone else and people look out for their neighbors. Our agency served 1,274 elderly clients last year (2016 Annual Report). Using the federal definition (HHS.gov), our clients range from age 55 and older; the oldest client we serve is 99 years old. Ninety percent of our clients worked in the copper mines, local schools, or up the road in high-end resort towns like Sedona. Twenty percent have at least a bachelor's degree and two percent hold graduate degrees. Eighty percent are white; 20 percent are non-white (Case Management Report, 2016). Seventy-five percent live solely on social security and Medicare benefits (Income source survey, 2016).

**How dire the problem really is:** Because the area we serve is remote and rural, many cases of elder abuse go unreported. Currently, we have no home wellness check program nor do we have the staff in place to conduct weekly face-to-face wellness checks. Coconino County is 8,127 square miles; more than one case worker can cover on her own — if we had even one case worker to spare. At this time, there are over 200 elderly persons on our waiting list for some level of home care. Last year, our agency had to transport 10 victims of elder abuse to an adjacent county for legal services. There is a dire need for an elder-specific legal services program in Coconino County. As more and more baby boomers reach retirement age and move to our region, the problems our staff faces on a daily basis will increase 100-fold. Unfortunately, we live in a country where the elderly are not highly respected or cared for by their loved ones or caregivers. More elderly people will die nationally and in Coconino County if the Avondale Area Agency on Aging cannot secure critically needed grant awards and contributions to create new elder support programs.

You know you've written a convincing and compelling statement of need when you get out your hanky to dab away a few tears after rereading your masterpiece!

**TIP**

If you have a summary of a needs survey or letters from organizations documenting that the demands for your services are greater than your resources to deliver the services, attach these documents to your application. Always reference such attachments in the narrative so grant readers can refer to them and get their full effect while reading the statement of need. These supporting documents allow a grant reader to verify the actual need for grant funding. (See Chapter 18 for guidance on how to organize your attachments.)

# Using Graphics When Allowed by the Funder

Presenting the problems in a way that doesn't bore the grant reader is important; reading nothing but sentences filled with demographics can get dull and confusing, and grant readers have a hard time awarding money when they're asleep. Luckily, graphics offer visual relief from chunks of text.

Charts, tables, and maps break up text and make the grant reader linger longer on a page. Why is that good news for you? Because the longer someone reflects on your particular problem, the better your chances for receiving funding.

I like to use comparison tables and maps to wow my grant readers, as I explain in the following sections.

## Understanding when and how to use informative graphics

Tables and other informative graphics are a great way to drive home a point about the target population and keep the reader interested.

A *comparison table* shows how your target population area compares to a similar area in the same targeted region. For example, Figure 14-1 shows a table that compares Nassau County against Suffolk County for total population by major communities and total population under the age of 18 years old. The table shows that there is a clear need for intervention in Nassau County.

| | Total Population | % of Population < Age 18 |
|---|---|---|
| **Targeted Community: Nassau County** | | |
| Hempstead | 52,526 | 36.2% |
| Roosevelt | 15,854 | 32.3% |
| Freeport | 43,144 | 46.4% |
| Westbury/New Castle Region | 14,263 | 33.6% |
| **Comparison Community: Suffolk County** | | |
| Huntington Station | 29,910 | 17.2% |
| Wyandanch | 10,546 | 12.8% |
| Central Islip | 31,950 | 20.5% |
| Brentwood | 53,917 | 11.8% |

**FIGURE 14-1:**
Use a comparison table to compare target populations.

*Illustration by Ryan Sneed*

TIP

Head to www.dummies.com/go/grantwritingfd6e for a comparison table template.

REMEMBER

Use more than one type of visual element if you have a lot of demographics on your target population. Mixing up your graphics is a great way to make your statement of need emit fireworks for the reader (and decision maker). You can always search the Internet for chart types and how to create them, and don't forget that a lot of spreadsheet programs also create graphs and tables of data.

Maps of the proposed service area are also great graphics tools to use in your statement of need. Maps tell the reader where your services will be targeted or how far the problem area spans. Maps are easy to find on the Internet and are available in color and black and white. You can use a map as a graphic insert, as in Figure 14-2, or as a watermark that appears in the background of your text.

TIP

If you use a map as a graphic insert, keep it contained to half a page or less. You can also add an arrow to point to the exact location of a county or town/city within a specific state.

**FIGURE 14-2:**
A map in a
manageable size
introduces your
service area to
the funder.

*Illustration by Ryan Sneed*

Look for maps that show the service area related to your problem or need. For instance, if the service area is statewide, use a state map; if the service area is regional, use a regional map. Also, remember that often federal grant-making agencies have online links to maps related to housing, crime, gang activity, and more.

## Dressing up your narrative texts

The preceding section points out the types of graphics you may use in your statement of need; this section shows you how to successfully use those graphics. Consider the following:

>> Limit your graphics to one per page or less.

>> Reserve tables for large amounts of information.

>> Use bar graphs and pie charts when you want to communicate age ranges by groups, income by groups, and numerical breakdowns of target population indicators.

>> When you use statistics or a figure created by someone else, always cite the source. You can insert a credit line directly below each graphic, or you can insert footnotes. In some funding documents in which the formatting guidelines bar the use of footnotes, you can create endnotes or a reference page.

**WARNING**

Failing to cite the sources of statistics can cause your request to lose peer review points or to be denied funding support. If the funding agency doesn't have specific instructions on reference citations, you can find all sorts of examples of various citation styles in writing stylebooks, online, or at the library.

>> When the funder limits the number of pages you have to develop your narrative, you must improvise when it comes to sneaking in much-needed graphics. Try wrapping text around a graphic or typing text over a watermark graphic. And remember, in most e-grant formats, graphics of any kind are not allowed.

>> Stay away from using photographs (including photo collages) of your actual clients. Without a permission to publish or a use-publicly sign-off statement from each person in the picture, you're liable to violate or breach a client's confidentiality.

>> Don't overdo it with colors in your graphics. If you opt for a shaded header row in a table, don't shade every row or column.

Chapter 15

# Using Best Practices to Build the Program Design Narrative

The program design section of the grant application narrative is by far the most important narrative section in your grant proposal. It's the section that divides the "I don't have a clue" grant writers from the "I have this in the bag" grant writers. The coaching and examples in this chapter show you how to write an award-winning program design section that's all about your vision — as in the positive changes you'll bring about when you win that grant award!

## Reviewing the Components of a Good Program Design Section

The *program design* section is where you roll out all the promising details about what will happen when the bucks are in place to actually create, implement, and evaluate your grant–funded program. The program design narrative shows funders that you have a well–documented project implementation and evaluation plan.

**REMEMBER**

To write a successful program design section, you need to be optimistic yet realistic and include the following main ingredients in this order:

>> **A purpose statement:** A one-sentence, direct explanation of why you're seeking funds.

>> **Goals:** Where your program or constituency aims to be when the grant funds are used up. There are two types of goals: outcome-focused and SMART. I give you examples of both later in this chapter.

>> **SMART objectives: S**pecific, **m**easurable, **a**ttainable, **r**ealistic, and **t**ime-bound benchmarks or specific steps that lead to the accomplishment of your goals. (I describe SMART objectives in the later "Plotting Goals and SMART Objectives" section.)

>> **An implementation plan with process objectives and timelines:** A plan listing the activities *(process objectives)* required to meet and exceed your measurable objectives and when they'll be implemented.

>> **A Logic Model with an impact objective:** Your Logic Model lays out a graphic road map with inputs, strategies, outputs, and outcomes. Adding an *impact objective* reflects the long-term benefit (seven to ten years) you believe your program will have on your target population and/or community.

>> **Evaluation:** Shows how you'll track the progress of the project's objectives, what data collection tools you'll use to gather information about the project, and who will conduct the evaluation. This section screams accountability!

Some grant applications may ask you to include evaluation plans separately, in a section following the program design or even in an attachment. However, many public and private sector funders are realizing the importance of having you, the grant applicant, integrate your evaluation plan into the program design.

The entire program design must give the grant reviewer a detailed explanation of the big picture. In other words, you must lay out each section as though you were placing the pieces into a large puzzle. The large puzzle is your program design, and the pieces are each of the elements in the preceding list.

# Starting with a Purpose Statement

As the first part of your program design narrative, the *purpose statement* tells the grant reader why you're asking for grant monies. You have two types of purpose statements to choose from: direct and indirect.

A *direct purpose statement* includes the amount of the requested grant award. Remember that even when you mention a dollar amount, the purpose statement shouldn't exceed one sentence. Get to the point and tell the grant reader the purpose of the grant request and the amount of funds needed. Use the following example as a guide for writing your own direct purpose statement:

> The Grant Writing Training Foundation is seeking your initial and ongoing financial support in the amount of $40,000 for its five-day public health-focused Grant Writing Boot Camp in Johannesburg, South Africa.

An *indirect purpose statement* simply tells the reader the purpose of the grant request — a program or project in need of funding. The example that follows shows you how an indirect purpose statement should read:

> The purpose of this request is to seek grant funding to conduct a five-day Johannesburg NIH campus-based residential grant-writing training program for Ministers of Public Health from 23 African countries.

I prefer to use a direct purpose statement in foundation and corporate funding requests because it more efficiently gets to the point for the reader who will make the final funding decisions. However, I use the indirect purpose statement for government grant proposals because government grant peer reviewers don't make those same final decisions; an agency staff person with authority over the grant-making initiative does. Therefore, no actual amount of monies requested should appear in the purpose statement of government funding requests.

# Plotting Goals and SMART Objectives

The first road-mapping tools in your program design narrative are goals (intent) and objectives (what, how much, when, for whom, and how your measurements will be proven). Your program's goals address the big-picture success of your program, and the objectives are the measurable ways (or *benchmarks*) you plan to reach those goals. Funding agencies view measurable steps as signs of accountability — showing how their money will make an impact on the problem and your organization's capability to solve the problem.

Always provide objectives for each goal and each year for which you're requesting funds for an activity.

The following sections help you differentiate between goals and objectives, craft goals worthy of funding, and design objectives that fit within the three classic types. Whether you're new to grant writing or you've submitted a few grant applications in your day, I strongly suggest you review the first of these sections. After multiple year-long stints as a grant application peer reviewer, I rated applications from school districts, colleges and universities, and nonprofit organizations that had received grant awards for years, and they all were very weak in the goals and objectives section. Most important, I never recommend applications for funding that have weak goals and objectives. It's never too late for failed grant applications to be turned around and resubmitted for funding consideration!

## Understanding the difference between types of goals and objectives

To keep the terms *goal* and *objective* straight, think of *goal* first and remember that it's the thing(s) you're attempting to accomplish. A goal is where you are when you're done implementing the activities associated with your measurable objectives. Grant application narratives must have goals to show the funder that you have a vision for solving the problem.

**REMEMBER**

A lot of things have changed since I first started writing *Grant Writing For Dummies* (roll your mind back to 2001). Back then I trained everyone in my grant-writing classes that goals are never measurable. However, there is a shift among some public-sector (government) and private-sector (foundation and corporation) funders. Some of these grant makers are not asking for *measurable goals.* I know, it's a bit confusing to all grant writers. To alleviate your own confusion, I provide definitions and examples of a goal and a SMART goal. *Remember:* SMART stands for specific, measurable, attainable, realistic, and time bound.

Okay, so what about an objective? An *objective* is simply a major milestone or checkpoint or benchmark on your route to reaching a goal. It's a place where you can say (and report to a funder, if necessary), "We've come this far, and we have this far remaining before we reach the goal." Award-winning objectives are **sp**e-cific, **m**easurable, **a**ttainable, **r**ealistic, and **t**ime bound (SMART); they also serve to keep goals realistic.

**TIP**

When I'm writing a government grant request, I develop my goals by using the funder's goals for the funding initiative. I always follow the funders' directions as to what type of goal they want to see in grant applications — nonmeasurable or measurable. I then create measurable objectives to track all the funding initiative's intended outcomes (also known as *performance measures*). Everything you need to cue you on how many goals and how many objectives to write is there in the grant application guidelines. On the other end of the spectrum, when I'm writing a proposal to a foundation or corporation, I have nothing to tip me off to what the funder wants to see or fund in terms of funder goals and objectives. In those cases, I keep it light and usually write one or two nonmeasurable goals. And each goal always has one or two measurable or SMART objectives.

That said, I don't have a magic number for goals and objectives. Just be sure your organization's goals are based on the vision of where you want the program or target population to be when the grant period is over. *Remember:* Your goals need to align with the goals of the funding. This verbiage will be provided on the funder's website or in its grant application guidelines.

## Following the funder's directions to write the right types of goals

There are two types of goals: nonmeasurable and measurable. Always read the funder's guidelines carefully and write the types of goals that it asks for. When you're in the process of writing any type of goal, be sure to write clear, concise, one-sentence statements. Nonmeasurable goals should be action-oriented and full of verbs (see Chapter 11 for more on choosing impactful words). Measurable goals are written much like SMART objectives.

TIP

I always start my nonmeasurable goals with the word *provide* until I get into a rhythm. After I have the magic nonmeasurable goal-language machine going, I venture out and use other starting action words such as *develop, plan, educate, create, build, empower, engage,* and so forth. Nonmeasurable goals truly mirror SMART objectives.

To be sure you've written effective and well-constructed goal statements of any type, ask yourself the following questions:

>> Did I follow the funder's guidelines for writing the *right* type of goal (nonmeasurable or measurable)?

>> Did I use one sentence?

>> Is the sentence clear and concise?

>> Do my goals align with the funder's priority areas and program-specific goals for awarding grants?

>> Does the grant reader know who the target population is and where the monies are needed (geographic impact area)?

Following are examples of both types of goals (nonmeasurable and measurable). I advise only using one goal-writing format in your grant application. In other words, don't mix nonmeasurable and measurable goals. Write one or the other — depending on the funder's specific guidelines for what it wants to see in your narrative.

Here are some examples of nonmeasurable goals:

**Goal:** Provide elderly disabled Brentwood Highlands residents with supervised physical fitness activities offered inside of their gated community.

**Goal:** Develop an obesity awareness campaign targeting Latino families residing in Genesee County, Michigan.

**Goal:** Create a women's business center incubator in Goodyear, Arizona, to train recent parolees from the Buckeye prison system in micro-enterprise entrepreneurship.

Here are some <u>examples of SMART (**S**pecific, **M**easurable, **A**ttainable, **R**ealistic, and **T**ime–bound) goals:</u>

**SMART Goal:** By June 30, 2017, elderly disabled Brentwood Highlands residents will increase their levels of physical activity in multilevel community-based exercise sessions by 25 percent as measured by pre- and post-declining health indicators.

**SMART Goal:** By August 31, 2017, create and carry out 13 weekly obesity awareness campaigns targeting 50 percent or more of Latino families residing in Genesee County, Michigan, as measured by the number of broadcast media PSAs in Spanish.

**SMART Goal:** By December 31, 2017, complete 100 percent of the women's business center incubator in Goodyear, Arizona, to facilitate micro-enterprise entrepreneurship training programs targeting recent parolees from the Buckeye prison system as measured by the number of building inspections passed, the number of months to complete the facility, and the number of post-parole agreements with regional correctional facilities.

**WARNING**

If the funding decision maker can't look at your goals and figure out from them what your entire program is about, you've failed to write clearly stated goals — measurable or nonmeasurable.

**TIP**

When you start writing your program design, remember to incorporate key words and phrases from the grant announcement's purpose of funding statement. During the grant review process, this strategy helps peer reviewers make a clear connection between the purpose of the grant and your statement of need and program design — which should fit like a soft leather glove to the announcement language. This approach of parroting the funding agency's own words results in receiving high review points — starting you down the road to getting a funding award! Just make sure your target population fits the one described in the purpose of funding statement.

# Recognizing and writing types of objectives requested by funders

Successful grant writing requires you to understand the three types of objectives (also known as *milestones* or *benchmarks*) and to know when to use them:

>> **SMART outcome objectives:** Measurable steps or benchmarks to reach a stated goal

>> **Process objectives:** Activities or tasks

>> **Impact objectives:** Benefits to end users that continue after the grant funding has ended

Using the right objective at the right time can help you rack up peer review points, which can also help you win big bucks for your program. (See Chapter 10 for further insight on the review process.)

**WARNING**

SMART goals (explained earlier in this chapter) do not mix with SMART objectives. Why? When funders require SMART goals, they simply want simple outcome objectives. There will be a **M**easurement term, like *increased* or *decreased*, without any **T**imebound or **T**imeframe language. These types of measurable objectives are merely performance indicators. I give you some examples later in this chapter.

**TIP**

Although you should definitely provide at least one objective for each goal and year of your funding request, some program designs have more than one objective for each goal. If this setup is the case with your design, make sure you number and alphabetize the objectives (for example, 1a, 1b, 1c, and so on) to eliminate confusion for the reviewer.

## Creating SMART outcome objectives

How do you recognize an *outcome objective?* It's an objective that shows that the project has accomplished the activities it planned to achieve. Always create outcome objectives for your programs or projects. They're the most common type of objectives funders ask for in their grant application guidelines.

When writing your own outcome objectives, use phrases that imply some sort of measurable change, such as *to increase* or *to decrease.* For example, you can write about an increase of 50 percent in the number of organizations receiving project services by the end of Year 1.

The easiest way to write outcome objectives is to use the SMART acronym:

>> **S:** Is the objective **s**pecific rather than abstract? The objective must point out who will benefit (students, patients, clients, or whatever applies) and specify what will be measured (behavior, participation, and so forth).

>> **M:** Is the objective **m**easurable? Can it be tracked easily with valid measurement tools, such as surveys, pre- and post-needs assessments, and more? Use measure-indicating words such as *increase, decrease, reduce, improve, lower,* or *raise.* Also include a percentage benchmark. You can't write, "By the end of Year 1, hire 10 teachers," because that doesn't specifically illustrate a measurable benefit to your target population.

>> **A:** Is the objective **a**ttainable? Can your organization really pull off the objective?

>> **R:** Is the objective **r**ealistic? Can the measurement actually be attained for the target population in the given time frame?

>> **T:** Is the objective **t**ime bound? Can your organization accomplish all the required tasks to achieve the objective in the given time frame? Make sure your objective contains a time-bound phrase, such as *by the end of Year 1,* or *the first semester, the second quarter, the grant-funding period,* or whatever time segment your project will occur in.

The following are some sample SMART outcome objectives for Goal 1, a non-measurable goal, in the examples in the earlier section "Following the funder's directions to write the right types of goals," ("Provide elderly disabled Brentwood Highlands residents with supervised physical fitness activities offered inside of their gated community"):

**Objective 1a:** By the end of Year 1, increase the number of residents inquiring about fitness events in the community room by 25% or more as demonstrated by pre-grant and post-grant award comparisons of incidences of interest among the target population.

**Objective 1b:** By the end of Year 1, increase the number of residents participating in one or more fitness activities by 25% or more as demonstrated by pre-grant and post-grant event attendance records.

**Objective 1c:** By the end of Year 2, increase the number of residents participating in two or more fitness activities by 50% or more over Year 1 as demonstrated by a comparison of Year 1 and Year 2 event attendance records.

In order to accurately measure any percentage increases for your target population (like measurements built into the example objectives), you need to know the baseline numbers (the starting point) for each type of measurement. For example, if the Brentwood Highlands community has 300 elderly residents, how many are participating in fitness activities at the time you're writing the grant request? You need a starting point in order to establish a reasonable (attainable) measurement. If you don't have baseline data, write that in the program design narrative. Explain to the funder that your data collection will include a pre- and post-assessment of the high-risk indicators to demonstrate that your intervention/implementation strategies will/did work.

If the program you're requesting funding for is new, you may not have baseline data to help guide the development of outcome objective targets (such as the percentage of charge you estimate will occur). In this case, be sure to build baseline assessments into the program enrollment process whenever possible.

REMEMBER

Why do I like to include the term *or more* in my SMART objective statements? Because if you meet or exceed conservative objectives, you'll look like a superhero in the eyes of the funder. On the other hand, if you set overly ambitious objectives and fail to meet them, you'll look like someone who didn't know how to collect baseline numbers or indicators for each SMART objective, and you probably won't be re-funded by that funder.

## Writing a performance indicator-based objective

When funders request SMART goals, you have to change up your objective language and write in a non-SMART format. Let's look at a SMART goal again and churn out some performance indicator-based objectives in the following example:

> **SMART Goal 1:** By June 30, 2017, elderly disabled Brentwood Highlands residents will increase their levels of physical activity in multi-level community-based exercise sessions by 25 percent as measured by pre- and post-declining health indicators.

Performance indicator-based objectives:

> **Objective 1a:** Increased physical and mental stamina in target population
>
> **Objective 1b:** Decreased critical health indicators in target population
>
> **Objective 1c:** Increased mobility in target population

Make sure not to overwhelm or convolute this section of the program design narrative by having timelines and measurements in both your goals and objectives. It's too much for the funder to digest visually and conceptually, and it's too confusing for the grant writer who has been writing traditional nonmeasurable goals for years.

When in extreme doubt or a state of confusion, call the funder and ask for a copy of a previously funded grant application. This will help you to understand how past or current grantees (the agencies receiving the grant awards) worded their goals and objectives. Don't plagiarize — just follow their template protocol from writing the requested types of goals and objectives.

## Producing process objectives

*Process objectives* are the implementation-related activities or tasks needed to reach your goals and meet or exceed your SMART objectives for your grant-funded program. For effective process objectives, write about the actual, chronological activities that need to occur from the time you receive grant funding until the monies have been spent.

The best way to present your process objectives is in a table format. Make sure to follow the funder's guidelines when setting up your timeline segments (which I explain in the upcoming section "Providing a Comprehensive Implementation Plan"). I like to use quarters; however, some funders ask for monthly timelines for all activities.

TIP

When writing process objectives, quantify your activities in numbers rather than percentages or words.

Following are two sample process objectives:

> **Process Objective 1:** Marketing outreach to 300 elderly residents in Brentwood Highlands.

> **Process Objective 2:** Enroll 75 Brentwood Highlands elderly residents in one or more fitness activities.

## Identifying impact objectives

*Impact objectives* demonstrate the achievement of the goal of the project or program when you or anyone else steps into the future and then looks back at what was accomplished and the differences that were made. In other words, what will the grant's impact on your target population be in three to five years?

TIP

If you come across a grant application in which the funding agency asks you to write about *benefits to participants,* respond by using impact objectives. Benefits to participants are really presumptions of how the funded program's intervention will change your participants. For example, you can write about changes in the target population's attitude about learning and achieving.

Impact objectives are easy to identify because they're written in past tense. They're futuristic glimpses into the past, your vision for what the program's future impact may be. Unlike process objectives, you don't have any common words to cue your writing. The funder is just looking for signs of significant change — change brought on by the interventions that the funder made possible.

Here is an example of an effective impact objective:

> **Impact Objective:** Brentwood Highlands residents who participated in Year 1 of the fitness activities have reported lower incidence of hypertension and a reduction in chronic disease progression.

# Providing a Comprehensive Implementation Plan

A *timeline* or *Gantt chart* tells the grant reader when major project milestones will begin and end during the grant's funding period (which is usually a 12-month period). The timeline also includes information about who's accountable for each activity and how you'll evaluate the program's accomplishments during that period.

When you develop a project timeline, keep in mind that the grant reader wants to see answers to the following questions:

>> What are the key tasks or activities that will be carried out to implement the program successfully?

>> Did the grant applicant include all tasks, from the day funding is announced or awarded to the last day of the project's funding time frame?

>> Can each task realistically begin and end in the proposed time frame?

>> Are evaluation activities included in the timeline chart?

>> Who is responsible for seeing that each activity is implemented and completed?

REMEMBER

You can use your word-processing software to create a simple timeline chart. Just be sure not to overdo it with color; use no more than four shading selections (and don't use red or black shading unless you change the font color to white).

Because I never know how many disruptions and malfunctions I'll encounter in implementing a grant-funded program, I prefer to set up my activity start and stop dates in quarterly increments. However, if you have total control over the activities, you can use monthly increments to show when they begin and end.

The sample activity timeline chart in Figure 15-1 clearly shows what the program plans to accomplish, when it plans to accomplish it, and who is responsible for seeing the activities (process objectives) through the completion phase.

| Brentwood Highlands Fitness Program Timeline Chart, Year 1 | | | | | |
|---|---|---|---|---|---|
| Activities/Milestones | Year 1 July 1 – June 30 | | | | Key Person/Group Responsible |
| | 1st Qtr. | 2nd Qtr. | 3rd Qtr. | 4th Qtr. | |
| Community Association governing body for Brentwood Highlands formally accepts the grant award by resolution adoption | 🚲 | | | | Community Association Board of Directors |
| Creation of fitness activity preference survey | 🚲 | | | | Activity Director |
| Distribution of fitness interest and past activity involvement survey via delivery to every occupied mobile home in the park's six block sections | 🚲 | | | | Block section captains |
| Free-of-charge community cookout to collect surveys and tour the new fitness facility | 🚲 | | | | Community volunteers Activity Director |
| Use survey data to identify fitness activity leaders from within and outside of the community | 🚲 | | | | Activity Director |
| Meet with interested fitness activity leaders to discuss their day/time/interest preferences | 🚲 | | | | Activity Director |
| Use survey data to develop list of indoor and outdoor classes and events to be offered weekly | 🚲 | | | | Activity Director |
| Email blast activity schedule to all residents (those residing in the park and winter visitors who arrive by October 1 annually) | 🚲 | | | | Activity Director e-Newsletter Coordinator |
| Classes and other activities begin | | 🚲 | | | |
| Develop retention incentives for all fitness activities | 🚲 | | | | Activity Director |
| Develop evaluation forms for residents to rate instructors and activities (type, time, day, intensity) | 🚲 | | | | Grand Canyon University Evaluation Intern |
| Administer evaluation forms halfway through each class and again at the end | | 🚲 | 🚲 | 🚲 | Activity Director |
| Monitor class enrollment records to track residents in more than one class | | 🚲 | 🚲 | 🚲 | Activity Director |
| Ongoing process and outcome monitoring and correction actions as needed | | 🚲 | 🚲 | 🚲 | Grand Canyon University Evaluation Intern |
| Winter visitor season-end fitness awards (most inches lost, most weight lost, most classes taken, and most health risk indicators reduced) | | | | 🚲 | Activity Director |
| Final reports to stakeholders (funders, Community Association Board, and park residents) | | | | 🚲 | Activity Director |
| Grant close-out | | | | 🚲 | Activity Director |

*Illustration by Ryan Sneed*

**FIGURE 15-1:** An example of a timeline of activities.

You can access a timeline chart template at www.dummies.com/go/grant
writingfd6e.

**TIP**

For programs that request funding for multiple years, you need to include extra timelines in the grant application showing each year's activities and the quarterly time frames for each activity. You can either create a multiyear timeline chart on one page that breaks down the four quarters for each year (do so in landscape format to make room for all the information) or create a separate timeline chart for each year. Figure 15-1 shows Year 1 for the Brentwood Highlands Fitness Program. Years 2 and 3 would take another two pages of table charts. Whether you choose to set up a multiyear landscape table chart or individual year charts that take up two or more pages depends on the funder's page limitations.

# Confirming Narrative Content Connectivity in Your Logic Model

The *Logic Model* is a graphic blueprint of the key elements of a proposed program. It looks at inputs, activities, outputs, outcomes, and impacts. If you live and work in the world of grants, avoiding the Logic Model is difficult. Just about every type of funder seems to want you to include a Logic Model in the program design of your grant application narrative.

Here's what the columns of your Logic Model graphic should contain:

>> **Inputs:** These are the human, financial, and physical resources dedicated to your grant-funded program. These resources include money, staff and staff time, volunteers and volunteer time, facilities, equipment, supplies, and community partners. (See Chapter 16 for information on personnel and organization resources.)

>> **Strategies:** These are what your program uses to organize the inputs. Using effective strategies helps the program to fulfill its mission. Basically, the funder wants a recap of your goals; I copy and paste the goals I wrote in the program design into this column of the Logic Model. Simplify your SMART goal (if that type of goal is required by the funder) and take out any measurement language.

>> **Outputs:** These are the direct results of your program's implementation activities. They're actually written as indicators of productivity. Outputs usually start with the phrase *number of* and reflect how you'll quantitatively track your program activities. You can extract output language from your objectives narrative (found earlier in your program design) and from your evaluation narrative as well.

>> **Short-, intermediate-, and long-term outcomes:** These are the benchmarks or measurements for your target population during and after program activities. For the outcomes, you can simply reuse your SMART objectives or SMART goals — extracting the measurements language only (see the earlier section "Plotting Goals and SMART Objectives"). Some funders want to see short-term outcomes (3-month SMART objective measurements), and others want to see intermediate outcomes (6-month SMART objective measurements). All funders want to see long-term outcomes (12 months or longer SMART objective measurements).

>> **Long-term impact or impact statement:** Funders want to know what long-term outcomes or impact (changes in systems and processes after the funding is expended) you anticipate for your target population.

Figure 15-2 shows the basic structure for the Logic Model with intermediate and long-term SMART objectives. Keep in mind, though, that this is only one example of how funders may instruct you to prepare your Logic Model form.

I provide a template of the Logic Model format at `www.dummies.com/go/ grantwritingfd6e`.

If you have a multiple-year program, you need to have multiple-year Logic Models. Each year's model should show a set of inputs, activities, outputs, outcomes, and impacts on its own page. Also, if the funder has its own logic model format, forms, or different components, follow those.

The Logic Model isn't a process you can pick up overnight. But reviewing the online materials at the W.K. Kellogg website (`www.wkkf.org`) can help with the learning curve. Type **logic model development guide** into the site's search box and download the *W.K. Kellogg Foundation Logic Model Development Guide* from the Show All Results menu. I suggest printing it out and using it as a desktop reference.

**Brentwood Highlands Fitness Program Logic Model**

| Inputs | Strategies | Outputs | Outcomes | |
|---|---|---|---|---|
| | | | Intermediate-Term (6 Months) | Long-Term (12 Months) |
| *Grant funding<br>*Grant applicant in-kind match<br>*Facilities (indoor fitness room and outdoor aquatic and trail walking area)<br>*Collaborative partner(s)<br>-Association Board<br>-Volunteers<br>-Staff<br>*Equipment<br>*Materials and supplies | Goal: Provide elderly disabled Brentwood Highland residents with supervised physical fitness activities offered inside of their gated community. | # of surveys distributed<br># of surveys returned<br># of residents touring the new facility<br># of activity leaders identified<br># of classes offered (inside and outside)<br># of days classes offered<br># of residents enrolling in one class<br># of residents enrolling in more than one class<br># of residents completing activity leader evaluation forms<br># of residents retained (halfway and at the end)<br># of residents receiving awards (by type of award)<br># of residents indicating interest in Year 2 Fitness Program | Increase the number of residents inquiring about community room fitness events by 12.5% or more as demonstrated by pre-grant and post-grant award comparisons of incidences of interest among the target population.<br><br>Increase the number of residents participating in one or more fitness activities by 12.5% or more as demonstrated by pre-grant and post-grant event attendance records. | Increase the number of residents inquiring about community room fitness events by 25% or more as demonstrated by pre-grant and post-grant award comparisons of incidences of interest among the target population.<br><br>Increase the number of residents participating in one or more fitness activities by 25% or more as demonstrated by pre-grant and post-grant event attendance records. |
| **Impact Statement** | *Brentwood Highland residents who participated in Year 1 of the fitness activities have reported lower incidences of hypertension and reduction in chronic disease progression.* | | | |

**FIGURE 15-2:** The Logic Model depicts your organization's planned work and intended results for a given project.

# Writing the Evaluation Plan for Your Program Design

The most important part of grant writing is the initial step of deciding which grants to pursue, but evaluating your project after it has been funded is a close second. The *evaluation plan* in the program design section of the grant narrative explains to the potential funder how you plan to evaluate the success of your project.

The evaluation plan includes

>> A review of your program's objectives and how you'll know whether you met them

>> The type of information you'll collect to use in the evaluation

>> How often you will collect the information

>> Who will collect the information

>> Who will analyze the information and report the results

To introduce you to the evaluation process, I explain evaluation terms and the types of evaluations your organization can perform in the following sections. I also show you how to put together an evaluation plan for your program design and how to write a dissemination plan.

**TIP**

The W.K. Kellogg Foundation has published a handbook describing how to actually go about conducting an evaluation. You can view or download the handbook on the foundation's website (www.wkkf.org) by searching for *evaluation handbook.*

## Making sense of evaluation plan terminology

Before you can write an evaluation plan, you need to have a basic understanding of the commonly used terms. The terms in the following sections are ones you should be familiar with and use when writing your evaluation plan for the program design.

### Data collection and analysis

You collect data in order to find out whether you're achieving the objectives you describe in the project design section of your grant narrative. You analyze the data to determine whether you met your goals. Both the data collection and analysis processes must be objective, no matter what the findings reveal.

# UNDERSTANDING EVALUATION STANDARDS

*Evaluation standards* are acceptable ways to measure various components of your project. The American National Standards Institute approved the following four nationally used standards in the 1990s. The entire evaluation process should incorporate these standards if you want funders and others in your field to accept your findings as valid:

- **Accuracy standards** are how you plan to show that your evaluation will reveal and convey technically adequate or sufficient information about your project.

- **Feasibility standards** are how you plan to ensure that your evaluation procedures will be realistic, prudent, diplomatic, and frugal.

- **Propriety standards** are how you plan to show that your evaluation will be conducted legally, ethically, and with due regard for the welfare of those involved in the evaluation as well as those affected by its results.

- **Utility standards** are how you plan to evaluate the information needs of the project's participants or end users.

*Data* is the information about your project gathered using measurement tools. *Measurement tools* can include surveys, pre- and post-questionnaires or tests, and oral interviews.

*Data analysis* occurs when you examine the information that you collect with the measurement tools. What you're looking for is whether the data produces information relevant to determining the progress of your project. If it isn't, you need to go back and design new measurement tools.

## Evaluators

The *evaluator* or *evaluation team* is the individual or group of people you select to determine whether your project succeeded or failed in meeting its goals.

Even if your project failed miserably (for example, your objectives said that, on average, 75 percent of the participants would gain one full grade point, but only 25 percent did so), you and your stakeholders, including the funders, need to know what went wrong and how the outcome could be reversed. Sometimes in this failed scenario, your funding source will actually give you a second grant to fix the problem, which equates to another chance to succeed. But you get the second chance only if your evaluation team is objective and accurate.

A *third-party evaluator* is an individual or company outside your program that designs and conducts your project's evaluation. (See "Taking the third-party evaluation route" later in this chapter for more information.) Remember to include an expense line in your project's budget to compensate the third-party evaluator for its services. The standard amount to set aside for evaluation is 15 percent of your total project budget. (See Chapter 17 for more about budgets.)

An *internal evaluation* occurs when you decide not to hire an outsider to conduct your evaluation and instead choose to gather stakeholders to assess the effectiveness of your program (see the later section "Keeping the evaluation process in-house").

You shouldn't evaluate your own project. You can be a part of the evaluation team if you decide to conduct an internal evaluation. However, refrain from coaching or coercing other evaluation team members (your co-workers, board members, volunteers, community members, or project participants). Everyone on the evaluation team needs to be able to talk openly about his perceptions of the data findings. Focus on being impartial.

## Types of evaluations

A *formative evaluation* occurs when you sit down with the project's stakeholders (community members, participants, and staff) and develop a list of questions the funders may ask about your project when determining whether the funding was well placed and used. Looking at several aspects of the project design (goals, objectives, and activities), stakeholders generate questions about how the project can become more effective or efficient. The formative process continues from the time you receive grant funding to the completion of the grant time frame. In light of this ongoing process, you should set a frequency for when the data will be collected to answer the questions you have posed.

Some funders give you due dates for evaluation and financial reports. Others leave the reporting frequency up to the grant applicant or grantee. If the latter is the case, I recommend giving quarterly reports — at a minimum — to all your funders. When you report quarterly, you find flaws or weaknesses in your program's implementation strategies quickly and have time to correct them — well within the funding period.

Always have progress reports or *raw data* (information collected but not compiled into summary form or typed in a formal report) on hand for funder queries or visits.

WARNING

If you can't make improvements to your project (that is, if your students just aren't improving their grade-point averages as quickly as you anticipated in your program design narrative), a formative evaluation may not be the right approach to measure the success of your project; instead, focus on using a summative evaluation.

The *summative evaluation* (also called an *outcome evaluation*) occurs near or at the end of the period for which you were funded. This type of evaluation should answer the following questions in a narrative format:

>> What did you accomplish?

>> How many participants were impacted and in what ways?

>> What overall difference did your project make?

>> Is this project worth funding again?

### Qualitative versus quantitative

*Qualitative evaluation* describes the approach you take when you want to understand the quality of your project's implementation process. You can use surveys and focus groups to determine the quality of the service delivery process, staff development training, partnership involvement, and other components of your program.

*Quantitative evaluation* (track the numbers) describes the approach you take to measure the progress of your SMART objectives. Did you reach your short-, intermediate-, and long-term outcomes as presented in the Logic Model (see the earlier related section)?

TIP

I like to collect data on both qualitative and quantitative approaches in order to analyze the progress and impact of the implementation process.

## Keeping the evaluation process in-house

When you plan to conduct an internal evaluation — meaning you aren't hiring an outsider to assist with or conduct the evaluation of your project — the best option is to propose a stakeholder's evaluation in the evaluation plan of your program design. In a *stakeholder's evaluation*, you don't need to identify the evaluators until you know your project is funded. You can then identify select stakeholders from your target population, board of directors, and community partners to sit on the evaluation team.

The easiest way to identify your project's stakeholders is to ask yourself the following question: "Who has a vested interest in our project and will be impacted by the project's success?" The outcome of the project definitely matters to your board of directors, if you have one, as well as to the staff assigned to work on the project. However, it matters most to the project's target population, which is why you should seriously consider inviting some of them onto the evaluation team.

A clue as to when you may need to propose a stakeholder's evaluation can be found in the grant application's budget instructions. If the budget instructions for the grant or cooperative agreement don't include a specific line item for evaluation or contracted services, and if your program implementation costs will require all the available grant funding, I suggest you consider a stakeholder's evaluation. It's less costly and keeps the entire evaluation process local and manageable. For example, suppose your organization proposes to operate a homeless shelter for veterans returning from overseas combat. The grantor requires that all proposed homeless prevention plans originate from the feedback collected at public meetings. At your public meetings, have a sign-in sheet that captures each attendee's name, mailing address, telephone number, and email address, as well as whether the person is a veteran or has a family member who's a veteran or on active duty. Each and every citizen who attends your public meeting and provides input on the need for housing for homeless veterans is a potential candidate for the evaluation team.

Be creative and bring together people who have different perspectives. Sometimes, opposing views bring out additional needs that weren't identified during the public meetings; having one or two devil's advocates on any team, including the evaluation team, can be good for flushing out the real needs and forcing team members to rethink their positions. The number of people you have on your stakeholder's evaluation team doesn't matter as long as everyone's point of view is welcomed, considered, and incorporated into your final intervention or prevention methodology for serving the target population.

Do you have board members who have wanted to work with your organization in a more hands-on way but who you're afraid will try to micromanage the program? Placing them on the evaluation team is an ideal way to divert their energy. They can really help shape the outcome of your grant-funded program — a program that may very well be the most important part of your organization.

When it comes to an internal evaluation team, you're not looking for groupthink. You want independent-minded people who can bring objective ideas to the table, giving you a credible evaluation process for your funded project. Also, remember that if you use your staff for the evaluation, they'll need time to oversee the data collection, interpretation, and reporting processes. In other words, the evaluation process will cost money and/or time whether you decide to use internal or external evaluators.

# Taking the third-party evaluation route

If you decide to bring in an outsider to conduct your evaluation, that person is referred to as a *third-party evaluator* in the grant narrative. Even though outside evaluators are costly (some need up to 15 percent of your total project budget to conduct the evaluation), the right outside evaluator can bring credibility and visibility to your project, which in turn attracts continued funding.

TIP

The grant application's budget instructions often provide clues that you need an outside evaluator. If the budget instructions discuss evaluation costs and ask you to provide information on third-party evaluators, plan to bring in an outside evaluator.

To find a qualified evaluator, first ask other organizations in your community that provide programs similar to yours about evaluators they've used. Their evaluator may have been a university research department, a college faculty member, or a retired government employee with expertise in the project area. However, be aware that you may have to look outside your home area for an evaluator.

You must choose an individual or organization that has experience in developing evaluation plans, creating monitoring guidelines that track the progress of a project's objectives, and conducting both simple and complex evaluations in the project's focus area.

During your telephone conversation or meeting with the prospective evaluator, work through a list of prepared questions and write down the evaluator's answers. You may have to decide from among several possible candidates, and having the answers on paper will help you review and make your decision. Keep in mind that the evaluator will need sufficient information about the program's design to respond intelligently to your questions.

Start off with the following questions:

>> What methodology will you use to understand the day-to-day operations of my project?

>> How much time will the work take, and how much will it cost?

>> How many on-site days can you provide in order to meet with project personnel and talk to representatives from the target population?

>> Are you willing to meet with my board of directors to provide progress reports on the evaluation?

>> At what points will you give me written evaluation reports?

Brainstorm with your staff to come up with even more questions. Selecting an evaluator is an important part of your project, and falling short in writing this part of the narrative can result in being denied funding.

TIP

After you select an evaluator, see whether that organization or person can help you write the evaluation plan for the grant narrative. Of course, you may have to pay a fee for the evaluator's time, but the money is well spent if you're going after a multimillion-dollar, multiyear grant with heavy competition. (When fewer than ten grants will be awarded nationwide in a major grant competition, that's what I call *heavy*.) And make sure you write this same evaluator into your budget to bring that person or group back for the full evaluation process when you have a funding award. (See Chapter 17 for more on how to incorporate the cost for post-grant award evaluation into your project budget.)

## Writing the evaluation plan

After you decide whether to conduct an internal stakeholder or external third-party evaluation, the next step is to start writing or incorporating your evaluation plan into the program design section of the grant application narrative. The evaluation plan goes at the end of the program design narrative if it's not a stand-alone section. The funder's formatting guidelines usually determine the length of each narrative section in the grant proposal. The program design is usually the largest section, so write succinctly but include sufficient details for the funder to see you have a comprehensive evaluation plan.

Your evaluation plan must always be written to address the funding agency's guidelines. A comprehensive evaluation plan includes a narrative on how the program will be evaluated (qualitatively, quantitatively, or both). It also tells the funder what type of data will be collected; who will be collecting, analyzing, and interpreting the data; and the frequency for the data collection process. Don't forget to add detail about each target population included in the evaluation process and tell how information or data will be collected from them (by way of survey, questionnaire, visual observation, and more).

REMEMBER

Most importantly, make sure all data to be collected is connected to determining your progress toward achieving your measurable objectives, which are presented earlier in the project design section of your application. And remember that your evaluation plan must be specific to your program goals and objectives.

TIP

Examples of evaluation plans abound online. If you do an Internet search for **sample evaluation plan** you find that just about every type of funder (foundation and government) has posted outlines and full narrative sections of its best or preferred type of evaluation plans. Don't forget to use the Kellogg Foundation's website to search for and use its Logic Model Development Process information.

The evaluation plan also needs to include information about how you'll share your evaluation findings with other organizations interested in replicating a successful model program. This sharing process is called *dissemination.* The dissemination plan, which is usually a paragraph or two, is written at the end of the evaluation plan.

Worried about giving away too many secrets? Don't be. When you receive a grant award, the funders expect you to share your findings with other organizations and associations. With government grants, everything you do — information and program activities — is subject to public access. Foundation and corporate funders want to maximize their investments, which means you're obligated to disseminate your evaluation findings. Practically all funders ask for your dissemination plans in their grant application guidelines.

When you write your dissemination narrative, include information on what you'll share and how you'll share it. List conferences, forums, website postings, and printed documents mailed out (and to whom they'll be mailed).

**WARNING**

When you're writing your grant applications, always, *always* follow the guidelines provided for preparing your narrative sections. In foundation funding requests, the dissemination plan can be short and to the point. However, in government funding requests, you may be instructed to write multiple pages on the dissemination process. Carefully reading and following the funding agency's guidelines can be the difference between a funded project and a rejected one.

Chapter 16

# Crafting Your Proposed Project Management Team Narrative

fter you tell the funding organization why you need its financial booster shot in your statement of need (see Chapter 14) and your project's implementation plan (see Chapter 15), you need to explain who's going to manage the grant-funded program. In this chapter, I show you how to write about existing and incoming staff in a way that convinces funders that you have the right personnel to manage their awarded monies. I also show you how to put together winning project-management profiles, an additional organizational resources narrative, and a federally guided approach to selecting diverse project personnel.

REMEMBER

You gain credibility when you outline the key personnel, organizational resources, and your equity process in hiring. Some funders call this section of the narrative *key personnel, adequacy of resources,* or *equal employment opportunity statement.* Regardless of the name, this narrative can range in length from one page to several pages. Developing narrative language that meets the requirements laid out in the funding source's grant application guidelines is important. Otherwise, the funder will likely reject your application for grant funding.

# Presenting the Project Management Team's Credentials

Just for fun, pretend for a moment that I'm your grant reviewer. I've already read the key opening sections to your application narrative, and now I'm *almost* convinced that your organization is worthy of the funding agency's award allocation. At this point, I just need to be taken to the finish line. In other words, before I can make a confident decision (fund this or reject this), I need to know who's in charge of your organization and the proposed project and who's going to carry out the day-to-day direct services. From a funder's perspective, I want written validation that competent administrators will manage the grant monies and highly qualified staff and/or contractors will manage the actual project's implementation, evaluation, and final reporting processes.

**REMEMBER**

You select and assign grant-funded personnel in one of two ways: by reassigning an existing staff person to the grant-funded project or by hiring someone after the project is funded. When you're writing about to-be-hired personnel, you don't know the specific qualifications of each individual, but you should know and be able to write about the minimum job specifications of those who will carry certain responsibilities.

Whatever specifics you include about your project management team, you'll be held accountable by the funder. For instance, if the funder's minimum qualifications for the project director or coordinator is a master's degree and your organization hires an individual with only a bachelor's degree, you aren't fulfilling the written promise that you made in your funding request. You must be conscientious about the qualifications required and the project team members selected or hired to fill the positions.

No matter how you assign project personnel, selecting individuals with project-specific qualifications can help you win a big grant award. And when you've identified qualified personnel for your project, your project's personnel profiles are a lot easier to write.

**WARNING**

As a regular grant peer reviewer, I can tell you that even if the rest of your grant narrative is perfect, you can easily lose peer review points if your project personnel aren't up to snuff. On a point scale of 100, projects scoring in the mid- to high 90s are recommended for grant awards, so losing even a few points can be fatal for your chances. Ninety-point projects just don't cut it anymore! (See Chapter 10 for more about the point system and review criteria.)

Before you start writing about staffing, resources, and equity in hiring, sit down with existing staff members or your human resources director and go over the project narrative you've already written. Look at your program design narrative and the implementation chart (see Chapter 15) to see what personnel you've committed to carry out the proposed activities. Highlight the job titles and any other information that gives you a clue as to how many staff members you need to implement the grant-funded project.

When compiling information for the project's personnel profile section, be sure to identify the following:

>> **A project administrator (or project manager):** This individual provides management oversight. In some organizations, this is the executive director or deputy director. This person should be able to allocate up to five hours per week of her work time to making sure the project meets its grant-funded conditions. The project administrator (along with the project director — see the next point) usually attends meetings with the project's community partners. (Chapter 13 covers establishing partnerships with other organizations in your community.)

>> **The personnel necessary to carry out the project on a day-to-day basis:** This entry usually means selecting a *project director* or *coordinator* who's responsible for the program's implementation and coordination. This individual reports directly to the project administrator. Identify a project director who has relevant and extensive experience in the same area as the project. In addition, for research projects, another day-to-day individual is the *principal investigator* (PI). This individual is responsible for the management and integrity of the program design as well as the direction and oversight of compliance, financial, and collaborative partnerships.

>> **All remaining personnel who will be paid from the project's grant-funded budget:** Work with your financial or business manager to review the project design and determine 100 percent of the staffing necessary to implement the project if funded. List all other personnel who will be hired for or assigned to the project in the adequacy of resources or management plan narrative of your grant application. This section of the narrative connects directly to your project budget. You'll either have direct costs or indirect costs. (More about the budget in Chapter 17.)

REMEMBER

Each project differs when it comes to the personnel needed to carry out activities, so spend some time with your human resources department to determine how much part-time/full-time equivalency should be dedicated to each staff role. See the later section "The basic profile" for more on full-time equivalency.

**WARNING**

The process of choosing personnel isn't the time to do a favor for your out-of-work, unqualified friend or relative! Not only does she have the potential to drag your project down, but she also drags down your funding request because decision-making readers shudder when they see unqualified personnel on a project they're considering funding.

# Articulating Qualifications

After you choose your staff, you can begin writing your personnel narrative. The grant reviewer looks for the key personnel narrative to answer the following questions:

>> What are the project administrator's qualifications? Is the time allocated sufficient? Who will report to the administrator? Is the line of accountability clear?

>> What are the project director's or coordinator's qualifications? Is the time allocated sufficient? Who will report to the project director or coordinator? Is the line of accountability clear?

>> Which project personnel will carry out the day-to-day activities? Is the time allocated sufficient for each position? Who will project personnel report to? Is the line of accountability clear?

>> Do the personnel members have extensive experience in the project's focus area? What percent of personnel have extensive experience?

>> What percentage of each position will be charged to the grant budget?

>> What percentage of all personnel costs will be *cash match* (cash that you have on hand and available to match the grant award for grants that require matching funds in order to receive the award) on the part of the grant applicant? (See Chapter 17 for further clarification on cash match and other budget-related terms.)

**REMEMBER**

Keep in mind that you absolutely must follow the funding agency's guidelines when it comes to writing about your project personnel. Your actual key personnel narrative may look entirely different from my examples in the following sections.

## The basic profile

For a basic personnel profile, write about what makes each person qualified for her proposed position. Give information on relevant work background, awards, acknowledgments, and special recognitions. Follow this text with educational information. End with a final sentence to blow the readers away — impress them with one more fact that qualifies the individual for the proposed position. If individuals filling some or all of the budgeted positions have yet to be hired, write a short description of the desired qualifications.

**REMEMBER**

Unless the funding agency has page limitations for this section of the funding request, write one paragraph for each budgeted personnel position. (Refer to the next section, "The profile with page limitations," to determine what to do when you have to watch how much you write.) This recommendation remains the same whether personnel costs will be charged to the grant or whether they'll be covered by your organization's cash match.

In the following example, I present the narrative language on the proposed director. Notice that I use boldface to highlight the individual's name, position, and expertise and that I use future tense. I want to plant the idea that this funding *will* be awarded and the proposed staffing-related tasks *will* occur. I also use the designation *FTE*, which stands for *full-time equivalent* (40 hours per week). An individual assigned to a project at 0.5 FTE works on it 20 hours per week; 0.10 is 4 hours per week, and so on.) Typically, you won't need to include an explanation of FTE, but you should spell out the abbreviation the first time you use it.

**Key Personnel**

**Project Administrator (0.05 FTE cash match):** Dr. Anne Mitchell **will be responsible for administering the grant-funded project. Dr. Mitchell is the founder and executive director of the Ready for the World Foundation and has functioned in this position since 2007.** She was the visionary who believed there was a need for a forward-thinking nonprofit in a historically static (little change in decades) community environment. Dr. Mitchell has 43 years of corporate management experience and 10 years of nonprofit management experience. She founded and managed the Women's Business Incubator in Burton, Michigan, for which she was awarded the Clairol Corporation's Entrepreneur of the Year award. She will report directly to the organization's board of directors. Dr. Mitchell is a bright ray of sunshine; everything she's involved in blossoms quickly and fully AND is sustaining.

Sometimes the expertise is in the team as a whole. However, in this example, Dr. Mitchell has the necessary qualities to fulfill this position all by herself.

## The profile with page limitations

If your funding request has page limitations and you can't write at least one full paragraph on all project staff members, you can include a brief list of key personnel, including volunteers, in the grant application narrative and note their responsibilities. Also, feel free to attach to the narrative more detailed information about your key personnel if the funder's guidelines allow attachments.

The following is an example of how to develop a list of key personnel:

**Project Director (1.0 FTE grant funded):** The organization will conduct a nationwide search for a project director who can **lead this project to a successful conclusion.** The individual hired will be *qualified to carry out the following responsibilities:*

- Assist the board of directors in fulfilling the organization's mission

- Have knowledge of the organization's target population

- Effectively carry out the grant-funded project's implementation plan

- Establish an annual program events calendar

- Identify qualified additional staff

- Secure new community partners

- Promote the programs via public forums

- Evaluate the effectiveness of community outreach and program services

This position will report to the project administrator.

**Volunteer Coordinator (1.0 FTE cash match):** One full-time volunteer coordinator will be assigned to this grant-funded project. Discretionary funds have been awarded from the organization's Regional Bank Association account to pay the salary and fringe benefits for this position. The volunteer coordinator will be responsible for recruiting, screening, training, and supervising adult mentors for our clients. This position requires ten years of volunteer coordination experience in either a paid or volunteer setting. The person assigned to this position must have a positive disposition, exhibit excellent analytical abilities, and demonstrate management-level skills. The Volunteer Coordinator will report directly to the Project Director.

# The profile for personnel paid by cash match

TIP

When you can provide personnel at no cost to the grant, you look *great* in the eyes of the grant reviewer. And when you look great, you score more points. For example, you may include the project director's salary in the grant proposal budget, but the project administrator's time will be cash match, so it won't be charged to the grant proposal budget. This setup shows the funder that you're focusing on the best use of grant funds and that you want to put the money toward providing services to the target population.

# INCLUDING THE PRINCIPAL INVESTIGATOR IN SCIENTIFIC OR RESEARCH GRANTS

In federal grant applications for scientific or research requests, you're asked to provide a biographical sketch for the principal investigator. In some cases, the *principal investigator* is similar to the project director (see the section "The profile for personnel paid by cash match") but usually holds a doctorate degree in the project's specialty field.

The form for a biographical sketch can change from agency to agency. The most common information fields found on the form are

- **Name:** Type in the first, middle, and last name of your principal investigator.

- **Position title:** Type in the project-assigned position title.

- **User name:** If you already have an agency log-in for the online e-grant portal entry, type it in this box.

- **Education/training:** List the colleges attended and locations, beginning with the baccalaureate degree. Fill in the degree column, the year earned or awarded, and the field of study for each institution of higher education attended.

- **Personal statement:** Write about the purpose of the proposed research and how it relates to the principal investigator's experience.

- **Positions and honors:** List, in chronological order, previous work or job positions, ending with the present position. List any honors, including present membership on any federal government public advisory committees.

- **Selected peer-reviewed publications (in chronological order):** List any publications in which work has been published and read or reviewed by professional peers.

- **Research support:** List all ongoing or completed (past three years) research projects (both federally and nonfederally supported).

Typically, biographical sketches range from five to seven pages, including its finished length after you add all the requested information. Government grant applications are often formatted for you to insert a page number at the bottom of the page, and the biographical sketch is no different. When you see the cue at the bottom of a form page, read and reread the funding guidelines to see whether your narrative and all accompanying forms must be numbered in sequential order from beginning to end.

**REMEMBER**

Grant reviewers are looking for answers to some hard-and-fast questions critical to the success of your project. Even if you aren't asking for grant funds to cover personnel, you still include a brief paragraph on the key personnel and include the résumé of the project director in the application's attachments.

When you have a volunteer advisory council, write a paragraph about the volunteers' individual commitments and how often the council will meet. In other words, you want to show that they have a vested interest in seeing your project succeed!

# Connecting Accountability and Responsibility to the Implementation Process

In addition to knowing who will be working on the project you're seeking funds for, the granting agency wants to know who reports to whom for your project. The funder wants to make sure that you understand the responsibility inherent in accepting the grant monies. You acknowledge these facts in the management plan and the statement of fiscal agency responsibility.

**REMEMBER**

If you're writing to foundations and corporations, some funders may ask for a separate narrative section on the management plan. If they don't, you can include it in the section for key personnel. However, state and federal funders usually ask for a qualification of key personnel section and a management plan; these sections are to be written separately and labeled clearly.

## Writing the management plan

The *management plan* tells the grant reviewer who's accountable to whom. It clearly shows where the buck stops when questions arise from the funder. You can integrate the management plan into the key personnel descriptions (as I did in the personnel list earlier in this chapter), or you can develop a separate graphic like the one in Figure 16-1.

**FIGURE 16-1:**
A sample management plan table.

| The Ready for the World Future Forward Initiative | | | |
|---|---|---|---|
| Position (# of personnel) | FTE | Reports To | Funded By |
| Program administrator (1) | 0.05 | Board of directors | Cash match |
| Program director (1) | 1.0 | Program administrator | Grant |
| Volunteer coordinator (1) | 1.0 | Program director | Cash match |

*Illustration by Ryan Sneed*

I like to show the management plan in black and white — no color graphics except a lightly shaded title row. The funder wants to see the position name, FTE allocation (which I explain earlier in the chapter), line of accountability (who reports to whom), and how the position will be funded (grant budget, cash match from funding applicant, or in-kind contribution). I prefer to list the project personnel in order of ranking, beginning with the highest administrative position and ending with volunteers, if any.

In your plan, the number in parentheses behind each position title indicates the number of individuals hired for each title position. For example, in Figure 16-1, the (1) behind each listed position tells you that The Ready for the World Future Forward Initiative will have one program administrator, one program director, and one volunteer coordinator. *Remember:* In an e-grant application format, you'll only be able to type this information in straight, plan narrative form. No graphics will be allowed in most cases.

You can access a customizable management plan template at www.dummies.com/go/grantwritingfd6e.

When the funder's management plan guidelines call for something that's not applicable or necessary to your project, write a response to indicate why that particular something isn't attached or discussed further in your application.

Always include a project organizational chart in the management plan — space permitting. A chart amplifies your key personnel narrative section and gives the grant peer reviewer a visual break from reading line after line of typed text. If the grant application's guidelines limit the number of pages you can write in the narrative and don't specifically request an organizational chart, leave it out; the organizational chart doesn't adequately capture position responsibilities or qualifications to serve as the entire management plan section on its own.

## Acknowledging your fiscal responsibility

The management plan should also include a *statement of fiscal agency responsibility.* This concise, one-paragraph written statement by the chief financial officer (CFO) of the applicant organization attests to the fact that the agency will take on the responsibility of accepting the grant award, managing the grant award monies, and preparing and submitting financial and evaluation reports. Basically, it's just one more affirmation to the funder of the grant applicant's internal accountability.

The statement of fiscal agency responsibility is presented depending on the type of funder:

>> **For foundation and corporate funding requests:** Written on the grant applicant agency's letterhead, signed by the CFO, and attached to the application and/or in the body of the grant application narrative in the grant applicant capability section. Read Chapter 13 for more on this section of the narrative.

>> **For government grant requests:** Included at the end of the management plan.

**REMEMBER**

Make sure to include the following accountability information in your statement of fiscal agency responsibility:

>> Legal name and corporate structures.

>> The year in which your organization was founded and whether it has any special recognitions.

>> Whether your organization will be the fiscal agent. (If not, provide information on the fiscal agent and tell the funder why you're using another organization to act as your fiscal agent.)

>> Who will monitor your fiscal activities.

>> A generic statement about your finances being managed prudently and effectively. (This statement sounds good, and it works to convince funders that you have a solid financial grip on handling all incoming revenues.)

>> Who conducts your financial audits and the frequency of those audits.

>> The amounts and sources of funds you've received from grant awards.

The following example shows you what a good statement of fiscal agency responsibility reads like:

The Ready for the World Future Forward Initiative (RWFFI), founded in 2007, is a pubic nonprofit charitable organization under IRS subsection 501(c)(3). RWFFI is the grant applicant and fiscal agent for this funding request. Finances are managed prudently and cost-effectively. Fiscal activities are monitored monthly by a CPA and reported to the board of directors within 30 days of receipt of accounting summary records. All financials are audited annually by CPAs, and audits to date have revealed no unfavorable findings. RWFFI has reported an income growth of 125% annually since its founding. Total revenues in 2016 were $2,257,000.

# Offering Up Cash and In-Kind Resources for Matching Funds

In government grants, you have to address something that's usually called *adequacy of resources.* In the adequacy of resources section, the funder looks at your organization's available resources — both the human and financial resources — and decides whether they're sufficient to successfully implement and support the project. In other words, it's a combination of the management plan and a portion of fiscal capabilities from your organizational background and capability narrative. (*Note:* You may be asked to address adequacy of resources solely in the budget section of your grant application; I fill you in on the budget section in Chapter 17.)

A graphic table is a great way to profile your resources for the funder; when you use a table rather than a narrative, you can show everything in one graphic. Figure 16-2 gives you an example of how to represent your adequacy of resources information. I like to use a three-column table with the following headers:

>> **Resource:** Record all the resources (monetary and in-kind) that will be available to help you implement a funded project successfully. If any collaborative partners are providing cash match or in-kind contributions, I list the partner agencies and what they'll be contributing to the funded project.

>> **Cash Committed:** Type in the actual cash committed to the funded project.

>> **In-Kind Value:** Type in the value of the in-kind donations from each partner. (You can find detailed explanations for in-kind donations in Chapter 17.)

| Resource | Cash Committed | In-Kind Value |
|---|---|---|
| Ready for the World Future Forward Initiative discretionary grant from the Regional Bank Association | $500,000 | |
| 25,000-square-foot training facility – fair market value based on the most recent appraisal conducted by the Exodus Nonprofit Facilities Appraisal Corporation | | $4,500,000 |
| Volunteers (100 adult mentors) valued at $22.14 per hour* x 20 hours per week x 50 weeks (closed for 2 weeks during the Winter holiday season) | | $2,214,000 |
| **Total resources to support funding request** | **$500,000** | **$6,714,000** |

*independentsector.org; 2012 (latest available) research on the value of volunteer time

**FIGURE 16-2:** An adequacy of resources table.

*Illustration by Ryan Sneed*

TIP

I also include an adequacy of resources table template at www.dummies.com/go/grantwritingfd6e.

If you choose to write a resources narrative rather than create a table, keep your narrative to one detailed paragraph.

When you use volunteers as resources, be sure to use the most current official research on the value of a volunteer. This hourly value amount changes every two years, and you can find a national and a state-by-state value. The Independent Sector's website (www.independentsector.org/volunteer_time) has a table for the national hourly value and for each state's hourly value.

**REMEMBER**

# Demonstrating Federal Compliance in Personnel Selection

*Equity* is created when you manage a program in such a way that no one is excluded. All the individuals hired with grant funds and all the members of the *target population* (those people the grant funds will help) must be given equal access to program opportunities — to be participants (target population) and to be hired (your project staff) without discrimination.

You show equity by opening your project to all who apply, providing they meet objective eligibility criteria. Funders want assurances that you won't violate federal or state antidiscrimination laws.

Federal and state funders mandate a grant application section on equity. Foundations and corporations usually don't have anything on equity in their guidelines, but including a paragraph on the subject to show your awareness of the issue doesn't hurt.

**TIP**

When evaluating the statement of equity, the grant reader asks the following key questions:

>> Does the grant applicant propose to assign or hire project personnel who reflect the demographics of the community and target population to be served under the grant funding?

>> Does the grant applicant embrace a sense of fairness to all human beings?

Use these quick-and-easy tips for writing the equity section without stress:

**TIP**

>> **Ask human resources for help.** Some grant application guidelines require that your equity statement actually cite the federal and state legislation that your organization adheres to in its hiring practices. Your human resources department can give you information on the acts you need to cite.

>> **Address equitable access for everyone.** The equity statement should include personnel (including the selection of volunteers for the project) and project participants.

>> **Be straightforward and make a statement.** Writing that discrimination will not be tolerated is important. Cite the federal and state antidiscrimination laws to which your organization will adhere.

The following example received high peer review points (see Chapter 10 for more on the peer review). Notice how the example addresses the makeup of program personnel and how the personnel will be recruited as well as makes a statement regarding discrimination and fair employment practices:

> The Ready for the World Future Forward Initiative will assign and/or hire staffing for the grant-funded project. All staff and volunteers having direct contact with clients will reflect the target population's demographics, culture, and have a demonstrated cultural competency of the individuals served. All staff and volunteers will complete a 16-hour cultural diversity training provided by Model State University. Following the training, staff will participate in role plays, trading the roles of mentee and mentor. The role plays will be observed and videotaped for affirmation of cultural competency.

> It is the policy of the Ready for the World Future Forward Initiative not to engage in discrimination or harassment against any person irrespective of gender, race, color, disability, political opinion, sexual orientation, age, religion, or social or ethnic origin. The center will comply with all federal and state nondiscrimination, equal opportunity, and affirmative action laws, orders, and regulations.

The federal government will require that all nondiscrimination forms be signed in the application submission package. Frankly, as a matter of best practices, all businesses (nonprofit and for-profit) should have these policies whether they apply for grants or not.

Chapter 17

# Creating a Budget That Includes All the Funding You Need

Many grant applicants create the budget section first, but it's actually one of the last sections you should tackle. After all, you can't develop an accurate budget for your grant request until you know all the costs involved in the funded project's implementation. Where do these cost clues come from? The program design narrative (which I fill you in on in Chapter 15).

I also find it extremely beneficial if you can develop your budget information in tandem instead of tackling it when your proposal narrative is complete. If you're working hand-in-hand with your finance staff or board treasurer or program administrator, you can work side-by-side in creating a budget during the narrative writing process.

**REMEMBER**

Your budget is connected directly to your project's goals, objectives, and implementation activities. And in order to achieve the goals and objectives, a series of implementation activities (also known as *process objectives*) must occur. The line items in your budget are the costs of carrying out the activities that lead to the achievement of your goals and objectives; these costs can include salaries, fringe benefits, travel, equipment, contracted services, construction, supplies, and more. Translation: Dollars are linked to activities and their resulting costs.

This chapter walks you through the budget preparation process for grant applications. It also tells you what the funder's expectations are when it comes to reading (or scrutinizing) your budget section.

# Reviewing Budget Section Basics

Most of the terms associated with the budget section of grant applications and cooperative agreements are everyday terms — no big deal. But when you thoroughly understand each section of the budget, you transform from the "I'm not so sure" grant writer to the "I know how to do this" grant writer who's ready to tackle the backside of the grant-writing mountain. As you start the final climb down, don't forget your enthusiasm (and don't forget to breathe)!

Your budget section contains two main parts, allocation and budget detail narrative:

>> **Allocation:** The dollar amount you assign to each line item. The *budget summary* is the short listing of each line-item expense category and the sum total for the category. At the bottom of it are the total expenses for all the line items listed in the summary. When a funder asks for a budget summary, it wants to see only a graphic table (created by you) or a completed short form (provided by the funder) with your main budget line-item categories and the total amounts for each category. Funders usually don't want to see narrative detail within a budget summary.

For example, if you're requesting funding for a staff position only, the two columns in your graphic table are Line Item (left-hand column) and Cost (right-hand column). The first line item is Personnel, and the second line item is Fringe Benefits. These two line items are flush left in the left-hand column. The total project budget, also flush left in the last row of the right-hand column, is the sum of these Personnel and Fringe Benefits columns.

>> **Budget detail narrative:** Funders require a detailed written explanation or narrative of how you plan to spend their monies if they choose to fund your project. So they typically request your *budget detail narrative* (also referred to as

your *budget justification* or just *budget narrative*). In the budget detail narrative, you explain and justify the assumptions or calculations you used to arrive at the figures in your budget summary. The budget detail narrative section isn't the place to spring surprises on the funder. You should have already discussed anything that shows up here in the program design section of the grant application (see Chapter 15 for guidance on crafting an award-winning program design section). Of course, always read the funder's guidelines and explanations for what should be included in each line-item explanation.

**REMEMBER**

As far as the order of your budget documents goes, the *budget detail narrative* section (the paragraphs that explain the details behind each expense) usually follows the *budget summary* (the overview of each line-item category and the total expense). Before you start working on the budget detail narrative, however, you need to research the funding source's preference for developing this section of your grant application. Some funders want only the budget summary, but others require the summary and detail narrative.

The organization I write about in the later budget detail narrative example (and that I use throughout this section) is a unit of municipal government — the City of Oz — that has existed since the late 1800s. The city needs additional money to create an energy-efficiency initiative that will save on utility expenses at city hall.

**TIP**

Don't forget to keep a copy of your proposal documents for your own files! For anytime access, I moved all my grant-related backup files from my computer's hard drive to cloud-based storage.

# Personnel

The personnel portion of the budget summary and budget detail narrative is where you indicate the costs of project staff and fringe benefits that will be paid from the grant funds and from your other resources. If your organization plans to assign existing staff to the grant-funded project but not draw the staff salaries from the grant monies, you need to create an in-kind contribution column to show the funder how you plan to support the costs of the project's personnel.

Funding for your project's personnel will either be requested from the funding agency or come as a cash match from your organization (the grant applicant):

>> **Cash match** refers to paid human resources or paid ongoing expenses for your organization allocated to the grant-funded program but not paid with monies from the grant funder. A cash match for personnel means that your organization isn't planning to request the salary and fringe benefit expenses from the funder; your organization's operating budget will continue to pay for

these expenses or one of your partnering agencies will plan to provide the funding needed to cover some of your implementation costs.

>> **In-kind contributions** refers to the donation or allocation of equipment, materials, and labor allocated to the grant-funded program but not requested from the funder. (I discuss in-kind contributions in more detail in "In-kind contributions [soft cash match]" later in this chapter.)

>> **Requested** refers to the funds you need to obtain from outside your organization — from the funding agency.

I recommend using *FTE* (which stands for Full Time Equivalent) throughout your budget forms. FTE is based on a full-time work schedule of 30 to 40 hours per week, depending on how an organization defines *full time.* For the following budget detail narrative example, I use 40 hours per week for a full-time employee: A 1.0 FTE is 40 hours per week; a 0.75 FTE is 30 hours per week; a 0.5 FTE is 20 hours per week; and a 0.25 FTE is 10 hours per week.

TIP

The federal government has published this definition for full-time employment: If an employee works an average of 30 hours a week or 130 hours a month or more, it is considered full-time.

REMEMBER

Because fringe benefits vary from organization to organization and from state to state, you need to check with your human resources department to find out your organization's fringe benefit calculation. This figure is always a double-digit percentage multiplied by the total salaries for the grant-funded and in-kind personnel.

Following is an example of the personnel budget detail narrative from the City of Oz's grant application:

**Personnel Budget Detail Narrative**

**Personnel:** One 0.5 FTE facilities manager will be assigned to the grant management duties and project oversight tasks. The operation manager's full-time salary is $90,000 annually. 0.5 FTE equals $45,000.

**Total Personnel Expenses:** $45,000

**Cash Match:** $45,000

**In-Kind Contributions:** $0

**Requested:** $0

**Fringe Benefits Budget Detail Narrative**

Fringe benefits are calculated at 40 percent of total salaries; fringe benefits include medical, dental, vision, short-term disability, worker's compensation insurance, unemployment insurance, and employer's FICA match for each salaried position.

**Total Fringe Benefit Expenses:** $45,000 × 40 percent equals $18,000

**Cash Match:** $18,000

**In-Kind Contributions:** $0

**Requested:** $0

WARNING

I want to emphasize that you shouldn't include cash-match or in-kind dollar amounts in the *Requested* line item of the budget summary or in the *Requested* line-item detail narrative. Your cash-match and in-kind items should appear in a separate column. Figure 17-1 shows an example from the City of Oz Project.

FIGURE 17-1:
The personnel section of a budget summary.

| City of Oz Energy Efficiency Initiative Budget Summary for Personnel and Fringe Benefit Expenses | | | | |
|---|---|---|---|---|
| Line Item | Requested | Cash Match | In-Kind Contributions | Total Line-Item Expenses |
| Salaries | $0 | $45,000 | $0 | $45,000 |
| Fringe Benefits | $0 | $18,000 | $0 | $18,000 |
| **Totals** | **$0** | **$63,000** | **$0** | **$63,000** |

*Illustration by Ryan Sneed*

## Travel

If you plan to reimburse project personnel for local travel, traditionally referred to as *mileage reimbursement,* include this expense in the travel line item of the budget summary and in the budget detail narrative. Be sure to use the current Internal Revenue Service mileage reimbursement rate in your calculations. Also, if you plan to send project personnel to out-of-town or out-of-state training or conferences during the course of the project, you need to ask for nonlocal travel expenses.

Your travel explanation in the budget detail narrative needs to include the number of trips planned and the number of persons for each trip as well as the conference or training program name, location, purpose, and cost. Don't forget to include the cost of lodging, meals, transportation to the events, and ground travel.

When reviewing the budget-related portions of the grant guidelines, you're likely to come across the term *per diem.* In this context, *per diem* refers to the daily allowance your organization gives employees to spend on meals and incidentals during their travel. Federal grant applications may have per diem limits, such as $105 per day.

REMEMBER

Keep in mind that setting a per diem amount may backfire when you or another employee travels to an area, such as Hawaii, the East Coast, or the West Coast, with a higher cost of living than the norm. Before you finalize your budget line items, contact the funding agency to see whether you can use higher per diem amounts for higher-cost locales.

TIP

If you want to set a per diem for your project but aren't sure what a reasonable amount is, you can check the federal per diem rates for your state at the General Services Administration website at www.gsa.gov/portal/content/104877. Enter the state, city, or zip code in the information input boxes to find hotel and other per diem amounts for the area.

Here's a portion of the travel budget detail narrative from the City of Oz's grant application. Notice that the purpose of the travel is clearly explained for the funder. The funds requested are clearly not for "luxurious" travel amenities:

### Travel Budget Detail Narrative

**Travel (Out of State):** Grant funding will enable our facilities manager to travel to six metropolitan southwest cities to meet with their facility environment directors and financial staff to determine the most cost-effective fiscal and management process to start this initiative. The following cities will be polled for their processes: Phoenix and Tucson (AZ), Albuquerque and Las Cruces (NM), Salt Lake City (UT), and Palm Springs (CA). Airfare from OZ (commuter airport) to each city is $600 (coach fare) times six flights. Each trip will be a one-day turnaround site visit. No money for meals or ground transportation will be needed.

**Total Travel Expenses:** $3,600

**Cash Match:** $0

**In-Kind Contributions:** $0

**Requested:** $3,600

Figure 17-2 shows you one way of graphically presenting the budget information for the City of Oz Project example.

**FIGURE 17-2:**
The travel section of a budget summary.

| City of Oz Energy Efficiency Initiative Budget Summary for Travel Expenses | | | | |
|---|---|---|---|---|
| Line Item | Requested | Cash Match | In-Kind Contributions | Total Line-Item Expenses |
| Travel | $3,600 | $0 | $0 | $3,600 |
| **Totals** | **$3,600** | **$0** | **$0** | **$3,600** |

*Illustration by Ryan Sneed*

WARNING

Be conservative yet accurate in calculating travel expenses. No funder wants to see its money pay for junkets or extended vacations. Looking for conferences in exotic places raises a red flag that can get your proposal tossed out during the review stages. (See the later "Plotting Ethical Expenses" section for more info about the right dollar amounts to include.)

# Equipment

The equipment line item of the budget summary and budget detail narrative is where you ask for grant monies to purchase a major piece of equipment, such as a computer, printer, or other critically needed operational equipment.

You can use government funds to purchase equipment when current equipment either doesn't exist or is unable to perform the necessary tasks required by the grant. Equipment purchased with government grant funds must be used 100 percent of the time for the grant-funded project.

TIP

Do your homework before requesting grant monies to cover capital (big-ticket) equipment. Sometimes, you're better off asking a local retailer or wholesaler to donate a big-ticket piece of equipment rather than bogging down the grant budget by adding it to your line items. (Head to Chapter 21 for help on asking for such donations.) Also, think about leasing capital equipment. Funders who don't allow you to use grant funds to purchase equipment may allow you to lease it instead. At the end of the lease, you have the option to purchase the equipment. Of course, you also need the funds to do so. Luckily, a lot of vendors have end-of-lease buyouts for $1.

Here's an example of the equipment budget detail narrative for the City of Oz Project:

> **Equipment Budget Detail Narrative**
>
> **Equipment:** The City of Oz will purchase heating and cooling leak-detection equipment. This equipment is highly specialized and comes with user training. The facility manager's staff will use the equipment in teams to check for heating and cooling leaks throughout city hall.
>
> **Total Equipment Expenses:** $80,000
>
> **Cash Match:** $0
>
> **In-Kind Contributions:** $0
>
> **Requested:** $80,000

Figure 17-3 shows you how to graphically represent your equipment expenses in an equipment budget summary. The table contains information from the City of Oz Project.

# Supplies

The materials and supplies needed for the daily implementation of the project go on the supplies line of the budget summary and in the budget detail narrative. Examples include office supplies, program supplies, maintenance supplies, training supplies, operational supplies, and so forth.

FIGURE 17-3:
The equipment
section of a
budget summary.

| City of Oz Energy Efficiency Initiative Budget Summary for Equipment Expenses | | | | |
|---|---|---|---|---|
| Line Item | Requested | Cash Match | In-Kind Contributions | Total Line-Item Expenses |
| Equipment | $80,000 | $0 | $0 | $80,000 |
| Totals | $80,000 | $0 | $0 | $80,000 |

*Illustration by Ryan Sneed*

The following is an example of the supplies budget detail narrative for the City of Oz Project:

**Supplies Budget Detail Narrative**

**Supplies:** Grant funds will purchase weather stripping, sealant, plastic sheeting, and other energy-saving supplies for all city hall windows and doors. City hall has 130 windows and 16 doors. The anticipated cost of these supplies is $97,000. The city has an additional $60,000 worth of these types of supplies already in inventory and will use these items first before initiating a purchase.

**Total Supplies Expenses:** $157,000

**Cash Match:** $0

**In-Kind Contributions:** $60,000

**Requested:** $97,000

Figure 17-4 shows a budget summary for the City of Oz Project. It shows the funds needed from the grantor or funding agency, the cash match (which is $0), in-kind contributions (which are $60,000 for this example because the city has supplies on hand), and the total line item for supplies.

FIGURE 17-4:
The supplies
section of a
budget summary.

| City of Oz Energy Efficiency Initiative Budget Summary for Supplies Expenses | | | | |
|---|---|---|---|---|
| Line Item | Requested | Cash Match | In-Kind Contributions | Total Line-Item Expenses |
| Supplies | $97,000 | $0 | $60,000 | $157,000 |
| Totals | $97,000 | $0 | $60,000 | $157,000 |

*Illustration by Ryan Sneed*

# Contractual

The contractual line of the budget summary and budget detail narrative is where you list the money needed to hire anyone for the project who isn't a member of the staff (staff expenses are listed under the personnel section of the budget that I cover earlier in this chapter). For example, you may plan to hire a construction contractor to build or renovate a room or building; an evaluation specialist to work on that portion of the application; or a trainer to work with your staff, clients, or board members.

**WARNING**

In some smaller nonprofit organizations, personnel hired with grant funds are considered contracted services because the term of employment is dependent on continued grant funding. The pro side of categorizing personnel as contractual is that doing so eliminates having project personnel file for unemployment compensation when they have to leave because the funding is up. The con side is that some really qualified individuals may want more of a commitment and may not remain with your project for the duration of the grant period. Also, constantly changing personnel can be a problem when it comes to the evaluation process. (Chapter 15 covers evaluation responsibilities.)

Here's an example of the contractual budget detail narrative for the City of Oz Project:

**Contractual Budget Detail Narrative**

**Contractual:** The City of Oz will create a "request for bid" document to identify a solar energy vendor. The city council has requested that 100% of city hall be heated and cooled with solar panels. The city has collected several estimates for this work. The most cost-effective bid specifications are $542,000 for 50 panels. This price includes installation and a 10-year warranty with guaranteed replacement at no additional charge to the city.

**Total Contractual Expenses:** $542,000

**Cash Match:** $0

**In-Kind Contributions:** $0

**Requested:** $542,000

To see a contractual budget summary for the City of Oz Project, check out Figure 17-5.

**FIGURE 17-5:**
The contractual line of a budget summary.

| City of Oz Energy Efficiency Initiative Budget Summary for Contractual Expenses | | | | |
|---|---|---|---|---|
| Line Item | Requested | Cash Match | In-Kind Contributions | Total Line-Item Expenses |
| Contractual | $542,000 | $0 | $0 | $542,000 |
| **Totals** | **$542,000** | **$0** | **$0** | **$542,000** |

*Illustration by Ryan Sneed*

## Construction

When you write a grant that's *exclusively* seeking funds for construction (also known as *building funds*), you don't need to bother with a budget summary and a budget detail narrative. Just insert a copy of the *bid*, which is the written document submitted to you by the construction company that lists all the costs involved in the project. Shortcuts are nice!

# Other

You may need to include this section in your budget summary and in the budget detail narrative if you have items that don't fit into any of the other categories. List items by major type and show, in the budget detail narrative, how you arrived at the total sum requested. Typical expenses that fall under the Other category are as follows:

>> Internet

>> Janitorial services

>> Rent

>> Reproduction (printing)

>> Security services

>> Stipends or honorariums for speakers or special project participants

>> Telephone

>> Utilities

>> Vehicles

>> Volunteers (check out the nearby sidebar for help calculating the value of volunteer hours)

>> Testing fees (for evaluations and other outcomes testing)

For the City of Oz Project, there are no additional expenses for the Other line item.

## Distinguishing between direct and indirect costs

*Direct costs* are expenses for most of the services and products mentioned in the previous sections — everything from the budget categories you've already listed.

**REMEMBER**

Direct costs and the category's corresponding line item are typically only allowed in government grants or contracts where you actually see direct costs (and indirect costs) in the application guidelines and on the preprinted budget forms.

*Indirect costs* — often called *overhead* — cover services and products essential to your overall organization that are consumed in some small degree by the project. Some indirect costs include things such as the telephone bill, rent payments, maintenance costs, and insurance premiums.

## ACCOUNTING FOR VOLUNTEERS' TIME

For decades, volunteers have rolled up their sleeves and stepped in to serve their communities. Volunteers are most often used where staffing shortages or gaps occur due to funding shortfalls. Nonprofits and for-profits that use volunteers in their organizations treat those volunteers as personnel; they have scheduled hours, they sign in and out of shifts, and they have job descriptions on file in personnel or human resources departments. Volunteers don't receive paychecks or contracted services fees for their volunteer work commitment; however, they're considered workforce or workplace contributors.

For federal and out-of-state foundation and corporate requests, use the national hourly rate to calculate the total value of volunteer hours. The national hourly rate is the number of volunteers on your project multiplied by their average hours each, annually. For state funding agencies as well as foundations and corporations in your state, use the hourly amount listed for your state to calculate the value of your project's volunteers.

Visit www.independentsector.org to access a state-by-state list of the dollar value for volunteer hours.

Indirect costs are usually calculated as a percentage of total direct costs. They can range from as little as 5 percent for a small nonprofit organization to as much as 66 percent for a major university. Your agency may already have an approved indirect cost rate from a state or federal agency, in which case the information is probably on file in the business manager's office. If your agency's business manager doesn't have that information, contact the US Office of Management and Budget or your state's fiscal agency. (Note that to recover indirect costs related to federal awards, you likely have to negotiate an indirect cost rate, or ICR, with the federal agency providing the majority of the funding. When this ICR is approved, it's referred to as a negotiated indirect cost rate agreement or NICRA.)

I've actually written federal grant applications with 50 percent indirect cost rates built in. This scenario means that if the application is funded and the direct costs total $500,000, another $250,000 gets tacked on for indirect costs. (Those are your taxes at work!) Additionally, many government grants limit or cap the indirect rate that can be charged for the project. Make sure to read the budget guidance carefully so that you adhere to any restrictions.

TIP

If you apply for a government grant and your organization has an indirect cost rate of 20 percent, you can choose not to ask for the entire 20 percent from the funding agency. Instead, because you want to look good and capable of managing a grant, you can ask for 10 percent from the funding agency and make up the other

10 percent as an in-kind contribution. (See the later section "Finding Matching Funds" for more.)

The following is an example of an indirect costs narrative. Note that the $86,712 requested for indirect costs covers project-related expenses for existing window and door energy-efficiency-related maintenance and repairs, utilities, office space for the facilities staff, and custodial costs:

> The City of Oz has been approved for an indirect cost rate of 12 percent by the US Office of Management and Budget. This approval was granted in 2010 when we applied for and received our first US Department of Energy grant to study the use of a wind-driven energy system. Indirect charges are calculated for the total government funds requested or $722,600 – $542,000 [contractual expenses] = $180,600 × 12 percent, or $21,672.

The reason I subtracted contractual expenses from the indirect cost calculations is because when you contract with outside consultants, your organization (the grant applicant) does not have indirect costs related to other entities' businesses.

**REMEMBER**

Federal government guidelines don't allow a grant applicant to include the cost of contractual expenses in the indirect cost rate calculations.

## Entire budget summary

**REMEMBER**

When you tally up the total amount of federal funds requested, you add the total direct costs to the total indirect costs. Then you calculate in your matching funds, which results in the total project budget:

> Total Direct Costs (Federal Request): $722,600
>
> Total Eligible Indirect Costs: $21,672
>
> Total Federal Request: $744,272
>
> Cash Match: $63,000
>
> In-Kind Contributions: $60,000
>
> Total Project Budget: $867,272

Figure 17-6 shows you how the entire budget summary for the City of Oz Project example looks when it's pulled together.

**TIP**

Visit www.dummies.com/go/grantwritingfd6e to access a budget summary template.

**BUDGET INFORMATION - Non-Construction Programs**

OMB Number: 4040-0006
Expiration Date: 01/31/2019

SECTION A - BUDGET SUMMARY

| Grant Program Function or Activity (a) | Catalog of Federal Domestic Assistance Number (b) | Estimated Unobligated Funds | | New or Revised Budget | | |
|---|---|---|---|---|---|---|
| | | Federal (c) | Non-Federal (d) | Federal (e) | Non-Federal (f) | Total (g) |
| 1. Corporation for National and Community Services - Capacity Building Initiatives for Nonprofit Organizations | 53.444 | $ | $ | $ 744,272.00 | $ 123,000.00 | $ 867,272.00 |
| 2. | | | | | | |
| 3. | | | | | | |
| 4. | | | | | | |
| 5. Totals | | $ | $ | $ 744,272.00 | $ 123,000.00 | $ 867,272.00 |

Standard Form **424A** (Rev. 7-97)
Prescribed by OMB (Circular A-102) Page 1

© *John Wiley & Sons, Inc.*

**FIGURE 17-6**
The City of Oz Project's entire federal grant application budget summary.

# Finding Matching Funds

If you're applying for consideration with a funder that requires matching funds, then this is the section for you. Push your fears aside and rev your engine, because finding matching funds is about to become a lot easier. First of all, read the grant application instructions regarding matching funds. Ask yourself how this funder defines matching funds. Can the match be an *in-kind contribution*, also referred to as *soft cash*, or are you required to identify actual cash (called a *hard match*) for the match?

In my travels across the country, I'm amazed at the feedback I get about how difficult it is for grant applicants to come up with required matching amounts in order to qualify for some state and federal grants. I've put together the following information to assist you in finding those much-sought-after matching funds.

TIP

When you're writing a grant application that requires matching funds, always show four separate columns in your foundation and/or corporate budget summary table (the feds no longer use this type of budget entry formatting on their revised budget forms) and explain the source of matching funds in your budget detail narrative. Follow these guidelines for the summary table:

>> Create your first column to list specific line-item categories.

>> Create a second column to input the amount of grant or contract funds requested for each line-item expense.

>> Create a third column to enter the cash match for each line-item expense.

>> Create a fourth column to enter the in-kind contributions for each line-item expense. If you have no in-kind funds, mark the amount as $0.

>> Create a fifth column for the total of columns one through four.

This setup is what I use in Figures 17-1 through 17-5.

## In-kind contributions (soft cash match)

The in-kind part of the budget summary and budget detail narrative is where you list the value of human and material resources your organization will make available to the grant-funded project (meaning you aren't asking the funder for all the resources needed to implement the project).

When a grant application requires matching funds, every dollar requested from the funding source must be matched with a specified percent of your own monies. The funder's guidelines tell you whether the match is 10, 20, or 50 percent. If the funding agency requires a 50 percent match (very high, but it often happens this way), if your organization requests $400,000 it must match with $200,000 in cash and/or in-kind contributions (the funder's guidelines will tell you if in-kind contributions are allowed for meeting its matching funds requirements).

REMEMBER

Following are line items where you may be able to pull out soft matching funds or in-kind contributions:

>> **Construction:** Eligible construction is any aspect of infrastructure work that will be donated by trade professionals or volunteers.

>> **Contractual:** Eligible sources are contracted consultants who will lend their expertise and time to the project after it's funded but whose expenses may not be requested from the grant-funder.

>> **Equipment:** Eligible equipment must be existing and you must document fair market value for each item.

>> **Indirect charges:** Eligible indirect charges can be a line-item request in the grant budget; however, if you're struggling to identify matching funds, use indirect charges as a matching contribution to be absorbed by your project.

Indirect charges range from 5 percent to 66 percent of the budget subtotal and are allowable in federal grant applications only. In some rare instances, foundations permit indirect charges as well, but they usually set a percentage cap, such as 10 percent of the total budget. Make sure you know and follow each specific funder's directions for how to include and calculate indirect charges.

>> **Miscellaneous:** Other eligible sources include utilities and telephone expenses related to implementing the project but that aren't allowable line items in the funding request; printing, copying, postage, and evaluation expenses not included in contractual or supplies; and any other costs your project will incur that haven't been requested from the funder.

>> **Supplies:** Eligible supplies must be on hand from existing inventory.

>> **Travel expenses:** Eligible travel must be grant-related for key or ancillary personnel, and money for the expenses can't be requested from the grant funder.

## Cash match (money on hand allocated for cash matching funds)

Inventory your cash on hand and work with your finance person or business manager to determine how much of the cash on hand can be used as cash match for the project, if funded. Remember that your cash match must be connected to grant-funded activities and related expenses:

>> **Equipment:** Equipment purchased by your organization with its own money that's connected to the grant-funded project.

>> **Fringe benefits:** Eligible fringe benefits for administrative, clerical, contracted, and facilities personnel are prorated based on the actual amount of time these staff members will contribute to funder-supported activities. Your organization pays these benefits.

>> **Personnel:** Personnel who will provide direct or indirect services for the grant-funded activities but who won't be charged to the project's budget expenditures as a line-item request to the funder. So, on a prorated basis, administrative, clerical, contracted, and facilities personnel (including custodial staff) can all be used as cash match line items. Salary for these personnel must be paid by your organization in order to count as cash match.

>> **Supplies:** Supplies purchased by your organization with its own money and connected to the grant-funded project.

>> **Travel:** Travel that your organization will pay for from its own funds connected to the grant-funded project.

TIP

When you're trying to find available money for a cash match, some places to look to first are

>> A *specialized allocation* (when your chief financial officer transfers cash from the general operating funds account into a specially allocated account to be used for cash matching funds).

>> Other state or federal grant funds. You can't use existing federal grant funds to match new/incoming federal grant funds; check with the funding agency for specific restrictions on matching funds.

>> Private sector grants for portions of the project.

>> Your general operating funds (unrestricted monies to pay the day-to-day operating expenses of your organization).

WARNING

Be sure to check with the funding agency to which you're applying to make sure that these types of matching funds are allowed.

# Plotting Ethical Expenses

Completing a project budget can be an individual effort or a team effort. Either way you go about it, however, developing thorough and accurate project budgets to present to funders involves more than just putting numbers down in a line and adding them together. Many factors affect how much you ask for in grant funding.

**REMEMBER**

When a grant is awarded, it's awarded in good faith and based on both your budget request and the funding source's grant-making capacity. So, your first goal in developing the budget section of your application narrative is to fine-tune your budget request to reflect the actual costs of your program needs. Your second goal is to get your program funded in full, of course!

## Gathering accurate cost figures

Not sure what kind of budget numbers to put down? Can't figure out how much you'll have to pay a program director? Unclear how much you'll have to spend on a copy machine? I have an easy solution: Use your telephone. Call the United Way in your area, for example, to find out its salary ranges for program directors, program coordinators, clerical support, accounting clerks, and other staff positions. Call vendors for specification sheets on equipment. It's amazing how quickly you can find answers by asking people in the know!

The Internet has a wealth of information on nonprofit organizations, including salary surveys. Run a quick Internet search, using your favorite search engine, for nonprofit salary surveys.

**TIP**

Network with other organizations in your community to locate purchasing cooperatives. With these co-ops, multiple agencies get together to place orders for like items in bulk, thus receiving a bulk purchase discount. All the members of the cooperative benefit by reducing their overall operating costs. Take notes and create a cooperative purchasing information file so you know whom to call or email for future cost-sharing opportunities.

**WARNING**

Funders often call applicants to get more information on a line item. So be prepared!

## Including all possible program income

If you anticipate having any program income at all, you must list a projected amount at the end of your budget summary table and subtract it from the total project costs; doing so means you need less money in grant funds. Examples of possible program income include the following:

>> **Interest:** You may earn interest on endowment funds you're allowed to use annually to assist with program costs.

>> **Membership or program fees:** A public library has late fees that add to its overall program income, for example. Likewise, a program may charge participants a small fee to enroll in program classes or services.

>> **Special events revenue:** You may be planning to hold a fundraising auction or raffle to collect additional monies for field trips, equipment, or other items or activities in the project's design.

>> **Ticket sales for planned events:** You may work within a performing arts organization that puts on three plays at the local community theater, and patrons purchase tickets to see your troupe perform.

>> **Tuition:** You may receive payment or reimbursement from a state or local agency for aiding a specific population. Your grant request may be for monies to develop additional programs, but you must account for the monies you already take in.

REMEMBER

Not reporting your income is unethical. Just think about the dozens, hundreds, or thousands of proposals a funder receives daily, weekly, and monthly. Ninety percent of the time, the funding source must send out letters to grant seekers regretfully stating that not enough funds are available to fund all the requests received. If you choose to omit the fact that you expect program income and greedily ask for the whole ball of wax, you're taking thousands of dollars out of the funder's annual grant-making budget. Your excess could have funded another grant, perhaps for a struggling start-up agency with no other resources. From an ethical standpoint, asking for grant funds means taking a private oath never to ask for more than you actually need.

## Managing expenditures to the penny

Asking for too much isn't looked upon favorably by any funding source. In fact, giving leftover money back at the end of the grant period may mean you can't go back to that funder, ever. No funder wants money back. Why? The funder has already worked the grant award or allocation into its annual giving budgets. Returned money is a hassle, from accounting to reallocation, if the funder has a specific amount of grant funds it awards annually.

To top it off, giving grant award money back may send one or more of these signals to funders:

>> Your organization (the grant applicant) didn't submit an accurate budget request — you overshot some of the line items and now you have more money than you know what to do with!

>> You aren't creative enough to find a way to use the leftover monies in your project to better serve the target population.

>> You failed to carry out all the proposed activities and had leftover monies.

Meet with your board of directors or project advisory council to brainstorm how you can (legally) spend the monies on project-related needs.

REMEMBER

Funders are often willing to work with you if you truly have a legitimate or unavoidable reason for not spending the grant funds as planned. Contacting the program officer as soon as possible when such issues arise is much better than having to send a check back at the end.

## Projecting Multiyear Costs

When you're planning to construct a building or purchase specific items of equipment, engineers or vendors can usually give you bids that are very close to the actual cost of the construction or equipment you'll need. However, when you're seeking funding for personnel or line items with prices that fluctuate, take care to account for inflation when preparing your budget.

REMEMBER

In a multiyear request, your line items should increase by at least 5 percent annually.

Here's how to create an award-winning multiyear budget summary table:

>> **Column 1:** Type your line-item categories (listed at the beginning of this chapter).

>> **Column 2:** Type your Year 1 in-kind contributions by category.

>> **Column 3:** Type your Year 1 cash contributions by category.

>> **Column 4:** Type your Year 1 amounts requested from the funder by category.

>> **Column 5:** Type your Year 2 in-kind contributions by category.

>> **Column 6:** Type your Year 2 cash contributions by category.

>> **Column 7:** Type your Year 2 amounts requested from the funder by category.

Continue this sequence for all remaining years in your multiyear budget support request. Only run your total at the bottom of each column, vertically. Don't run horizontal totals (at the end of rows); it's too confusing for the funder to nail down the actual costs and requests for any specific year. Use an Internet search engine to find examples of multiple year budgets.

# Building Credibility When You're a New Nonprofit

If your organization is a new nonprofit, you can increase your chances of winning a grant award by applying through a fiscal sponsor. A *fiscal sponsor* is usually a veteran agency with a long and successful track record in winning and managing grants; of course, the sponsor must have 501(c)(3) nonprofit status awarded by the IRS.

The role of a fiscal sponsor is to act as an umbrella organization for newer non-profit organizations that have little or no experience in winning and managing grant awards. Your new organization is the grant applicant, and the established agency is the fiscal sponsor. It acts as the fiduciary (financial) agent for your grant monies. In other words, your fiscal sponsor is responsible for depositing the monies in a separate account and for creating procedures for your organization to access the grant monies.

Why would you use a fiscal sponsor instead of applying directly for grant funds yourself? Because some foundations and corporate givers don't award grant monies to nonprofit organizations that haven't completed the IRS advanced ruling period — typically a 36-month time frame during which the IRS is monitoring your nonprofit-related activities and finances to make sure you're fulfilling the mission, purpose, and activities stated on your nonprofit status application (Form 1023). No funder wants to award substantial grant monies (more than $10,000) to a nonprofit in the advanced ruling period. *Note:* Government agencies don't have advanced ruling period–related requirements.

When selecting a fiscal sponsor, do the following:

» Find a well-established nonprofit organization with a successful track record in financial management.

» Ask your local banker to make a recommendation for a suitable fiscal sponsor.

>> Look for community-based foundations set up to act as umbrella management structures for new and struggling nonprofit organizations.

>> Choose a sponsor you're on good terms with and one you have open lines of communication with. Otherwise, your grant monies may be slow in trickling down.

**REMEMBER**

Creating a written agreement between you and your fiscal sponsor regarding how you'll use and access the money is essential to prevent any misunderstandings.

When it comes to your relationship with your fiscal sponsor, keep the following points in mind:

>> The fiscal sponsor is responsible if your organization mismanages the money.

>> The fiscal sponsor is responsible if the fiscal sponsor mismanages the money.

>> If an audit for financial expenditures is in order, the funding source can audit the fiscal sponsor, and the fiscal sponsor can audit your organization.

Sometimes a fiscal sponsor wants you to include expenses for accounting services or grant management in the Other section of your budget summary and in the budget detail narrative. This practice is acceptable to funding sources.

**TIP**

If your fiscal sponsor indicates that it will provide the fiscal management services at no cost, mention this point at the end of your budget detail narrative. Also present the fact upfront, in the grant applicant credibility section of the narrative (see Chapter 13 for more details).

The following is an example introduction of an organization that plans to use a fiscal sponsor:

> The Ready for the World Future Forward Initiative (RWFFI) will use the Entertainment Industry Foundation as its fiscal sponsor. Although our organization is a recognized nonprofit organization in the state of Wonderland and approved by the IRS for nonprofit tax-exempt status, the RWFFI has never managed a grant in excess of $1,000,000. Our board's executive committee has met with the financial manager at the Entertainment Industry Foundation and has obtained a written fiscal agent agreement. For this request, the grant applicant is RWFFI; however, the fiscal agent will be the Entertainment Industry Foundation. We have attached a profile of the foundation as well as its signed fiscal agent agreement. IRS letters of nonprofit determination for both organizations are attached.

# 5

# Triple-Checking Your Application, Submitting, and Following Up

**IN THIS PART . . .**

Wrap up your submission by checking that you've met all the funder's requirements, proofreading the entire application (or having a second set of eyes proof it for you), compiling necessary attachments in the proper order, and sending off your baby according to the funder's submission protocol.

Organize all the records of your grant application with the help of cloud-based file-storage services. Figure out how best to follow up on your request based on whether you appealed to a public or private funder.

Prepare to officially accept a grant award via a resolution signed by the leadership of your organization's board of directors. Learn from a failed grant application by requesting the peer reviewer's notes from federal reviewers or by convening a stakeholders' meeting to brainstorm following a corporation or foundation's rejection notice.

Use a corporate request letter to ask Fortune 500 companies and smaller corporations for matching funds or donations of equipment and supplies. Make initial contact with corporate funders.

# Chapter 18

# Checking Off the Mandatory Requirements

B efore you can call your application a done deal, you need to look at what goes into finalizing your grant application package. Putting on the finishing touches is so important because if you fail to adhere to the funder's packaging (meaning how it wants to receive your grant application) and formatting guidelines, you may lose technical review points (I fill you in on this peer review in Chapter 10). And if you lose sacred review points, your grant application may be eliminated before it starts the race for a competitive monetary award. This chapter tells you the final steps you must take before submitting your grant application for funding consideration.

## Double-Checking All Required Components

Practically all government grant applications and even a few foundations and corporations are now using an application package or online upload checklist — a list of everything you need to prepare and submit a complete application package.

Use this checklist to make sure you include each section of the grant application the funder expects to find when its program staff opens your submission. Some funders even ask you to include the checklist in the funding application package. Read carefully for instructions on where to place the checklist in the final application package.

Not all private sector funders (foundations and corporations) have these easy-to-follow checklists. If you're working on a project for a funder that doesn't provide a handy checklist, I suggest you create your own. Based on what you read in the funder's instructions, type your own list showing the order of the application materials. In other words, what's the first document the funder needs to read when opening your funding package? Continue the list until you have a completed listing for the forms, narrative sections, and attachments. (Be sure to hash out the recommended length for each section or for the entire narrative.) Creating your own checklist gives you peace of mind and cues you as to when the funding package is complete and ready for submission to the funder.

In the following sections, I outline the information peer reviewers expect to find in your application.

**REMEMBER**

Make sure you follow the order that the funder presents in the checklist, which may or may not be the same as the order I present here.

**TIP**

You can also find this checklist at www.dummies.com/go/grantwritingfd6e.

## Cover materials

The cover materials are the first things grant reviewers see when they pick up your application, so make sure each part listed here is finished, well done, and in its proper place. (See Chapter 12 for more details about these items.)

- ❏ A **cover letter,** if required, typed on the grant applicant organization's letterhead and signed by the president of the board or the executive director.

- ❏ All **pre-narrative forms** in place, with empty information fields filled in with the requested information. Examples of pre-narrative forms include cover page fill-in-the-blank forms and federal grant application cover forms (SF-424A and SF-424B).

- ❏ The **abstract or executive summary,** which typically has page or word limits, appears on a separate page. This section is merely a brief overview of

**REMEMBER**

the application's contents and should be placed before the grant proposal narrative.

The executive summary is the same as the abstract; it just has a different title. The executive summary or abstract is frequently used in government grant applications, and some regional grant-making forums have designed applications that call for an executive summary. Private sector funders usually ask for an executive summary.

❑ The **table of contents,** which is required by most federal and state grant applications.

## Organization history and capability

The section about your organization's history and capability, which is part of your grant application narrative, introduces the funding agency to your organization and what it does. This section is a formal "this is who we are" type of written introduction (go to Chapter 13 for more about building your organization's credibility as a grant applicant). Double-check what you've written in this section, making sure you address the following points:

❑ **History of the organization:** Why it was founded and how long it has been around. Mention the organization's purpose and mission statement as well.

❑ **Major accomplishments relevant to the proposed grant-funded project:** Successful capital campaigns, major grant awards, award-winning programs, and successful outcomes for your target populations.

❑ **Current programs and activities relevant to the proposed grant-funded project:** A simple list of what you do in chronological order with the newest programs and activities listed first and the oldest ones listed last.

❑ **Target population demographics that mirror the types of populations the funder wants to support in its current funding cycle:** A brief look at your service population over the past five years.

❑ **Collaborations with local, regional, and statewide nonprofit and for-profit partners:** The who's who in your stakeholder group.

**TIP**

If you refer to any attachments in the introduction, keep a running list of attached documents so you can double-check that they're in place before submitting the application.

# Statement of need

Make sure your statement of need touches on the following topics:

- ❏ The problem within the community in critical need of grant funding
- ❏ How you identified the problem
- ❏ How the problem looks from national, regional, and local perspectives
- ❏ The current national and local research that proves the existence of the problem
- ❏ The gloom, doom, drama, and trauma that justify the need for grant funds

If you refer the reader to any attachments, list them for double-checking later. Check out Chapter 14 for the scoop on how to convey a hopeless situation for your statement of need.

**TIP**

Take another look at the first two narrative sections in your funding request. If you didn't include at least one or two graphics, go back and look for key pieces of information you can present in a table or chart; even a simple map of your location helps give the grant reviewer's eyes a visual break.

# Program design

The *program design* (also referred to as the *case statement*) is the real meat of your grant application. Consequently, making sure you've hit all the right points in it is crucial. Check that your program design contains the following (and refer to Chapter 15 for more details on this section):

- ❏ **One concise statement expressing the purpose of the program:** What the program will do for your target population
- ❏ **Goals that shadow the funder's specific funding goals:** Non-measurable or measurable statements that create the vision for what the funding will do for your target population
- ❏ **SMART or outcome objectives written in quantifiable terms: S**pecific, **m**easurable, **a**ttainable, **r**ealistic, and **t**ime-bound commitments to show the steps to achieving your goals
- ❏ **Process objectives:** A list of activities (tasks) that will occur when the grant funding is awarded (timelines)
- ❏ **Impact objectives expressed in terms of their benefits to end recipients:** The "step away for five years and look back" statements

- [ ] **The Logic Model graphic (see Chapter 15), which helps the grant reader connect the dots between goals and objectives:** The road map for lazy readers that is included in the narrative or as an attachment and is a "one page tells the story" document with input, strategy, output, and outcome columns

- [ ] **The time frame for starting and ending all proposed grant-funded activities:** The timeline table that connects the process objectives to when they will start and end during the grant-funding time frame

- [ ] **Integration of the evaluation plan into the overall program design or plan of operation:** Accountability language to demonstrate your process for tracking the SMART or outcome objectives and to show funders that all your performance measurements will be monitored and reported

- [ ] **A dissemination plan:** How you'll get the news out about how your grant-funded program succeeded and share your success with other grant seekers and organizational stakeholders

- [ ] **A sustainability plan:** How your organization will keep all or a portion of the grant-funded program running when the grant-funding cycle has ended

Did you refer the reader to any attachments or appendixes? If so, remember to add them to your running list so you can check them later.

## Evaluation and dissemination

If the funder requires you to submit a separate evaluation section with your application, make sure yours addresses the following information points:

- [ ] **The methods your organization will use to evaluate the progress of your objectives:** Surveys, pre- and post-documentation, observation, and more. See Chapter 15 for more about the evaluation process, which is a part of the plan of action.

- [ ] **How you plan to share (or disseminate) your findings with others:** In some Common Grant Application (CGA) formats, the evaluation belongs in the attachments section, not in the grant narrative. You must follow the formatting instructions for what goes in the narrative and what must be added in the attachments.

If you refer the reader to any attachments, add them to your attachments checklist for double-checking later.

# Management plan, assets, and your equity statement

In this portion of your application, make sure you provide details on the following elements of your program:

❏ **Key personnel, including each person's qualifications and the amount of time he will allocate to the project:** Experience and education should match position assigned in the grant-funded project. Make sure you include who each person reports to and thereby demonstrate accountability at every level in your management plan.

❏ **Resources that your organization and its partners bring to the program:** Technical assistance, financial, facilities, executives on loan, and more.

❏ **A demonstration of equity (fairness/equal opportunity for all) in hiring staff and recruiting program participants:** Proving you can find qualified personnel and follow federal and state equal opportunity legislation.

REMEMBER

In most Common Grant Application formats, key personnel (management plan) information belongs in the attachments, not the grant narrative. If you refer to any attachments, don't forget to add them to the attachment checklist.

Head to Chapter 16 for more on how to present your fiscal, human, and physical assets and show fairness.

# Budget summary and narrative detail

The budget portion of your application is where you must be as accurate as possible. After all, money's a pretty serious thing — especially to the funder handing it over! Be sure to do the following:

❏ **Double-check your budget summary totals and make sure your formatting follows the guidelines.** Are you supposed to round to the nearest dollar? Are you supposed to omit decimal points?

❏ **Write a detailed narrative to support the budget summary's line-item amounts.** You need to defend every line item. For further information on connecting the information in your budget to the plan of action, refer to Chapter 17.

As you've done for the other sections of your application, note references to any attachments so you can ensure the attachments are in place.

# Avoiding Editing Red Flags

Even after six editions of *Grant Writing For Dummies* and more than $430 million in funded grant and contract awards, I absolutely can't see my own blatant writing errors! Don't be surprised if you experience the same thing. After putting so much time and energy into your application, your eyes and brain may be too strained or fried to spot fatal writing or formatting errors. Unfortunately, the individuals who review and evaluate your grant application (program officers and peer reviewers) are trained — like hawks with trifocals and magnifying glasses — to find your mistakes. And when they do, your application is at high risk of not being funded. That's why recruiting a fresh pair of eyes is so important for making sure your writing, formatting, and adherence to the funder's guidelines are spot on.

To get the most from your final edit, you have three options:

>> **Finish your funding proposal early (five to six days before it's due) and lay it aside for 24 hours before rereading.** Taking a break from your text allows you to look at it with fresh eyes and spot mistakes you may not have noticed if you'd kept chugging along nonstop.

>> **Have a colleague proof and edit all your work.** Be sure to pick someone who doesn't feel intimidated or shy about marking up your mistakes. Give this person a copy of the guidelines you followed. After all, it's very easy to miss a narrative section response.

>> **Secure the services of a professional proofreader or editor.** Remember to give any outside eyes a copy of the grant application's guidelines. Your hired helper needs to know the purpose of the funding, the funder's instructions for writing and formatting the narrative, and the required supporting documents. You can locate professional editors by searching the Internet and typing in *professional editor for grant applications.*

REMEMBER

For the last two options, you may need to allow a little more than three or four days, so don't wait until you finish the application to pick a path. Figure out ahead of time what you're going to do so you can line up the resources you choose to work with and then build the needed time into your deadline schedule.

TIP

Whether you choose to proofread your application yourself or hire someone to do it for you, always run the spell-check feature on your word-processing program. Doing so takes only a few minutes, but fixing spelling errors early in the proofreading game saves you time later on, when you may be working to fix more prominent errors.

If you decide to proofread your own grant application, just toss it in the wastebas-ket now! No, I'm not kidding. Get some help! Here's a list of the types of bloopers and blunders that we grant writers often make and never seem to find until it's too late:

>> **Nonmeasurable goals:** When the funder's guidelines require measurable or SMART goals and you fail to incorporate **S**pecific, **M**easurable, **A**ttainable, **R**ealistic, and **T**ime-bound language into your goals, you won't be funded.

>> **Nonmeasurable objectives:** Failing to write SMART objectives is one of the most common reasons proposals lose peer review points and end up being eliminated for funding consideration.

>> **Narrative section headings and subheadings that aren't the same as the funder's review criteria headings:** If the funding agency has specific formatting guidelines for headings and subheadings and you omit these, the peer reviewer won't be able to find the corresponding information for each narrative section.

>> **Unpaginated (unnumbered) pages in the narrative:** If peer reviewers have to match the last sentence on the previous page with the rest of the sentence on the next page because you leave off the page numbers, your application won't be recommended for funding.

>> **No sequential pagination from the cover form to the last attached or appended item when the funder has requested total document pagina-tion:** Some funding agencies publish specific paginating guidelines that require first page to last page sequential pagination. If you don't follow the instructions, your application won't be funded.

>> **Different font types and sizes when the funder instructs you to use only one particular font type and size:** Government funding agencies typically publish formatting guidelines that include a font type and size. If you use a different font from the published required font, your application won't be funded.

>> **Incorrect spacing between sentences when the funder indicates a specific spacing:** Funders will publish the line-spacing requirements (single- or double-spaced) in their grant application guidelines. These are mandatory formatting instructions that must be followed.

>> **Orphan lines, headings, or subheadings left hanging alone at the bottom of a page:** For visual continuity, bump orphan lines to the next page. Also, always check the bottoms of your pages for stand-alone lines of text. Reformat accordingly.

>> **Blatant spelling errors or misused words (for example, using *there* rather than *their, hour* rather than *our,* and so forth):** Use a hard-copy dictionary

and a thesaurus or your word-processing program's spelling and grammar check options to ensure you've used the correct words.

» **Omitted heading or subheading responses that you believe don't apply to your organization:** Be sure to type "Not Applicable" under the heading or subheading or in the information field box.

» **Grammatical, punctuation, and sentence-structure errors:** When a grant reader (program officer or peer reviewer) starts finding these types of mistakes, he wants to start reading your application over again from the beginning to look for more mistakes and reasons not to recommend your application for funding consideration. Don't give him this opportunity!

» **Character and spacing errors:** When you're copying and pasting word processing text into online e-grant information fields, if you fail to count the words or characters or spaces and characters combined, your application section won't upload into the funder's portal. You'll get multiple error warnings that can cause you to miss the grant application deadline (not just the day it's due, but the time limit for submission).

Check out Chapter 10 for more about the importance of formatting your application properly.

REMEMBER

Different funders have different rules. You can win the grant-seeking game if you read and adhere to each funder's specific formatting rules.

# Assembling the Proper Attachments in the Right Order

The attachments to your grant narrative go in a specific order. For most government grant applications, the attachments are compiled in the same order you refer to them in the narrative. So, read through the narrative from beginning to end and put your attachments in that order. Each attachment should be numbered in the narrative — for example, *attachment 1, attachment 2,* and so on. Make sure you type the attachment number on each attachment (I like to put it in the upper right-hand corner).

WARNING

Only include additional information in attachments if the funder permits them — otherwise, you've wasted your time because the additional material won't be read or considered.

The types of attachments you may need to include generally fall into two categories: capability-related documents and financial documents. However, you may also need to provide supporting documentation. I help you figure it all out in the next sections.

## Capability-related documents

A funding agency may request lengthy information on your organization's structure and administration processes. If you don't have sufficient space in your grant application narrative, you can refer the grant reader to the attachments.

Make sure to follow the funder's guidelines for what should be included in the attachments. See Chapter 16 for the personnel information that can be expanded on in the attachments:

>> **What are the responsibilities of the board, staff, volunteers, and (if a membership organization) the members?** Write a brief paragraph giving the reader a one- or two-sentence description of each group's responsibilities. Sometimes for a new, nonprofit organization, I insert a copy of the bylaws to fulfill this attachment requirement.

>> **How are these groups (the board, the staff, and so on) representative of the communities with which you work?** What are the general demographics of the organization? I usually provide a board roster that includes each board member's name, address, occupation, gender, ethnicity, and term on the board. I also attach a list of key staff members and give gender and ethnicity information for each individual. Your board and staff should be reflective of the target population served by your organization.

>> **Who will be involved in carrying out the plans outlined in this request?** Include a brief paragraph summarizing the qualifications of key individuals involved. For this attachment requirement, I put in one-page résumés for each key staff person.

>> **How will the project be organized?** Include an organizational chart showing the decision-making structure (see Chapter 16). Make sure the chart is up-to-date and includes a box for volunteers (if your organization uses any). Titles are more important than names, especially given that the staff may change over the duration of the grant's funding period.

## Financial documents

The attachments in the finance section should cover or include specifically what the funder is asking for in the grant application guidelines. Here are some typical financial-related attachments:

>> **The organization's current annual operating budget:** Show your current and next fiscal year's operating budget; detail the line-item expenses for the grant reader.

>> **The current project budget:** Be realistic here. Develop a budget that clearly shows you've budgeted adequately to achieve the program goals and objectives.

>> **A list of other funding sources for this request (foundations ask for this information):** Include the name of each funder, the amount requested, the date you sent the grant proposal, and the status of your request (whether the request has been funded or rejected or is pending). I like to use a four-column table to present this information in an easy-to-read format. See Figure 18-1 for an example.

You can find a template to help you create your potential funding sources table at www.dummies.com/go/grantwritingfd6e.

>> **The financial statement for the most recent complete year (expenses, revenue, and balance sheet):** Use the audited version, if available. If your organization has one of those 20-pound financial reports, pull out the comments and breakout budgets for each department and just attach the overall organization expenses and revenue along with the balance sheet.

>> **A copy of your IRS 501(c)(3) letter:** If you don't have 501(c)(3) status, check with the funder to see whether it's willing to fund through your fiscal sponsor (I talk about fiscal sponsors in Chapter 17). You may need to submit additional information and add information on your fiscal sponsor to the portion of your grant narrative that introduces your organization. Another possibility is that the funder may be willing to exercise expenditure responsibility.

**TIP**

| Funding Sources Receiving This Request | | | |
|---|---|---|---|
| **Potential Funder** | **Amount Requested** | **Date Request Sent** | **Status** |
| US Environmental Protection Agency | $50,000 | April 2016 | Pending |
| Green Building Foundation | $100,000 | January 2016 | Pending |
| US Department of Agriculture | $250,000 | November 2016 | Funded |
| Save a Tree Foundation | $50,000 | December 2016 | Funded |

**FIGURE 18-1:** A table neatly lists other funding sources, amounts, dates sent, and request statuses.

*Illustration by Ryan Sneed*

Refer to Chapter 17 for details on the budget information that goes directly into grant applications.

## Supporting documentation

Other miscellaneous materials funders may request include letters of commitment (up to three). Having some handwritten letters of commitment from your constituency is okay; handwritten letters have a lot of impact on the reader. And don't correct spelling or grammar errors; they make the letters more authentic.

Additional relevant materials include your most recent annual report (an original, not a photocopy), recent newsletters sent out by your organization, newspaper clippings about your programs (make sure they're dated), and previous evaluations or reviews (up to three). Don't go into overkill with too many non-relevant attachments. When in doubt, call and ask the funder!

Finally, this section is the one where I put the supporting documentation I've referenced throughout the grant application narrative that doesn't fit in any of the other attachment sections. *As always, only include items the funder requests.*

# Meeting Submission Requirements

You have likely labored for upward of 20 hours or more on your grant application narrative, the forms, and the other mandatory attachments. Don't exhale yet! It's time to get ready to submit your prize funding-request package. Read the submission requirements two or three times and highlight any technical requirements such as special packaging, the date and time the application is due, and the number of copies needed if you're mailing your application to the funding agency.

## Paying attention to submission protocol

These days, most government agencies prefer to receive grant applications digitally. What does that mean for you? That you must upload all your documents, likely in PDF format, via a federal e-portal such as Grants.gov.

TIP

Make sure your Adobe Reader PDF software is compatible with the federal government's version by logging onto the e-portal website and looking for frequently asked questions or submission guidelines.

If you're applying to one of the few government agencies that still accepts hard-copy submissions, review the government grant application guidelines for guidance on how to secure and submit your final grant application package (the cover forms, assurances, certifications, budget forms, narrative, and required attachments). Usually, you're instructed not to staple or spiral bind the finished document. Practically all government funding agencies need numerous copies for the peer review process, and it's easier to make copies of a document that hasn't been stapled together or bound. Even if an agency's grant guidelines tell you to send one original and two copies, the funder will still make additional copies for the review process.

TIP

For hard-copy submissions, anything other than a simple black metal binder clip looks (and is) wasteful. Unless instructed otherwise, stick with what's unobtrusive and effective. Also, don't create fancy graphics-filled covers; no one asks for them and no one looks at them!

Targeting private sector funders? The split is about 75-25, with the majority preferring e-grant submissions via e-grant application portals and others requiring paper copies submitted by regular mail services.

## Uploading applications on time

REMEMBER

If a foundation or corporate funding source sets a deadline, your application must reach the funding source by that time. Similarly, government agencies make no exceptions for late grant applications. If the grant application is due on a specific date, you should be uploading on Grants.gov at least 72 hours before the due date and time (be on alert for the time zone listed in the grant application guidelines). All the pleading, whining, and cajoling in the world, including calls to the funder from your congressional representatives, won't make a difference if your application is late. Only a natural disaster is a valid excuse.

Personally, I don't work 20 to 40 hours on a grant application and then leave the application to regular mail. I prefer a guarantee stronger than a mere postage stamp, so when I have to resort to mailing a grant application, I use an express courier service. I always get the application to the courier three weekdays before the date by which the package must be postmarked. Using an express mail service may cost a little more, but it ensures that your application will make it to its destination and enter the review process.

## Clicking Submit without panicking

The Grants.gov website is the main gateway for federal e-grants — and one of the most comprehensive e-grants systems. Chapter 5 covers Grants.gov in detail, but I guide you through uploading your completed application to the site right here.

The Submit button on the application package cover page becomes active after you download the application package, complete all required forms, attach all required documents, and save your application package. Click the Submit button after you do all these things and you're ready to send your completed application to Grants.gov.

Review the provided application summary that pops up after you click the button to confirm that your application will be submitted to the program you want to apply for. You need to log onto the Internet and log onto Grants.gov if you haven't already. When you log on, your application package is automatically uploaded to Grants.gov, and a confirmation screen appears when the upload is complete. Note that a Grants.gov tracking number is provided to you; record this number so you can refer to it if you need to contact customer support.

The Track My Application section (found on the Applicants tab of the homepage) of the site lets you log into Grants.gov to determine whether you've registered successfully with Grants.gov, check the status of your grant application submissions, and manage your applicant profile.

Chapter 19

# Knowing What to Do after Submitting Your Application

Y ou clicked the Submit button or mailed your grant request. Now you have to face a number of cleanup questions: How can you store these documents where you will have access 24 hours a day, seven days a week in the event a problem arises and you need to view the submitted application document and submit a clarification or a missing attachment? In this chapter, I show you how to deal with all the housekeeping issues you need to take care of after you submit a grant application.

## Keeping Accessible Copies of Electronic Files

You have multiple options for storing your electronic files. Using cloud-based storage services is as secure as printing out your notes and other documents and putting them in a file box for later use. These services are encrypted and easy to access from any mobile device. Some are free up to a maximum storage level; after that, there's a small fee, which varies from provider to provider. I've used each of these cloud-based storage options for electronic files, and all are compatible with both PCs and Macs:

>> **Dropbox** (www.dropbox.com)**:** I like the folder-sharing options of this service and the feature that allows me to see when one of my clients is accessing a shared project folder to retrieve or deposit information. A small window pops up on the lower-right corner of my computer screen to give me the heads-up on any actions in the folder.

>> **Google Drive** (http://drive.google.com)**:** This service has file storage and synchronization capabilities. Documents can be shared, and Google Drive has collaborative editing options. You need a Google account to use this service, but signing up is free.

>> **Onehub** (www.onehub.com)**:** After you subscribe to this collaborative file-sharing cloud-based storage service, you can add Onehub Sync to your desktop and keep all your files handy. There is also a mobile application to add and view files away from your office or home.

>> **Microsoft OneDrive** (http://onedrive.live.com)**:** I use this service on my Windows-equipped computers. It works the same as Dropbox and Google Drive. The only distinct feature that I have found is that it only works on computers that have Windows installed.

*Note:* New cloud-based storage services are emerging on a regular basis, so keep checking to see what's out there and what best fits your needs.

# Staying Connected to Your Stakeholders

Before you write a grant request, you convene your staff, volunteers, community partners, and other interested parties to help your organization develop the plan of action (covered in Chapter 15) and provide the information for the statement of need (see Chapter 14). (If you need more information, Chapter 9 covers your work with stakeholders and how to involve them in the planning phase of your grant proposals.) After you turn in your grant request, you need to bring the stakeholders back together for a debriefing in which you pass on the key information in the following sections.

## Providing updates on what's been completed and what to expect next

A few days after the grant application deadline, schedule a debriefing conference call or face-to-face meeting online or in your office with your program-level staff, board members, community partners, and any advisory board members who were involved in the planning process of developing the grant application's focus. The debriefing can occur simultaneously online, but a meeting is really best. Regardless, follow these debriefing steps:

1. **Review the group's efforts and explain how the information they contributed in the grant-planning meetings was included in the final grant application.**

**REMEMBER**

2. **Give each person or agency a complete electronic and/or paper copy of the final grant request.**

   Blacken out any personnel salaries before distributing.

3. **Answer questions and propose some what-if questions to find out whether the stakeholders understand their roles and responsibilities if and when the grant application is funded.**

   Consider asking the following questions, in addition to others appropriate for your project:

   - What if we're funded for less than we ask for?
   - What if we're not funded at all?
   - What if the needs of our constituents change before we're funded?

4. **Provide a general overview of the process from here and when the funder will make a decision.**

**REMEMBER**

Even though you may have worked as a group when putting together the narrative information, people present at the debriefing meeting may not have been present at the meeting for the document's final draft review, where your stakeholders were given a chance to critique and/or approve the final document for submission to funders. Some feelings may be hurt when a writing contributor sees massive changes in the final document. Remind anyone who seems upset of the ultimate goal: to get funded and help a segment of the community.

## Keeping your partners in the additional-information loop

Give your collaborative partners a list of the funding sources and contact people. Someone on your team may know a foundation trustee or a corporate giving officer personally. And sometimes a simple telephone call or an email to a connected friend can make the difference between getting funded and not getting funded.

Share other critical information with your partners, too, such as the following:

>> Timelines for funder decisions

>> A master list of partners with contact information and make sure that you have clearance from all partners before distributing their information

>> Other projects or programs your organization is planning (this info opens the door for future partnering opportunities)

What can partners do for you as a result of the sharing process? They can commit seed monies to begin program implementation on a small scale. Partners who know your needs can unexpectedly make donations of needed equipment, program space, or other items and services. Partners can also give you leads on other funding sources for the project. They can also recommend an internal staff person or an affiliate colleague for your board of directors.

REMEMBER

Always strive for increased involvement from the team leaders at your partnering organizations.

# Tracking the Status of Your Submitted Application

You submitted your grant application. You know the funder received it, but you don't know whether anyone has actually looked at it yet or how to find that out. This section gives you the postsubmission protocol of when and whom to call to check on your application's status and when to just chill out and wait for notification. The rules are different based on the type of funding source you send your application to, so the next sections look at each type individually.

## Requesting elected official tracking for government grant requests

As soon as you send your grant application off to a state funding agency or upload it via a federal e-grant portal, start the tracking process.

## THE WAITING IS THE HARDEST PART

How much patience do you need to have when you're waiting for communication from a funding source? It depends on the funding source:

- **Federal:** Expect to wait three to eight months from the date you turn in the request. The length of time between when you submit the grant application and when the funder decides on funding varies from agency to agency.

- **State:** Expect to wait up to nine months from the date of submission. Some state agencies have rather quick turnarounds on decision making, while others take forever.

- **Foundation:** Expect to wait a minimum of 3 to 6 months and as long as 18 months from the date of submission.

- **Corporate:** Expect to wait a minimum of three to six months from the date the request was submitted.

REMEMBER

Now's the time to use those great political contacts you've made in your state's capital and in Washington, DC. (Head to Chapter 4 for guidance on alerting your elected officials to your needs.) Because the money you're requesting comes from public funds, keep these political do's and don'ts in mind:

>> **Do** email a complete copy of the grant application to your elected officials.

>> **Do** email the funding agency head (state or federal) any letters of support from elected officials that were written too late to submit with your grant application. Often, your elected officials' offices will email their letters of support directly to the secretary of the federal funding agency (a cabinet appointee appointed by the president and approved by Congress).

>> **Do** email or call your senators' or representative's local and Washington, DC, offices to remind them that you need their assistance in tracking the grant application.

>> **Don't** scream at or threaten elected officials. You really need their influence to help you get this and future grants funded.

>> **Don't** count on getting your grant funded just because you ask your elected officials to get involved in the tracking process. Using the elected official tracking process helps, but it does not guarantee a grant award!

## You get a grant award notification

At the state level, you receive a funding award letter or email when your project is selected for funding. Monies are transferred electronically into your organization's bank account. Some monies are awarded and transferred in advance; other monies are released on a reimbursement basis.

At the federal level, you may receive a telephone call or email from one of your elected officials in Washington, DC, who notifies you of your funding award and issues the official press release to your local newspaper. If your official doesn't contact you, you can expect to receive an email from the Office of Management and Budget, known as the OMB. In some instances, the press release from elected officials is published before the grant applicant organization has been notified by the feds.

REMEMBER

If you agree to a lesser amount, you need to rewrite your goals, objectives, and timelines to match the reduced funding. Here's my logic: If you're going to receive less grant money, your promised program design (goals, objectives, and timelines) shouldn't remain at the same level as a fully funded program. Reduce your promises by serving fewer members of the target population. Decrease your objectives to take the heat off of having to hit 80 percent or higher. Do less with less — that's the rule! (See Chapter 15 for details on setting up goals, objectives, and timelines.)

## You receive a standard form rejection email or letter

At both the state and federal levels, you receive a rejection letter when your project is denied funding. No call, no advance warning, just a cold, very disappointing rejection letter or email.

REMEMBER

If you're not funded, request a copy of the peer reviewers' comments using the language of the Freedom of Information Act, the law that entitles you to such public information. Some federal agencies send you the peer review results automatically. In other instances, you may have to call a federal program officer to request the peer review comments. If you don't receive these comments within 90 days of receiving your rejection notice, use the Freedom of Information Act to request them. And don't forget to check out Chapter 20 for more on what to do after your grant request gets denied. (For full details and advice on how to make a Freedom of Information Act request, visit www.foia.gov.)

# Following up on foundation and corporate grant requests

Some foundation and corporate funders use their websites to post information on procedures for grant proposal awards and declines. If you can't locate the funder's guidelines, it's okay to email or call the funder for more information on your funding application's status. However, wait three to six months after your submission date to make this call or to send an email because the board of directors for these private sector funders often don't meet monthly and often have a lot on the agenda to cover when they do meet. This meeting schedule often delays the grant-funding announcements.

REMEMBER

These funders want you to be involved in the process that eventually leads to either your success or your failure. Communicating with funders is a key to getting your project or program funded — and if not this project, the next one!

You can expect foundation and corporate funders to notify you that

>> The status of your request is pending.

>> Your request has been rejected for funding.

>> Your request has been awarded funding.

*Note:* Of all funding sources, corporate funders are the most likely to fail to notify you when your grant request is rejected. Eighty percent of the time, communication from a corporate funder means you have a check in the mail.

## Round one: Determining whether your request is under review

When you submit a foundation or corporate grant application, you may soon receive an email, a postcard, or a call letting you know your application's review status. The most-desirable immediate communication from a funder tells you that your funding request has been received and is under review. For example, you may receive something that sounds like the following:

> We recently received your request for funding. Our board of trustees meets four times per year. Our next meeting for your area is scheduled for June. If we need additional information, someone from our office will contact you via email or telephone. After we have had the opportunity to fully review your proposal, you will be advised of the board's decision.

A response like this one means you're in the running for the money. Don't call this funder; someone will let you know when it has a decision.

The least-desired communication from a funder tells you that your grant application was received and that the funder isn't considering it for a grant or other type of funding award. Here's an example:

> Your recently submitted grant proposal was reviewed by our program staff and then forwarded to our board of directors. The board met on December 1 and reviewed over 200 grant proposals seeking foundation funding. Regretfully, your grant proposal was not selected by the board for funding consideration. There simply was not enough money to fund every great funding request.

**REMEMBER**

Sometimes, a rejection letter comes with a further stipulation that you not submit another grant request for at least one year. This is a standard funder policy. Most corporate and foundation rejection letters are sent to you within 90 to 120 days of the funder's receipt of your grant request.

## Round two: Finding out whether you're funded

After your first positive communication from the funder indicating that your request is under review, expect a letter within several months (some come in 90 days; other funders can take up to 18 months) that tells you the outcome of the funder's review. The most desired letter from a funder includes information on the amount of your funding award and how to begin the process of transferring funds. Consider this example:

> The board of Directors for the Grant Writing Training Foundation met on June 30 to review your grant proposal. I'm pleased to notify you that the board is awarding $150,000 for your Five-Days to Grant Award Magic Boot Camp Program. We ask that the money be spent exclusively to ensure that the goals and objectives of your project will be achieved. The grant will be paid to you in one lump-sum payment and processing will begin as soon as the grant agreement is signed and returned to us. On behalf of the board, I wish you every success.

**REMEMBER**

Many foundation and corporate funders, as well as state and federal funders, require that *grant agreements* (contracts signed by the grantee and the grantor indicating that you'll spend the money as promised in your funding request) be in place before the funder releases the money. This step is standard procedure. Failing to sign a grant agreement means no grant. However, always have your legal department or attorney examine the language before you sign on the dotted line as a precaution. Call the funder if you have questions.

The least desired letter, however, is a rejection letter stating that although your proposal was recommended for funding, no funds are available in this fiscal year to fund your project. The preceding section shows an example of a typical rejection letter (for an application that wasn't even considered for funding). Read on to find out how to proceed after you've been rejected.

## Round three: Following up after a rejection

When your project is denied funding by a foundation or corporate funder, your options for what to do next are similar to your options when dealing with a state or federal funding agency (see "You receive a standard form rejection email or letter" earlier in this chapter).

First, contact the funder to determine why your grant proposal was rejected. Then ask for a face-to-face meeting if the funder is located within driving distance. If meeting in person isn't a viable option, ask for the best time to discuss the weaknesses in your funding request with a program officer over the phone. This step gives you the opportunity to learn from the experience and to evaluate whether to attempt another submission the following year.

When you consider the time spent researching and writing your grant proposal, you owe it to yourself to find out why you failed. You can't correct narrative weaknesses based on the feedback from a standard form rejection — you have to talk to a real person.

Never become argumentative with a foundation or corporate funder about your grant proposal's rejection. After all, you may want to submit another grant proposal to the funder in the future. Remember to say thank you for all feedback.

Chapter 20

# Winning or Losing: What's Next?

H ave you heard the saying, "It's not over until the fat lady sings?" Well in the world of grant seeking, it's not over until you know the fate of your grant request and have carried out the post-notification tasks. I have seen many grant writers, administrators, and boards of directors drop the ball after finding out that a request for funding was rejected. When I fail, I want to have a major meltdown and just cry. However, there is no time for a pity party or speeding through a box of tissues. Grant writers must decide on (or at least have a thorough process for) a *win* or *lose* communications plan. This chapter guides you through the steps you should take — win or lose.

# Handling Funding Status Communications from Grant Makers

When the word finally reaches you that your grant proposal has been selected for funding, shout, do a happy dance, call colleagues and community partners, and plan a celebration! But then get ready to hunker down and begin the post-award process. First and foremost, your governing body needs to know so they can enter a resolution to accept the grant award. Next, you need to let the granting agency know that you accept the monies. Most important, you need to know how to report the windfall to your external stakeholders and set up a process for managing the money if you don't already have one in place.

## Drafting a resolution

Any agency with a board of directors (such as a nonprofit, school district, or hospital) or trustees, or any government agency with a decision-making body (such as a city council, town board, or county board of supervisors) may be required to adopt *resolutions* to apply for and accept grant funds after an official letter has been received announcing a forthcoming award. Even if the funding source includes a check with the award announcement letter (foundations and corporations occasionally do this), government organizations need a formal resolution before the check is deposited. Make sure to check with the funding agency and your governing body to see if any of these resolutions are required, if they are on file, and if they must be attached to your grant application or signed grant agreement.

The resolution should include the name of the agency receiving the grant funds, the name of the funding agency, the amount of the funding awarded, and the intended use of the funding. Here's an example:

> The What Do You Know Institute hereby resolves to accept $10,000 from the International Association of Advanced Braniacs for the 2017–2021 Five-Year Institutional Support Initiative. These funds shall be used exclusively for this project. Approved unanimously by the What Do You Know Institute's board of directors on 11/1/2016.
>
> Signed by Brighter Now, Founder and Executive Director, What Do You Know Institute

**REMEMBER**

The funder absolutely needs to see the original signature on the resolution, so either mail the *original* resolution or email a scan of the original resolution to the funding source. Be sure to keep a copy for your own files as well.

## Accepting the award

During the post-award process, you must inform the funding source that you accept its offer of funding before you can share the good news with the world. The following steps secure your role as the grant recipient:

**1.** **Notify all your administrators, including the chief financial officer (CFO), of the award.**

2. **Add the item "Accept grant funds" to the agenda of your board of directors' next meeting.**

3. **Prepare an overview of the grant request document for board review prior to the meeting.**

   In the overview, include the purpose, objectives, timelines for program implementation, project budget, and a copy of the official award letter from the funding source.

4. **Prepare a brief oral presentation to give to the board, and draft resolution language.**

   The resolution is to accept the grant award. See the next section for more on drafting resolutions.

5. **If grant agreement forms need to be signed, have these documents ready for the board.**

6. **Prepare a press release (provided the funder doesn't want anonymity) for board approval.**

   As I note in Chapter 19, your senator or representative may take care of the press release if your grant is government funded. Before you make any in-house press release public, verify whether the funder (specifically, foundations and corporations) requires prior approval. Many funders stipulate that they must approve grantee press releases before a release is officially issued.

7. **Create or purchase a certificate of appreciation for foundation and corporate funders, and get it signed by your board officers.**

   Your CEO or board president can also write a formal letter of thanks. Skip this step if you're dealing with government agencies.

8. **Meet with the CFO to discuss fiscal accountability, including creating a clear or single audit trail.**

   See the later section "Reviewing post-award guidelines for help with financial reporting" for more on these audits.

## Tackling the grant management process

What is *grant management*? First, it's making sure you keep all the promises you wrote in the program design narrative of your grant application (see Chapter 15 for details on the program design section). Second, it's handling all the funder's reporting requirements. Sometimes the grant writer assumes this responsibility; other times, these tasks are divvied up between the grant program manager or project director and the person who makes the financial decisions for your organization (the CFO or business manager). In smaller organizations, the CFO may be a bookkeeper working in concert with an executive director. In larger organizations, entire departments may handle the finances, including fiscal reporting.

The *grant program manager* or *project director* is the person responsible for overseeing the implementation of the grant-funded activities. This person brings the program design narrative in the grant proposal to life. She is responsible for ensuring that all the tasks (process objectives) outlined in the program design's timeline table are accomplished on time.

Other tasks for the program manager or project director include the following:

>> Meeting with collaborative partners to let them know the grant request was funded and working with them to plot out the action steps needed from partners

>> Meeting with the human resources department to start the recruitment, screening, and hiring or reassigning of the grant-funded project's staff

>> Meeting with the third-party evaluator (if applicable) to begin strategizing the monitoring and evaluating process for the SMART or outcome objectives (which I cover in Chapter 15)

>> Orienting project staff to the purpose of the grant-funded project and giving them a copy of the program design narrative so that they can see how the project should unfold during the implementation process

>> Sharing the evaluation process with the project staff and the collaborative partners so that everyone knows what will be monitored, how the data will be collected and reported, and the role of each stakeholder in the feedback process

>> Making sure that staff adheres to all task/activity timelines, and developing a corrective action plan to assure that the SMART or outcome objectives will be met before the end of the grant-funding period if the timelines go off-track

>> Working with the CFO or business manager to compile interim and final financial reports for the funder (see the next section)

>> Preparing an end-of-project report for all stakeholders, including the board of directors and collaborative partners

## Reviewing post-award guidelines for help with financial reporting

In federal grants, the Office of Management and Budget (OMB) works cooperatively with funding agencies to establish government-wide grant management policies and guidelines. These guidelines are published in circulars and common rules. At the federal level, these documents are first introduced in the *Catalog of Federal Domestic Assistance* (CFDA). New circulars and common rules are published in the Federal Register. (Head to Chapter 4 for guidance on using the CFDA.)

Table 20-1 lists the most commonly used federal grant management OMB circulars. The circular numbers are the keys to locating the document on the OMB website. To explore the circulars yourself, visit `www.whitehouse.gov/omb/circulars`.

**TABLE 20-1**     ## Office of Management and Budget Circulars

| Circular Number | Applicable Agencies |
|---|---|
| **Cost Principles** | |
| A-21 | Education institutions |
| A-87 | State, local, and Native American tribal governments |
| A-122 | Nonprofit organizations |
| **Administrative Requirements** | |
| A-102 | State and local governments |
| A-110 | Institutions of higher education, hospitals, and other nonprofit organizations |
| **Audit Requirements** | |
| A-133 | State and local governments and nonprofit organizations |

At the state funding level, the funding agency provides you with the funding stipulations, including the regulations for accessing, spending, reporting, and closing out grant funds.

Foundation and corporate funders give you their funding stipulations and/or regulations, if any, when the funds are awarded. Other than asking you to sign a *grant agreement* (a contract indicating that you'll use the awarded funds as promised in your grant application), most private sector funders don't have a ton of regulations and usually spell out any stipulations in the grant agreement.

As you read the circulars and guidelines, you may come across some unfamiliar terms. *Fiscal accountability* is the obligation to ensure that the funds granted are used correctly. Fiscal accountability lies with the entity responsible for managing the grant funds — usually, that's the grant applicant, but in some instances it's the fiscal sponsor. (Chapter 17 explores what it means to be a fiscal sponsor for a nonprofit organization.)

Fiscal accountability means establishing an audit trail. A *clear* or *single audit trail* is an arrangement that allows any auditor, whether internal or from the funding source, to track the grant monies from the money-in stage to the money-out stage without finding that grant funds have been commingled with other organizational funds.

**REMEMBER**

Any grant funds received should be deposited into a separate account and tracked individually by using accounting practices that enable tracking by date, by expenditure, and by line-item allocation against the approved project budget (which is the budget that was approved by the funding source).

# Handling Multiple Grant Awards

Suppose you've applied for grants with 20 potential funding sources. One of the 20 funding sources funds you in full. The money has been deposited, and your project is up and running. But more mail comes in, and guess what? Your project has received two more grants, totaling an amount equal to the full funding request. You must have written one fabulous narrative!

If your project is overfunded, here's what to do:

>> Immediately contact each funder and explain your predicament.

>> Ask the funders' permission to keep the funds and expand your project's design.

>> Ask the funders' permission to carry grant monies over into another fiscal year.

The worst-case scenario is that all funding sources except for the first funder ask you to return the additional funding. The best-case scenario is that you're allowed to keep the funding and create a bigger and better project or program.

**REMEMBER**

The best way to avoid the predicament of having too much money is to write a letter to each outstanding funding source (sources that haven't communicated with you on their decisions to fund your grant requests) immediately after you know that you have full funding. Be honest and quick. It's the right and ethical thing to do — even though having too much money *sounds* like a good thing. (Chapter 17 talks more about the ethical approach to grant seeking.)

# Failing to Get a Grant Award

Failed efforts in the grant-writing field are upsetting, but remember that they don't signal the end of your grant-writing career. After all, just because a grant proposal isn't funded doesn't mean it doesn't have some salvageable parts. This section helps you look at why your application failed and then plan how to fix it.

## Requesting peer review comments when your government application is rejected

If your grant application was rejected by a state or federal funding agency, you're entitled to review the grant reviewer's comments under the Freedom of Information Act (FOIA). Unfortunately, if you're rejected by a foundation or corporate giving entity, you probably won't receive any reviewer's comments, and you can't use the FOIA to get them. (Chapter 19 covers the type of communication you can expect from a foundation or corporation when you aren't funded.)

Government agencies, especially federal ones, typically send a summary sheet with the section scores and an overview of strengths and weaknesses for each application section. If you receive a rejection notice from a state or federal funding agency that doesn't include such a summary, or if the summary doesn't give you enough information, write a letter requesting the peer reviewers' comments (each federal grant application usually has three peer reviewers). When you use the FOIA, you receive the federal peer reviewers' actual written comments and scores (the points they bestowed on each narrative section in your grant application). (For more information on the federal peer review process, head to Chapter 10.)

**TIP**

In order to invoke the FOIA, your letter should include the following information, at a minimum, to assist the funding agency in locating your requested documents:

>> **The name of the federal funding agency from which you're seeking the information:** This name must be in the address section of the letter and on your envelope. You can also email your letter to the granting agency's contact person. You can usually find the contact person's email address in the grant application announcement or on the funding agency's website.

>> **The letter must include the application identification code:** At the federal level, when your application is uploaded to the Grants.gov system, you'll receive a notice that it has been received by the agency. This notice contains an identifying number for tracking your grant application. If you don't receive this notice or lose the email, you can log in to Grants.gov and click the Applicants tab to see the drop-down list. Click Apply for Grants and scroll down to Step 4: Track Application. When you click this link, you see the information shown in Figure 20-1.

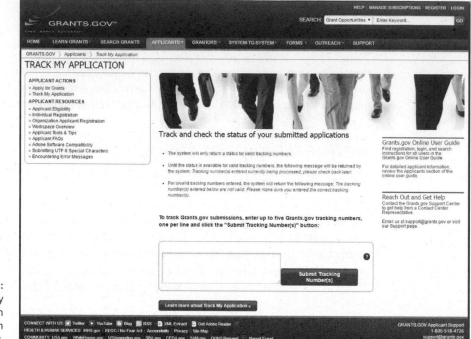

**FIGURE 20-1:**
The Track My
Application
Package on
Grants.gov.

Source: www.grants.gov/web/grants/applicants/track-my-application.html

Address your letter to the funding agency program officer listed as the contact person in the grant application guidelines. On the envelope and at the top of your FOIA letter or in the subject line of your email message, write "Freedom of Information Act Request." Keep a copy of your request; you may need it in the event of an appeal or if your original request isn't answered.

Federal agencies are required to answer your request for information within ten working days of receipt. If you don't receive a reply by the end of that time frame (including mailing time, if applicable), you may write a follow-up email attaching your FOIA letter again and reminding them of the date on the letter or call the agency to ask about the delay. Other government agencies have their own set time frames for replies. Calling and asking before writing your letter is the best way to find out how long you should wait for a reply.

**REMEMBER**

You can try to contact the funding agency's program officer to request written feedback on your failed grant application. However, if you don't receive your feedback in 90 days or less via email or mail, begin to formulate your FOIA letter.

# Acting fast to reuse a failed government request

After you receive the peer review comments for a rejected public sector grant application (see the preceding section), use them to find out what your peers found wrong with the application's narrative sections. Correct the weaknesses, and if parts of your sections were confusing or incomplete, rewrite them. If other people helped you put the application narrative together, now's the time to reconvene the grant-writing team.

If you're stuck holding a failed grant request, why are you doing all this work? Here's why:

>> To get the grant ready for resubmission to the same federal or state grant competition when it cycles again, which is usually once per federal or state fiscal year

>> To make sure you have a great working document for cutting, pasting, and reworking into state, foundation, and corporate grant application formats

However, face the facts. You went to the feds or the state government because you needed mega monies for your project. No other single funding source can fill the gap that a federal or state grant award would have filled. Consequently, you need to scale down your project design and project budget when you take your request to private sector funding sources. Base your adjustments on each funding source's limitations, which you uncover through research.

For example, say you asked for $450,000 to clean up contaminated soil near a city playground in your government grant request. Of the $450,000, $50,000 is needed for soil sampling and preparation to decrease surface level contaminants. Look at all your line items. Which ones can be stand-alone line items? Can the project be started in phases? If yes, then target funders to fund each specific phase. Although this will be a much slower start-to-finish process, at least the project will be completed and eventually benefit an entire community.

In Chapter 4, I tell you how to find state- and federal-level grant opportunities. Chapter 6 covers how to find out about foundation and corporate funding sources.

# Dealing with failed foundation or corporate funding requests

Program officers from local foundations are usually more than willing to discuss the reasons a proposal was denied. However, some foundations and corporations that fund throughout the nation explicitly state that due to the volume of grant applications anticipated, they won't provide feedback on declined applications.

Never, ever throw a rejected foundation or corporate grant request into your files, walk away, and give up. Instead, do the following:

>> Go back and do another funding search to identify a new list of foundation and corporate funders you can approach with your grant request (see Chapter 6 for more about private sector funds).

>> Convene your stakeholders' planning team to discuss the failed attempt with the first funder or funders. Sometimes, other people in the community have funding leads to share with you. After all, they want to see your project funded as much as you do.

>> Beef up your original foundation or corporate proposal to meet the requirements of state or federal funding opportunities. This means writing more narrative and adding more research to support your statement of need. You also need a new project budget based on federal or state funding limitations.

REMEMBER

Foundations or corporate giving entities probably won't provide reviewers' comments; the Freedom of Information Act applies only to grant applications submitted to local, county, state, and federal government agencies.

Chapter 21

# Requesting Matching Funds and Other Goodies from Corporate Grant Makers

Many Fortune 500 corporations and smaller corporations reduce the taxes they pay on their bottom-line profits by creating *community reinvestment programs* that give away money, goods, and services to nonprofits and units of government located in or near corporate headquarters and operating locations. When a company's end-of-financial-year profit is $5 million, it can give away 5 percent of the profits in the form of deductible contributions (according to Uncle Sam). In many regions across the country, this annual transition of taxable to non-taxable dollars drives big bucks into small and large communities. Grassroots nonprofits, mid- to large-size nonprofits, and units of municipal government can request matching funds and a myriad of program-related items.

How can your organization get a piece of a corporation's philanthropy pot? In this chapter, I walk you through building long-lasting relationships with potential corporate funders and show you quick and easy steps of using the corporate request letter format to request funding support and other types of donations from a corporate grant maker.

# Recognizing What Corporations Are Willing to Fund

Before you can ask for goodies from the nearest corporate giver, you first need to understand what corporations will fund. You can ask for any of the following in a corporate request letter or a funder's specific online e-grant request format. Sometimes, their online template is referred to as a *sponsorship request form*. (I provide you with the format for the corporate letter request later in this chapter.)

>> **Equipment:** Copy machines, computers, fax machines, printers, all-in-one machines, assistive devices for hearing- and visually impaired persons, new or used vehicles, appliances, audiovisual items, phased-out specialized equipment (for example, body cameras or night-vision glasses), or other new and used items.

>> **Matching funds:** Cash grant award to provide matching funds to one or more current or pending grant requests that require a cash match. See Chapter 17 for more information on cash match funds.

>> **Materials:** Training videos, curriculum packages, and project-related materials (such as canvas, easels, and so on).

>> **Supplies:** Copy paper, printer or copy cartridges, standard office supplies, or special project supplies. These supplies may include ink pens, paper clips, computer software, or other age-specific or target-group-specific supplies.

>> **Professional development:** Registration fees and travel-related expenses. Most training programs and conferences require registration fees for each attendee. In addition, the training may be offered in a nearby city or state, which means you'll either drive (fuel expense) or travel by airplane or train (ticket expense).

>> **Professional services:** A capacity building trainer for your board of directors, an accountant to prepare your organization's annual audit statement, someone to evaluate your funded project, and more.

# Making Initial Contact and Building a Relationship with Funders

In Chapter 1, I tell you about the importance of building relationships with potential funders. Here, I go into specific to-do's for contacting potential funders.

## Building relationships with funders

I can't write this enough: Prepare, prepare, prepare! If you don't prepare and cultivate the relationship before asking for money, you and your organization have a double loss when it comes to winning grants from newly identified potential funders.

In order to build a relationship with a potential funder, you need to start by researching corporate funding sources thoroughly. Chapter 6 is all about how to find corporate funders.

When you've thoroughly researched funding sources, you're ready to review all the language in the funder's profile to find its initial contact information. Typically, funders will state one of two possible initial contact preferences: a phone call or a letter of inquiry. Calling to introduce yourself and your organization or ask for a face-to-face meeting is preferable, but the funder may prefer that you write an email instead — and if that's the funder's preference, you should honor that request.

If you contact your funder by email, follow these steps:

1. **Introduce yourself and your organization to the funder.**

2. **Explain why you are contacting that funder.**

   For example, maybe you have a shared mission, you've gotten funding from it in the past, maybe you know someone on its board of directors, you've attended one of its technical assistance meetings or webinars, or you have some other attention-grabbing connection.

3. **State your problem.**

4. **Give the solution.**

5. **State the amount of funding you need.**

6. **Ask for permission to submit a full funding request based on the funder's guidelines.**

7. **Thank the person you are speaking with for his or her time.**

8. **Proofread and send your official request.**

9. **Follow up in five days.**

TIP

If you're able to make telephone calls to potential funders, here are some tips:

>> **Write a script of what you want to say on the call.** Your script should provide the same information you would provide if you were sending an email.

>> **Time yourself and make sure to keep your spiel under three minutes.** Keep that timer in front of you during your phone call so you don't start to ramble.

>> **Keep it simple.**

>> **Speak with a smile.** It's true: When you're smiling, people can hear it.

>> **Take copious notes.**

TIP

If you get lucky and score a face-to-face meeting with a potential funder, take advantage of that opportunity! Write a script before the meeting and practice it over and over until you can say it naturally, without referring to your notes. Your script should communicate all the same things you would by email or over the phone.

# Writing a Corporate Letter Request

When you've completed the relationship-building process with potential funders, including corporate giving prospects, you'll likely be asked to write a corporate letter request.

TIP

Keep your corporate request letter to one-page maximum, not including your attached supporting documentation (description of equipment, project budget, and so on). Corporations don't have the time to read cumbersome or lengthy requests. Also, make sure you use your organization's letterhead and that the letterhead includes your organization's name, address, telephone and fax numbers, email address, and website address. (If the letterhead doesn't include this information, simply add it to the end of your letter.)

The following steps explain how to construct your letter and what it should contain; check out Figure 21-1 for a complete example of a corporate request letter:

**Action for Women Institute**
5555 E. Milky Way Lane
San Luis, NM 44444
Voice: 555-555-1212, Fax: 555-555-1214
Email: executivedirector@awi.org
Website: www.awi.org

October 1, 2016

Dr. Bev Browning
Founder and Director
Women's Support Foundation
777777 North 7th Street
Oz, Wonderland 77777

Dear Dr. Browning:

➲ Over the past decade, women have increased their political visibility as frontrunners in state and national campaigns for office by 75% over the 1990s. (Emily's List, 2016)

➲ 50% of women running for an elected office with their state legislature DO NOT win their campaigns due to a lack of know-how about how to run a campaign and insufficient financial backing. (New Mexico List, 2016)

➲ 40% of women who campaign successfully are elected for only one term and lack the internal and external support mechanisms to successfully run for another term. (Action for Women Institute, 2016 Survey of Elected Female Officials)

The Action for Women Institute (AWI) was founded in 2000 by Hillary Roswell Cromfield, a local corporate CEO and mother of five female local elected officials. She served as campaign manager for each of her daughters and experiencing the ongoing obstacles her daughters encountered led her to found AWI with the funds from a second mortgage on her family's childhood ranch. AWI's mission is to support women in politics with no strings attached. This support includes training in circulating and validating petitions for office; launching a campaign; rounding up the right volunteers; securing financial support; accepting office with grace; and planning for additional terms in office.

Our staff meets daily with women who want to run for public office; however, with no finances or solid plan for executing their dreams of public service, they come to AWI seeking anything and everything. AWI's resources are limited to contributions and a few small grants under $5,000. There is a critical (no, dire) need to secure funding support in order to change the landscape of male-majority politics in city councils, county commissions, state legislatures, and most importantly, in Congress! We have highly capable women on the waiting list for our support services.

AWI is requesting $50,000 per year for five years from the Women's Support Foundation. This generous gift will enable us to assist 25 women annually to fulfill their plans to become elected officials. In addition, we will train mentors to assist the potential legislators from our growing waiting list in exploring public office as a career option. Most importantly, 50% of the women trained will likely be elected (based on past tracking of AWI's impact). We are asking the Women's Support Foundation to become our initial and ongoing financial partner because your founder, former Supreme Court Justice Sandra Night O'Connell, was one of the first contributors and mentors for our program in 2000. Re-involving Sandra would give AWI the public acknowledgement needed to support our mission and branding in the world of philanthropy.

I can meet with you at any time and cordially invite you to be my guest at one of our monthly "Women in Politics" forums. We are excited about the possibilities of opening up more training programs before June 2014. Thank you, in advance, for expediting your funding decision.

Many women are awaiting your positive response,

*Hillary Roswell Cromfield*

Hillary Roswell Cromfield, Founder

Attachments (3)

*P.S. "Any woman who understands the problems of running a home will be nearer to understanding the problems of running a country." —Margaret Thatcher*

**FIGURE 21-1:**
This sample corporate request letter tells how the receiver can help a nonprofit program with a donation.

*Illustration by Ryan Sneed*

1. **Record the date.**

   Use the current date if you're mailing or emailing the letter immediately; otherwise, postdate your letter to match the actual mailing date. If you stagger the mailing for multiple letters, be sure to change the date on each letter before mailing it.

   TIP

   Give the corporation plenty of time to respond to your request. Send your letter three to six months before you need the item or money so the corporation has enough time to consider your request (and ideally say yes).

2. **If you're mailing a letter rather than emailing one, write the opening address for the letter's recipient, including his name, job title, the company's name, and the complete mailing address.**

   TIP

   Be sure to use the correct personal title (Ms., Mr., Messrs., and so on) or professional title (Dr., the Honorable, and so on). Call or email the company to double-check the gender of the contact person, the proper job title, and the company's current mailing address.

3. **Use a professional salutation before the recipient's title and surname.**

   I use the word *Dear*. If you know the recipient personally, you can use his first name after the salutation, rather than the more formal title and last name. Because this letter is business correspondence, follow the salutation with a colon, not a comma.

4. **Start your letter with three bulleted introductory sentences.**

   One approach to these initial bullets is opening with accurate, startling facts about your target population or the beneficiaries of the goods or services you're requesting. (Check out the example in Figure 21-1 for this approach, and head to Chapter 14 for info on how to research target populations.) Another approach is to try stirring the memory of the reader and quickly connecting him to a past event that he or a loved one experienced personally. If you go this route, make sure the memory-jogger starts out sad but ends happily.

5. **Introduce your nonprofit organization or unit of government in the next few sentences.**

   REMEMBER

   You don't have to include your organization's geographic location because that info is elsewhere in your letter. However, you do need to share your organization's structure (nonprofit, membership association, or private operating foundation) and target population. Provide enough detail on your organization to put the recipient at ease about giving to your agency for the first time. (Browse Chapter 13 for suggestions on how to profile your organization for a funder or donor.)

**6.** **State your problem in the next few sentences.**

Tell the recipient what's wrong at your organization that requires you to seek outside funding support, equipment, supplies, or consulting assistance. Give sufficient information on the problem to answer all the recipient's questions about why assistance is needed. (See Chapter 14 for more tips on writing a winning statement of need.)

**7.** **In one sentence, ask for the money (specify the amount), services (list the services), or equipment (give the piece of equipment's name — the name most commonly used by the company) you need.**

Tell the recipient why you need the requested item(s). (Note that asking for money is very similar to drafting a purpose statement, so head to Chapter 15 for advice on how to write one.)

**8.** **In one to three sentences, explain the measurable objectives the donation will help you achieve.**

This section is your chance to show the recipient that you plan to take steps to prove your organization lived up to its end of the donation. See Chapter 15 for help crafting futuristic goals and measurable outcome objectives.

**9.** **In one or two sentences, tell the recipient why you chose his company and point to your knowledge of the organization.**

**TIP**

Use the Internet to do your homework on the recipient's organization. First, read all the press releases on its website. Then search the web for the company or foundation name to see what outside information surfaces. Look for the positives and share, in writing, your knowledge of any awards or accolades.

**10.** **Tell the recipient that if his company helps your organization, the contribution will mean much more than the money, goods, services, or equipment donated.**

Stroke the recipient's ego by explaining how a donation from his organization makes you partners in promoting community change.

**11.** **Close your letter with a sentence that tells the recipient whom to contact with further questions and when you need to have the funds, goods, or services in place.**

**WARNING**

Don't forget to provide this deadline for the giver's decision making. Otherwise, you may receive a response to your request long after you actually need the donation.

**12.** **Say goodbye.**

I usually use one of these phrases: "Sincerely," "Hopefully," "Awaiting Your Response," "Praying for Support" . . . you get the idea.

**13.** **When mailing a hard-copy letter, space down three lines and type the name and title of the administrator authorized by your board of directors to sign legal documents. When emailing the letter, simply add your email signature box with all your contact information.**

Although the letter that you're mailing isn't a legal document, it *is* a formal request and should be signed by the individual authorized to sign other types of accountability documents for your organization. Make sure to give your letter, in draft form, to the official signatory for review and approval before showing up at his or her door with a finished letter.

**14.** **If you're attaching any supporting documents, type the word *Attachment* and the number of documents after the administrator's typed name and signature.**

I recommend including the following basic attachments to give your letter's recipient an in-depth look at your organization's internal components and nonprofit status:

- A total project budget

- Your organization's most recent financial statement

- A brochure listing your programs and activities

- Your IRS nonprofit letter

- A catalog page that features the item you're requesting (if applicable)

**15.** **At the end of your hard-copy letter, add a handwritten postscript (P.S.) of no more than three sentences that appeals to the reader's emotions.**

TIP

The handwritten postscript is your last chance to get the recipient to identify with your organization's values. Recipients who can relate to your need because of personal experience will be the first ones to respond favorably to your request. The postscript is important because it takes the recipient from the typed wording in your letter directly to your handwriting. This level of personalization gives your letter the edge over any others the recipient may receive. (If you want to add some winning words to your postscript to impart the importance of your request, you can find several options in Chapter 11.)

If you're planning to send letters to multiple recipients, you're welcome to use the corporate request letter template I provide at www.dummies.com/go/grant writingfd6e.

TIP

When a board member personally knows the recipient of a letter, give the finished letter to that board member and ask him to cross out the typed salutation and write in the recipient's first name. For example, in Figure 21-1, you can cross out "Dr. Browning" and replace it with "Bev." Doing so shows Bev, the recipient, that someone at the requesting organization knows her personally. Just make sure the board member is the official signatory so Bev knows who's calling her Bev!

# Following Up with Potential Corporate Funders

After you send your letter requesting funds, goods, or services, wait 90 to 120 calendar days and then call the individual to whom you addressed the letter. Ask the person whether he received your request and offer to answer any questions. This important courtesy can speed up the recipient's decision to help your organization. In some instances, the funder may, in fact, follow up with you in as little as 30 days. If not, please wait and be patient.

TIP

If a member of your board of directors handwrote the salutation and signed the letter (as suggested in the preceding section), he needs to make the follow-up call because he has a personal relationship with the recipient. This action can increase your chances of receiving what you ask for in your corporate request letter because a more personal connection is being made between the executives.

REMEMBER

Always express gratitude for contributions at any level. Write a thank-you letter and have your board president sign it. Also, ask someone at your organization to invite the donor or representatives of his corporation to public events, grand openings, ribbon cuttings, and more. Essentially, invite the donor to witness firsthand the impact of his organization's contribution on your group and on your target population. Such actions show the donor that your organization really does want a long-term partnership, not just a donation.

# 6

# The Part of Tens

Chapter 22

# Ten e-Grant Tips

Today, e-grants are the norm for most funders. Unfortunately, grant writers and others working in e-grant limitations tend to have the misconception that e-grants are a piece of cake. The reality is that e-grants aren't easy to write.

In this chapter, I give you some tips to stay on top of the e-grants game and reduce common errors (and stress!) when the grant application submission time rolls around.

## Log In and Set Up a Password Immediately

The first step in writing an e-grant application is to log in so you can see what the requirements are. Read over all the questions and note how many characters you're allotted for your answers. Then, as you work on your application offline, you can make sure that all your answers fit. (The last thing you want to do is try to write your grant application on the fly in the online system.)

REMEMBER

Make a note of your password and keep it someplace safe where you'll be able to find it if you forget. Also, set your online calendar alert with the due date so you don't forget.

# Fill In Routine Organizational Information

The first step in most e-grant applications is to provide routine information about your organization. Before you log in again, assemble all the following:

>> Your organization's name

>> The year for IRS 501(c)(3) incorporation

>> Your organization's physical address

>> Your organization's mailing address

>> The name of the contact person and that person's job title

>> The contact person's telephone and fax numbers and email address

>> Your organization's employer identification number

>> Your organization's DUNS number

>> A copy of your most recent annual operating budget

Have all this organizational information within eyesight because the e-grant portal may automatically log you out after a certain number of minutes of inactivity.

**REMEMBER**

The organizational information fields required can differ from funder to funder. If you don't have some of the requested information on hand and ready to enter into the online e-grant application template, start looking at previous grant applications and have these files open on your screen with all possible organizational contract information.

# Review the Entire Online Application Template

Now that you have access to the online grant application template, it's likely that you'll be viewing one page of instructions at a time from a multipage grant application template (a set of questions that you must fill in the answer for online). In some e-grant systems, you can't advance to the next screen until you fill in the requested information on the current screen. In other e-grant systems, you can advance and see every page remaining in the online template without entering anything.

Review as much of the e-grant application template as possible. Take notes on the information you need to assemble to complete the rest of your grant application.

If you can't advance to the next screen or page until you fill in the information on the current page, stop and log out. Call the funder to see if you can get a Word or PDF copy of the entire blank application template via email.

## Copy and Re-Create the Template in a Word Processing Program

When you access the first page of the e-grant application template, copy and paste what you see on the screen onto a blank word processing page. Save your word-processing file early and often, in case your power goes out or the computer freezes up. When you've copied and pasted everything required in the online e-grant template, log out and get ready for the next step.

If you're timed out of the grant application website, you can always log back in. Any information that you've entered and saved will remain intact.

## Determine If You're Counting Characters or Characters and Spaces

Look at the instructions for each information field box. There will likely be limits on the number of words, characters with spaces, or characters with no spaces that you can enter. As you type your responses in the same word processing document, monitor or track what you're typing so you can make sure you're fitting within the space allowed.

Stop your writing at about 50 characters less than what's allowed. That way, you have a little wiggle room. Also, check with the funder to see if your understanding of the formatting requirements (spaces and characters) is correct.

## Live without Traditional Graphics

When you work in an e-grant application template, you can't insert graphics. You're going to have to ditch your use of tables, maps, charts, and figures. In the coveted space that you're allowed to respond, everything will need to be in narrative format. The first few times you create your narrative for this type of limited uploading environment, it may be challenging to communicate your point with words alone. But after you have a few e-grant applications under your belt, you'll know the true meaning of the term *plain and simple.*

## Live without Traditional Formatting

All the e-grant submission systems I've worked with haven't been so good about special formatting — stuff like bold, italics, underlining, and different font colors. You just have to settle for plain text. Typically, the font doesn't matter either, because when you paste it into the e-grant system, it's all the same.

**TIP**

Convert your text into RTF format before pasting it back into the online application. This will prevent formatting issues that can come up with Microsoft Word and the HTML interface.

## Recheck the Funder's Website Daily for Modifications to the Guidelines

Just like the federal funding agencies that post endless modifications and amendments to their initially posted grant application package, foundations and corporations that use e-grant application systems can also post changes. If you're registered and you've started your grant application by entering the organizational information, you'll likely receive an email notification of any changes that are made. Still, I recommend you develop the habit of logging on every day to look for notes or changes posted and follow their instructions accordingly. That way, you don't have to change your narrative content or find out that you're missing another required financial document at the last minute.

# Confirm the Due Date Time and Time Zone

This snafu happened to a colleague of mine. She planned to enter her e-grant application text and submit it the same day it was due. The deadline was published as 12 a.m. on Saturday, March 1. In her mind, she thought she had until Saturday night before midnight. But the deadline was actually Friday night. It took some frantic weekend communications to get the funder (someone she knew) to extend the portal's submission system to accept her grant application on Saturday morning. You may not be that lucky, so always double-check with the funder on the due date time and time zone. Your funder could be located out of state across three time zones. If you want to be even safer, plan to submit your application a couple days before the deadline, to reduce your chance of problems.

# Hit Submit

You're ready to submit your online e-grant application. Sweat is pouring down your forehead and you're letting every doubt possible enter your mind. *Did I? Should I? What if?* If you've followed the funder's instructions, read and reread and reread (yes, read your text three times or more) your entries and edited them, you're ready to hit Submit. Just do it!

Make sure to look for a receipt confirmation in your email or in the viewing window after you submit, indicating that the application was received by the funder.

What's next? Either onto the next grant application or a well-deserved day off of work!

Chapter 23

# Ten Steps to Becoming a Grant-Writing Consultant

P ractically every grant writer dreams about quitting his or her full-time job with an employer and jumping into the self-employment arena to become a grant-writing consultant. But dreaming about something and actually doing it are miles (sometimes years) apart. The good news is, with the right tools, you can make it happen! In this chapter, I show you how to build your professional assets and launch a successful grant-writing consulting business.

## Getting Trained

Even if you have work or volunteer experience as a grant writer, there's always more to learn in this field.

When I made the leap into freelance grant writing, I was already writing award-winning grant applications as a consultant, but my clients keep asking for specific credentials or evidence of training in grant writing. At first, I was stymied.

But I quickly discovered a national training company that presented its multiday grant-writing workshops around the country. So, after paying the fee, I flew to Michigan's upper peninsula for a five-day training program. I was so bored having to listen to information that I already knew, but I also reminded myself that at the end of those five days, I would have a coveted certificate of completion from a credible and reputable training corporation. It worked, and today I'm a grant-writing consultant with 43 years of success behind me and some good years of consulting ahead as well.

**TIP**

These are the training options I recommend:

>> **ed2go** (www.ed2go.com**):** Click Writing and Publishing, and then scroll down to Grant Writing. I teach Advanced Proposal Writing and Becoming a Grant Writing Consultant. These easy six-week courses are graded on a pass/fail basis.

>> **A local community college or university:** Many colleges and universities offer classroom-based grant-writing courses.

# Collecting and Reading Resource Materials

I'm constantly online looking for new reports related to demographics on specific populations or tips on how to write effective evaluation plans. You can set up Google Alerts (http://alerts.google.com) for a subject that you want to read up on. I cull data from the Kids Count Data Center (http://datacenter.kidscount.org). I also subscribe to several e-newsletters published by universities that include information and links to emerging topics and statistics. You never know when you'll need something quick and you won't have the time to scour the Internet trying to find that information.

# Joining a Professional Association

There are several professional associations related to grant writing, but I personally only recommend joining the Grant Professionals Association (www.grantprofessionals.org), which has local chapters in most states (although you can join no matter where you live — there are members from around the world). The local chapters have frequent monthly professional development training programs, there are annual regional conferences, and the national association has an annual conference with hundreds in attendance. Not only have I attended most of their conferences, but I also have been selected as a workshop presenter for local, regional, and national conferences.

# Writing without Errors

If you're going to build your reputation as a qualified grant-writing consultant, you must have some grant wins in your career track record. To win a high number of grant applications submitted for funding consideration, you have to learn to write everything error-free — from your grant-related documents to your web content to your marketing materials.

I've used an editor for decades — almost since I started my consulting business — and I recommend that you hire an editor, too (on a per-project basis), to assist you in catching errors. A good editor will polish your writing and help you put your best foot forward every time. If you allow grammatical errors to slip through the cracks, your grant proposals will be rejected, and you'll have a hard time building a business. Your potential clients will think that you can't write if any of your published writing has glaring errors.

The editor I use is Sara Shopkow (`www.linkedin.com/in/sshopkow`). My grant application win rate is high because I make sure she reviews all my documents before I submit them to my clients. Sara isn't the only editor out there — not by far! To find an editor, try typing **editor grant applications** into your favorite search engine.

# Subscribing to Grant Research Databases and Directories

In Chapters 5 through 8, I give you my list of go-to grant research databases and directories for government and private sector funding sources. These databases all have profiles of grant makers or grant-funding programs. Having everything that you're looking for related to new clients and project areas come into your email inbox daily will save you time.

**TIP**

Decide early-on what databases will be the best based on your types of clients. For example, if you specialize in working with units of government, they'll most likely only be interested in federal and state agency grant-making opportunities. On the other hand, if your clients are nonprofit organizations, they'll most likely want you to find money from foundations and corporations. Only one or two databases cover all types of funders, so you're going to have to subscribe to multiple databases to cover 100 percent of your client base.

## Keeping Track of Your Wins and Losses

Keeping track of your grant writing wins and losses is a sore spot with some grant writers. Why? Because when you work for an employer as its devoted (and sometimes only) grant writer, you often can't control what applications you're required to write and submit. Your research may tell you that your employer has no chance of winning a certain grant-funding competition, but your supervisor says, "Just apply for it!" So, you dutifully fill out the application and press Submit. Three months later, you get a rejection notice from the funding agency. Is this your fault? Did you do something wrong in the application? Probably not.

Don't fret if you wrote 20 grant applications last year — at the direction of your supervisor — and only 2 got funded. When you set up your consulting business, start keeping track of your wins and losses at that point. Why? Because you have total control over what you write. If your client wants you to apply for a specific grant competition and you know that the application won't be funded, speak up! Save yourself and your reputation. After all, you're the expert!

**REMEMBER**

The client contracted with your new consulting firm because you have expertise, education, experience, wisdom, and insider knowledge on the entire grant process. Use all of this to firmly tell your clients why they shouldn't apply for this specific grant competition — and suggest some alternatives you think they'd be more likely to succeed with (so they don't lose out, and neither do you!).

## Asking to Join a Grant-Writing Team

If you're wondering how to jump-start your consulting business, consider volunteering your skill sets by sitting on a local nonprofit organization's grant-writing team or in its grant-writing planning meetings. Ask to write a portion of the application narrative or to work on gathering the critically needed research information. This strategy will give you some experience in working with team members on a grant application and allow you to let a potential client know of your cooperativeness and willingness to help that client win a grant award. Even if the client doesn't contract with you in the near future, still ask for a letter of recommendation on the work that you contributed to the organization.

# Getting a Consulting Coach

Many veteran grant writers (those with a decade of experience or more) offer coaching or mentoring services. Consider looking for a virtual or face-to-face coach to help you get started on the right track in preparing to transition from full-time employment to part- or full-time consulting. For example, I offer a tuition-based coaching program for up to six months for people who are interested in becoming grant writers and consultants. You can ask your local Grant Professionals Association chapter for a referral to members who may be interested in offering you some sage guidance.

# Branding Your Business

Set up a website for your new business. The first step is to choose your web address. Don't choose a web address that's too long or difficult to remember. I use my name for one of my websites (www.bevbrowning.com) and the name of my grant-writing training program for my other website (www.grantwritingboot camp.us).

**TIP**

These days, you don't have to be a computer programmer to create your own website. Companies like Squarespace (www.squarespace.com) allow you to build your own professional-looking website for not very much money.

If building your own site seems like more than you want to deal with, you can always hire someone to create your website for you. Some designers can do both *branding* (for example, creating a logo) and web design. One of the best ways to find web designers is to spend time looking at websites of writers and other creative people whose work you admire. When you find a website you really love, look around to see if you see a link to the web designer. If you don't, email the person whose site it is and ask who designed her site.

# Networking Like a Pro

If you create a website and no one knows about it, your business can fall flat. Joining large professional networks like LinkedIn (www.linkedin.com) and Referral Key (www.referralkey.com) can be a great way to connect with people. Here are some other ways to network:

>> **Attend Grant Professional Association meetings and conferences.** You may meet other grant writers who have too much work or who work for employers that are looking for intermittent outside help. When you form honest and sincere relationships with your peers, they may send work your way! Just be sure to repay the favor when you've built up enough work of your own.

>> **Attend meetings of the Association of Fundraising Professionals (**www.afpnet.org**).** Most of their members are decision-makers for nonprofits — in other words, potential clients.

>> **Attend conferences sponsored by a state Alliance of Nonprofits.** Just type *your state name* **alliance of nonprofits** into your favorite search engine to find your state's alliance or association. These events are attended mostly by nonprofit executive directors and board members, all of whom are decision-makers when it comes to contracting grant writers.

Chapter 24

# Ten Ways to Continue Building Your Grant-Writing Skills

n this chapter, I offer ten great tips on how to continue building your grant-writing skills. All the advice I offer comes from the school of hard rocks and hard knocks. I hope my carefully thought-out list helps you avoid closed professional doors.

## Take on New Challenges

How many times have you looked at a grant application and said to yourself, "No way. I can't do this! It's too difficult! There are way too many pages of instructions to read! Goodness, the grant-making agency wants 50 pages of single-spaced narrative. The application is due in ten days!" And in your mind, the list grows. It's important to take on new challenges. Say "yes" to something completely outside your comfort zone. You'll be surprised at what you'll learn and how much more confident you'll feel. The sky is your only limit!

# Become a Grant Research Specialist

If you don't want to work on your writing skillsets yet, consider working on being the best-ever grant researcher. You can work on researching undiscovered grant-funding opportunities and presenting them to your supervisor, employer, or client, or you can focus on researching demographics and best practices for grant application topics. New reports or studies are published online every day. Do you have the most up-to-date set of information? When will you need it and can you store it in electronic folders for future use? Work ahead, be prepared, and write like the wind when you find new grant programs and updated research information. Everyone in your work setting will look to you as the grant research specialist.

# Volunteer Your Services

If you're a member of a nonprofit board of directors or of its "friends of" group (volunteers who raise funding through special events), consider volunteering your services as a grant writer for one or more projects. If you have a full-time day job, you can do your volunteer work in the evenings or on the weekends. Cast your net wide and start giving back to the community where you live.

# Become a Peer Reviewer

Open your web browser, go to your favorite search engine (like Google), and type **call for peer reviewers**. Scroll through the findings and look for state and federal grant-making agencies that have published calls for grant application peer reviewers. (Chapter 10 gives you more detailed information on becoming a peer reviewer.) You'll gain so much more experience and knowledge about what it takes to win a government grant award.

# Do Copyediting for Other Grant Writers

You can learn a lot by reading grant applications written by other grant writers and editing their content. Copyediting entails reading the formatting and content guidelines published by the funder and then reading the completed grant application narrative to see if the grant writer's work is in compliance. You'll learn formatting and graphic techniques, pick up new research websites for your own growing list, and contribute to your employer's or the grant writer's client's success. This is a great way to build your own skillsets and become a successful grant writer.

# Work with an Experienced Grant Writer

One of the most mind-opening experiences is to ask another grant writer if you can help her with her overage work. I work, silently, in the background for another grant-writing consultant. Before I started working with her, I had grown so used to only taking clients with government grant-writing projects that I completely forgot what it felt like to work on the more whimsical, less technical grant proposals to foundation and corporate giving grant makers. I enjoy this work — it's refreshing, fulfilling, and much less stress for me. Working with an experienced grant writer can help you improve and broaden your own grant-writing skills.

# Attend National Professional Development Training

Find a conference with workshops of interest to you, register, attend, and take copious notes. If you're working in an environment where you're a grant writer and you also manage the funded grant awards, your list of potential conferences just doubled. Check out these national conference possibilities and see what looks interesting to you:

>> **Grant Professionals Association Annual Conference:** www.grant professionals.org/conference

>> **American Grant Writer's Association Annual Conference:** www.agwa.us/ agwa.us/grantconference2015

>> **National Grants Management Association Annual Grants Training:** http://ngma.org/annual-grants-training

# Review Successful Grant Applications Online

Search the Internet for previously funded grant applications that have been posted online by the *grantee* (the organization that received the grant award). I love to look at a mixture of grant applications that were funded by the federal government, foundations, and corporations. Rarely will you find a high volume of grant applications funded by state agencies posted online.

# Write and Publish Articles That Require Extensive Research

When you decide to become an author of articles that will be read by the public, you might panic first and then hunker down and start to research your topic before you begin the writing process. Whom can you write articles for? Your own blog (if you don't have a blog yet, try `www.blogger.com`, `www.squarespace.com`, or `www.wordpress.com`) or for other publications and companies that continually update their websites with contributions from guest writers.

I write a monthly blog article for `www.ecivis.com`. It's one of my clients, so I also do much more than just write a blog for its website. I also reciprocate when I receive requests to write for associations, chambers of commerce, and other national publications. Why? Because it takes research and due diligence in writing articles to meet looming deadlines. In addition, it's a great way to brand my name and my consulting expertise.

# Continue Your Formal Education

Across the country and around the world, there are lots of community colleges and universities that offer degrees in nonprofit management. When I searched the Internet for examples, I found the following (not naming the institution, just the degree program):

>> Masters in Grant Writing, Management, and Evaluation

>> Grant Writing Certificate Program

LearningPath.org has a list of possibilities for master's and doctoral degrees in grant writing at `http://learningpath.org/articles/Grant_Writing_Degrees_Masters_PhD_Online_Class_Info.html`.

# Index

# About the Author

**Dr. Beverly Browning** brings more than four decades of grant expertise — including grant writing, contract bid responses, and organizational and program development — to her role as a *For Dummies* author. She is the author of hundreds of grants-related publications, including online articles. Dr. Bev (as she's known to her colleagues, students, and *For Dummies* fans) holds an honorary doctorate in business administration, a master's degree in public administration, and a bachelor's degree in the management of human resources. She is a former member of the Grant Professionals Association and was a frequent workshop facilitator and keynote speaker at its national conferences as well as for state chapters.

Dr. Bev has won more than $430 million in grant and contract bid awards. She finds both solace and elation in the hundreds of thousands of *Grant Writing For Dummies* readers who have purchased each new edition of her book. In 2011, Dr. Bev joined eCivis as the Vice President of Grant Professional Services. With this corporate undertaking, she launched a new division to serve existing and new clients from all public and private service sectors. In 2016, Dr. Bev was appointed Vice President of Client Capacity Building. Today, her role is to carry out grant-related training sessions on the company's behalf.

Dr. Bev is also involved in her Grant Writing Training Foundation. She has developed trademarked curricula for several customized Grant Writing Boot Camps and for her Nonprofit Board of Directors Boot Camp. Dr. Bev's foundation work takes her around the world (in 2015, she and Kimberly Richardson, GPC, conducted a five-day grant-writing program for the US Department of Health and Human Services in South Africa), facilitating adrenaline-filled training programs. Her personal philosophy is, "If I can touch just one person while passing through life, then my mission will be fulfilled."

Dr. Bev loves to hear from *Grant Writing For Dummies* fans and former students. Contact information is on her website: www.grantwritingbootcamp.us.

# Dedication

I dedicate this book to all of my *Grant Writing For Dummies* fans. I've read your published and emailed feedback on this book. I've also spent countless hours on the telephone listening to your suggestions for deletions and new content for this updated edition. You are truly the wind beneath my wings or my earth angels (one of my favorite terms for endearing friends). When my energy is nearly drained, it's your very kind words that come to mind and revive me even more. I am asking a huge favor of you with this edition. Can you please share the news about *Grant Writing For Dummies* worldwide with your entire network of professionals? The words and examples in this book come from my mind, and most important, from my own experiences. I want to help the entire grants industry step up their skill sets and win, win, win! Thank you, in advance, for making this book a number-one selling reference book for the grants industry worldwide. I am grateful!

# Author's Acknowledgments

This book wouldn't have been possible without the tenacity and ongoing support of my literary agent, Margot Maley Hutchison at Waterside Productions. Margot and her family are my family because we've been together since 2001. I am forever grateful for her wisdom, her vision, her commitment, and the love that she has for her authors.

Next, I'd like to thank the dedicated professionals at John Wiley & Sons, Inc., including my team: Tracy Boggier, acquisitions editor, and Elizabeth Kuball, project editor and copy editor. I'd also like to thank Bahíyyah Maroon, my technical reviewer. Together, this group guided my revision efforts from a mere table of contents to what I hope will be the most comprehensive and best-selling grant-writing reference book to date.

Special thanks are also in order for my family. To John Browning, my husband of 50 years in 2016, and my daughter, Lara Suzanne Scott, as well as her husband, Charles Scott, and my precious special-needs granddaughter, Aaliyah Raine Scott. You're always there when I need you, and you, too, help me to remember that family time is important!

I'm going to be 68 years old in November 2016, and I've been a grant writer for more than 43 years. I still love what I do. I thought I was slowing down, but I'm in my second and uplifting wind!

## Publisher's Acknowledgments

**Senior Acquisitions Editor:** Tracy Boggier

**Project Editor:** Elizabeth Kuball

**Copy Editor:** Elizabeth Kuball

**Technical Editor:** Bahíyyah Maroon

**Production Editor:** Siddique Shaik

**Cover Photos:** xefstock/Getty Images, Inc